MW01031054

"An extremely valuable book at a crisis point in our culture—a must-read for those on both sides of the issues that are tearing our country apart."

Ravi Zacharias, Ph.D.
Bestselling Author and Speaker

"This is a powerful message for these feeble times. Geisler and Turek have mapped out how we can get real answers to long-perplexing questions: Should morality be legislated? And if so, how and by whom? This book is the new standard for resolving debates over the nature and necessity of legislated morality among civilized societies."

D. James Kennedy, Ph.D.
Bestselling Author and Speaker

"*Legislating Morality* goes to the heart of America's growing social crisis because it shows the inseparability of law, morality, and order. Required reading for most lawyers and all judges."

William B. Ball
Noted First Amendment Attorney

"This book will challenge your thinking about 'legislating morality.' Geisler and Turek's thorough critique of conventional wisdom will force you to reevaluate just about every aspect of this topic."

William C. Adams, Ph.D.
Professor of Public Administration,
George Washington University

"*Legislating Morality* is a powerful and readable explanation of how the same Moral Law exists today that was the ground for the American Revolution—as the Declaration of Independence says—and for the United States Constitution."

Wendell R. Bird
Lead Attorney for U.S. Supreme
Court Creation Case

DR. NORMAN & FRANK
GEISLER&TUREK

LEGISLATING MORALITY

IS IT WISE?

IS IT LEGAL?

IS IT POSSIBLE?

BETHANY HOUSE PUBLISHERS
MINNEAPOLIS, MINNESOTA 55438

Legislating Morality
Copyright © 1998
Norman L. Geisler & Frank S. Turek III

Published by Bethany House Publishers
A Ministry of Bethany Fellowship International
11300 Hampshire Avenue South
Minneapolis, Minnesota 55438

Printed in the United States of America

Library of Congress Cataloging-in-Publication Data

CIP data applied for

ISBN 0–7642–2094–2   CIP

ACKNOWLEDGMENTS

We wish to express our deep appreciation to our wives, Barbara and Stephanie, for their love and support during this project as well as their helpful comments on the manuscript. We also are grateful to Wendell Bird, Bill Adams, Bob Knight, Rose Marie Turek, Rachel Buss, Randy Hough, and Francis Beckwith for taking the time to review sections of the manuscript and for suggesting specific improvements. Their insights were indeed very beneficial.

Finally, we extend thanks to Steve Laube, Kevin Johnson, and all of the fine people at Bethany House Publishers for having the courage to take on this sensitive subject and for their hard work in seeing the project through. We hope the nation will be better for it.

A Selection of Books by Norman L. Geisler

Legislating Morality (Bethany House, 1998)

Creating God in the Image of Man? (Bethany House, 1997)

When Cultists Ask (Victor, 1997)

Love Is Always Right (Thomas Nelson, 1996)

An Encyclopedia of Christian Evidences (Victor, 1996)

Roman Catholics and Evangelicals (Baker, 1995)

In Defense of the Resurrection (rev. by Witness Inc., 1993)

Answering Islam (Baker, 1993)

When Critics Ask (Victor, 1992)

Miracles and the Modern Mind (Baker, 1992)

Matters of Life and Death (Baker, 1991)

Thomas Aquinas: An Evangelical Appraisal (1991)

In Defense of the Resurrection (Quest, 1991)

The Life and Death Debate (Greenwood, 1990)

When Skeptics Ask (Victor, 1990)

Gambling: A Bad Bet (Fleming H. Revell, 1990)

Come Let Us Reason (Baker, 1990)

Apologetics in the New Age (Baker, 1990)

The Battle for the Resurrection (Thomas Nelson, 1989)

Christian Ethics (Baker, 1989)

The Infiltration of the New Age (Tyndale, 1989)

Knowing the Truth About Creation (Servant, 1989)

World's Apart (Baker, 1989)

Christian Apologetics (Baker, 1988)

Signs and Wonders (Tyndale, 1988)

Philosophy of Religion (revised, 1988)

Introduction to Philosphy (Baker, 1987)

Origin Science (Baker, 1987)

The Reincarnation Sensation (Tyndale, 1986)

A General Introduction to the Bible (revised, Moody Press, 1986)

False Gods of Our Time (Harvest House, 1985)

To Drink or Not to Drink (Quest, 1984)

Explaining Hermeneutics (ICBI, 1983)

Is Man the Measure? (Baker, 1983)

Miracles and Modern Thought (Zondervan, 1982)

What Augustine Says (Baker, 1982)

The Creator in the Courtroom—Scopes II (Baker, 1982)

Decide for Yourself (Zondervan, 1982)

Biblical Errancy (Zondervan, 1981)

Options in Contemporary Christian Ethics (Baker, 1981)

Inerrancy (Zondervan, 1980)

To Understand the Bible, Look for Jesus (Baker, 1979)

The Roots of Evil (Zondervan, 1978)

A Popular Survey of the Old Testament (Baker, 1977)

From God to Us (Moody Press, 1974)

PREFACE

PLEASE READ THIS FIRST!

As Judge Robert Bork's book aptly put it, America is "Slouching Towards Gomorrah."[1] Indeed, an alarming number of moral and cultural problems have exploded in our country since 1960. According to William Bennett's index of leading cultural indicators, violent crime has risen 550 percent; births to unwed mothers are up 400 percent; teenage suicide has risen 300 percent; divorce has doubled; and the average S.A.T. score has fallen 73 points (this despite a doubling in education funding). Meanwhile the population of the United States has risen only 41 percent.

Over this same period, standards of morality expressed in our laws and customs have been relaxed, abandoned, or judicially overruled. And our leaders have been besieged by scandals and charges of immorality. President Nixon, Gary Hart, Senator Packwood, and President Clinton, among others, have been accused of everything from lying to adultery to unethical, if not illegal, activities. "Watergate," "Donna Rice," "Whitewater," and "Monica Lewinsky" have become household names.

Why have we been experiencing this moral free fall? Should Americans be concerned about falling standards and rising crime? Should we care about the moral lives of our leaders? Is a common standard of morality even possible, and if it is, how important is it to the nation?

Since America's moral standards began changing, it seems that most of us have been too weak or too scared to make a case for our lost standard of decency, our lost common morality. That is, until now. Whether you consider yourself liberal, moderate, or conservative, this book is sure to challenge your thinking about right and wrong and your ideas about what the moral future of our great nation should be. For the issues that divide us as a nation—abortion, family values, gay rights, euthanasia—are all moral issues. Yet conventional wisdom dictates that morality cannot be legislated. In fact, those who raise the prospect of legislation on any of these topics usually encounter a host of objections:

- The government can't legislate morality.
- No one should force their morals on anyone else.
- As long as I don't hurt anyone else, the government should leave me alone. Whatever consenting adults do is OK.
- We're a pluralistic society. We fundamentally disagree on values, so there are no common values to legislate.
- Legislated morality is not enforceable because the government can't force people to be good—just look at Prohibition!
- We can't legislate morality because doing so involves religion, and that's a violation of the separation of church and state.
- Laws can't change hearts.

In the following eleven chapters, we will provide direct answers to these objections and present our thesis, which is: (1) Legislating morality is literally unavoidable (morality is *always* legislated), and (2) Americans should legislate the morality common to us all—the one expressed in our *Declaration of Independence*, the Constitution, and, until recently, the laws of our land and decisions of the Supreme Court.

The book is divided into four parts. Part I addresses the question "Can we legislate morality?" Chapter 1 will deal with the question "Is legislating morality constitutional?" Chapter 2 will tackle the problem of enforcement. And chapter 3 will address ethical questions about legislating morality; specifically, should the government be permitted to "cram morals down your throat"? *Along the way, we will show that all political groups—liberals, moderates, and conservatives—are trying to legislate morality.*

Part II examines "How has morality been legislated?" Chapter 4 will uncover the roots of the nation's recent moral decline, tracing the seed back to Charles Darwin. Chapters 5 and 6 will show how this moral decline has been legislated in our country since 1961 without the vote of a single citizen or member of Congress.

Part III explores the question "Whose morality should we legislate?" Chapter 7 settles the argument of whether my morality or your morality should be legislated. The answer, fully presented in chapter 8, is neither mine nor yours—the morality common to all of us (*our* morality) should be legislated!

Part IV explains how we should legislate "our" morality on the most controversial issues of the day. Chapter 9 applies "our" common morality to homosexuality, chapter 10 applies it to abortion, and chapter 11 applies it to euthanasia. The epilogue wraps it all up by answering the question "Where should we go from here?"

We realize that we're marching through what seems like a minefield of objections. Nevertheless, it is our hope that you will proceed through this book with an open mind, receptive to examining all of the chapters rather than giving in to the temptation to jump to a preconceived conclusion. In fact, we *dare* you to do so, and we will welcome any reasoned rebuttal!

We hope that this systematic approach to our nation's moral problems will help get our country back on track again. For we agree with French historian Alexis de Tocqueville, who predicted that *America will cease to be great when it ceases to be good.*

DR. NORMAN L. GEISLER is author or coauthor of some fifty books and hundreds of articles. He has taught at the university and graduate level for nearly forty years and has spoken or debated in all fifty states and in twenty-five countries. He holds a Ph.D. in philosophy from Loyola University and now serves as Dean of the Veritas Graduate School in Charlotte, North Carolina.

FRANK S. TUREK III holds a Master's in Public Administration and has taught courses in leadership and management at George Washington University. He is a professional speaker and consultant who creates and conducts training programs for businesses nationwide. He is completing a second Master's degree, this one at the Veritas Graduate School.

CONTENTS

PART I

CAN WE LEGISLATE MORALITY?

1. IS IT CONSTITUTIONAL?

2. IS IT ENFORCEABLE?

3. IS IT ETHICAL?

CAN WE LEGISLATE MORALITY?

1. IS IT CONSTITUTIONAL?

"If men were angels no government would be necessary."
—James Madison

AMERICA'S MORAL FREE FALL

It's no secret that America has been experiencing a moral crisis over the last few decades. As we documented in the preface, an alarming number of moral and cultural problems have exploded in our country since 1960.[1]

This moral free fall has both liberals and conservatives joining hands to express their concerns. In fact, former Secretary of Education William Bennett, one of the leading conservative voices in the nation, recently teamed up with liberal leader C. Delores Tucker, head of the National Political Congress of Black Women, to protest violent and sexually explicit rap music that was being sold under Time-Warner record labels. Bennett and Tucker challenged Time-Warner executives to stop putting out such morally offensive and violence-inciting material. But despite their direct and passionate pleas, these two high-profile, concerned citizens got no commitment from the company's

Board of Directors to self-censor their products. In fact, after the executives refused even to answer whether they thought the music in question was below some minimum line of human decency, Bennett aimed right for the heart by asking them if they were "morally disabled."[2]

This refusal to conduct self-censorship should come as no surprise. We're living in a society in which people feel no obligation to control their own actions. Instead, we rationalize and justify every aberrant behavior under the umbrella of freedoms granted by the First Amendment, never admitting that freedom without reasonable and responsible limits destroys individual lives and ultimately destroys the fabric of a civilized society. Since many in our country seem to have "disabled" their sense of morality, that fabric has been unraveling over the last generation.

WE CAN'T LEGISLATE MORALITY?

People are looking everywhere for answers, including the government. In fact, the Republican revolution of 1994 that swept away forty years of Democratic control in Congress was largely the doing of the religious and social conservatives who said they wanted the government to provide the moral leadership necessary to help get this country back on track. But, of course, if you believe the popular wisdom, the so-called "religious right" is going to be disappointed because everyone knows that "you can't legislate morality."

Just think ... those religious and social conservatives went through all that organizing, all that fund-raising, and all that campaigning for nothing. They made it to the big show and now they can't deliver. What a shame. If they had only known, like the rest of us, that *you can't legislate morality*, maybe they could have saved themselves all that trouble!

Of course, clichés rarely impart the whole truth. Just ask Democratic members of the House Agriculture Committee, who lost a battle over food stamps early in the new Republican Congress. On March 7, 1995, Republicans on the committee voted to reduce $16.5 billion from the $149 billion that had been designated for food stamps over the next five years. Committee Democrats were furious. Earl Pomeroy from North Dakota said the food stamp proposals were "God-awful"; Representative Kika de

16

la Garza of Texas boldly asserted that "we have a responsibility as a nation and as a people—a *moral* responsibility—to see that in this, the greatest nation in the world, there is no hunger." Others echoed de la Garza by calling the bill "*immoral* and mean-spirited."[3]

One of the proposals considered but rejected by the committee would have prohibited the use of food stamps to buy coffee, tea, cocoa, candy, and other snack foods. Mark Foley, Republican from Florida, said that it was *wrong* for the government to subsidize "people's appetite for popcorn, potato chips, ice cream, Coca-Cola, and Gatorade." But Sam Farr, a Democrat from California, said that the committee was not authorized to "enforce morality."

Wait a minute—there seems to be an inconsistency here. On the one hand, committee members called the bill "immoral," yet, on the other, they said morality can't be legislated. How can a bill be "*im*moral" if it can't be moral? And how can our representatives fulfill their "moral responsibility" if it's impossible to legislate morality? Since the Democrats considered the cut in food stamps to be "immoral" legislation, wouldn't it stand to reason that they would regard an *increase* in funding as "moral" legislation? If they weren't fighting for moral legislation, then what were they fighting for? It appears that something's not right with the "you can't legislate morality" cliché. Let's take a closer look.

A COMMON SENSE OF JUSTICE

Do you remember how you felt the last time you were wronged—the last time someone took advantage of you and, for their own selfish gain, profited at your expense? Certainly that feeling of being treated unfairly came to you immediately. You knew intuitively that the other person was wrong, and any impartial observer—even a small child—would have agreed with you. You had an undeniable right to be upset, seek justice, and demand restitution from the guilty party.

After you went to that insensitive person and pointed out his error, maybe he realized he was wrong, confessed, and your friendship was restored. On the other hand, maybe the other person was so hardheaded that he refused to admit that he was wrong, and you felt so strongly about his despicable behavior that you ended the friendship.

Whatever finally happened in your situation, one thing was clear to you from the very beginning: You had no trouble distinguishing between what was fair and what was unfair. The instant you understood the situation, no one had to tell you to feel angry or betrayed—your sense of injustice came to you naturally.

"We hold these truths to be self-evident. . . ."

That same sense of injustice also came naturally to Thomas Jefferson and our other Founding Fathers over two hundred years ago. They, of course, felt wronged by the way the king of Britain had been governing the thirteen American colonies. In fact, Jefferson listed in the *Declaration of Independence* more than twenty-five of the king's offenses which, in Jefferson's view, had established "an absolute tyranny" over the colonies. According to Jefferson and the other signers of the *Declaration*, the king should not have taxed people without their representation and consent; he should not have cut off their trade with other parts of the world; he should not have burned their towns, plundered their seas, and ravaged their coasts, etc. And since the king refused to confess to those charges and change his ways, the colonists felt justified in ending their relationship with Great Britain by declaring their independence. (See the complete *Declaration of Independence* in Appendix I.)

When you really get down to the heart of the matter, the primary reason the colonists declared their independence was because they believed that the king of Britain was not legislating morally. In other words, the colonists believed that the edicts of the king were simply wrong. Unable to tolerate the situation any further, the colonists sought to replace the king's unjust legislation with their own just legislation. Their objection was not about legislating morality—they realized that all laws declare one behavior wrong and another right. Their objection centered around *whose morality was being legislated.* The colonists believed that the king was legislating the wrong morality—his edicts and actions were unfair and violated basic human rights.

When Thomas Jefferson pointed out the alleged violations of the king in the *Declaration of Independence*, he didn't appeal to the Bible or some other holy book to prove that the monarch was wrong. Instead, he recognized that the same sense of fairness

18

that came instinctively to him also came instinctively to the rest of the world. In fact, Jefferson was so confident that the king was obviously at fault that he began the long list of offenses with these words: "To prove this, let Facts be submitted to a candid world." In other words, Jefferson believed that the rest of the world—understanding this same sense of fairness—would agree that the colonists were clearly right and the king was clearly wrong.

Since this sense of fairness came naturally to all people, Jefferson appropriately referred to it as part of the "Laws of Nature." This was also known as "Natural Law," or the "Moral Law," or more commonly called "Conscience." From the Moral Law, Jefferson observed that the "self-evident," "unalienable Rights" of all people should be protected by a government established by the people. He wrote:

> We hold these truths to be self-evident, that all men are created equal, that they are endowed by their Creator with certain *unalienable Rights,* that among these are Life, Liberty and the pursuit of Happiness—That to secure *these rights,* Governments are instituted among Men, deriving their *just powers* from the consent of the governed (emphasis added).[4]

Notice the phrase "they are endowed by their Creator with certain unalienable Rights." In other words, the Founding Fathers believed that rights are God-given and, as such, they are universal and absolute—they are the rights of all people in all places at all times, regardless of nationality or religion. And since everyone is equal, no person has the moral authority to rule over or take away the rights of someone else. Governments are established to protect these rights of the people, and when a government fails to do so, according to the Founding Fathers, "it is the Right of the People to alter or to abolish it, and to institute new Government...." That is what our Founding Fathers believed, and it is the basis on which our country began.

In other words, Jefferson and the other Founding Fathers believed that there was a higher authority—the "Creator"—to whom they could appeal to establish objective moral grounds for their independence. Had they begun the *Declaration of Independence* with "We hold these *opinions* as our own..." they wouldn't have had an objective moral justification for their declaration. It simply would have been their opinions against those of the king.

So the Founding Fathers appealed to the Creator because they believed His Moral Law was the ultimate standard of right and wrong that would justify their cause.

In a sense, the Founding Fathers were in the same position as the Allied countries after World War II. When the Nazi war criminals were brought to trial in Nuremburg, they were convicted of violating the Moral Law (which is manifested in international law)—the law that all people inherently understand. If there was no such international morality that transcended the laws of the secular German government, then the Allies would have had no grounds to condemn the Nazis. In other words, we couldn't have said that Hitler was absolutely wrong unless we knew what was absolutely right.

Like our World War II leaders, our Founding Fathers had the Moral Law to tell them what was absolutely right, and they indicated as much in the *Declaration of Independence*. In effect, the *Declaration* was the moral statement that would later become the foundation for the Constitution of the new nation. Through it, our founders confirmed that establishing a morality was unavoidable, for the declaration itself establishes a morality, and that morality was derived from the Moral Law—the law not everyone obeys, but the law by which everyone expects to be treated.[5]

Since they believed that the king had violated the "self-evident" morality, the founders were ready to pay the ultimate price to restore it. The last line of the *Declaration* contains these words: "And for the support of this Declaration, with a firm reliance on the protection of divine Providence, we mutually pledge to each other our Lives, our Fortunes and our Sacred Honor." In other words, the founders believed so strongly in the right to establish morality through legislation that they promised to die for it. However, it is critical to recognize that the founders were pledging their lives to restore not *someone's* revealed religion, but *everyone's* self-evident morality. That's a critical distinction we need to talk more about.

RELIGION, NO! MORALITY, YES!

Many of the world's governments have been based on either religious doctrine or secular ideas. Religious governments get their charge from someone's sacred scripture, while secular governments simply codify the beliefs of whoever happens to be in power. Both types have significant disadvantages: religious governments frequently experience doctrinal struggles and often create an environment of intolerance toward those of other faiths; and secular governments—since they are based on nothing more than the personal opinions of their rulers—have a tendency to lose stability and violate the rights of the people when corrupt rulers take power. The Founding Fathers wanted to avoid these two extremes.

Since they had firsthand experience with the first extreme, the founders wanted to steer clear of a government-mandated religion for the United States. In England, government religion led to acts of religious intolerance that violated unalienable human rights. The Founders wanted to ensure that the citizens of this new nation did not make the same mistake as their mother country. They realized that since God doesn't *force* anyone to adhere to one set of religious beliefs, neither should the government do so.

On the other hand, the Founders were realistic people who believed that absolute power corrupts absolutely. Neither did they want the instability and abuse of power characteristic of a secular government. As a result, they brilliantly developed the perfect third alternative to the religious/secular dilemma. Instead of creating their own secular system, or adopting laws directly from an existing religion, the Founders wisely based the laws of the United States on the Moral Law. After all, the government's function is not to create rights or to settle theological debates, but, according to the *Declaration of Independence*, it is "to *secure* [the unalienable] rights" of the people (emphasis added).

Again, it is critical to recognize that they based our government and its morality on God, not on religion. You may be thinking, "How could they invoke God without invoking religion?" Simple. They believed that since all people, regardless of culture, have this same "Moral" Law imposed on their minds, *someone* had to impose it. After all, since every effect has a cause, the Moral Law must have a Moral Lawgiver. Our Founding Fathers didn't need religion to figure that out.

It is also important to note that even though the Founders believed the Rights of the people came from God, they did not insist that every citizen *believe* in God; they simply saw no way to *justify* those natural moral Rights unless there *was* a God.

CAN WE LEGISLATE MORALITY?

Hence, they set up a form of government that would recognize and protect God-given Rights without establishing a government religion or creating an environment of intolerance. This was important to the founders because they considered religious freedom to be an "unalienable Right," even though they didn't specify it in the *Declaration of Independence*. (They did so in the First Amendment to the Constitution.)

"Congress shall make no law. . . ."

After Thomas Jefferson identified the Moral Law as the foundation of the nation's laws in the *Declaration of Independence*, James Madison and other Founding Fathers legislated those laws and "unalienable Rights" in the Constitution. The First Amendment, of course, is the one that deals with religion. It reads: "Congress shall make no law respecting an establishment of religion, or prohibiting the free exercise thereof; or abridging the freedom of speech, or of the press; or the right of the people peaceably to assemble, and to petition the Government for a redress of grievances." (See the complete Constitution: Appendix II.)

The key point is this: While the First Amendment clearly forbids the federal government from establishing a national religion, it does not prohibit the government from establishing a national morality. In fact, the First Amendment itself is a law that helps establish a national morality: it clearly implies that it is *wrong* for Congress to establish a religion or to prohibit the free exercise of religion; it also implies that any congressional attempt to abridge freedom of speech, the press, or assembly is morally wrong. The Founding Fathers obviously were convinced that it would be immoral for Congress to restrict these freedoms. In other words, they believed these freedoms were morally *right* and needed to be protected through legislation.

The same holds true for the other amendments adopted by the Founding Fathers, commonly known as the Bill of Rights: Unreasonable searches and seizures are *wrong* (the Fourth Amendment); it is *not right* to deprive people of life, liberty, or property without due process of law (the Fifth Amendment); cruel and unusual punishments are *wrong* (the Eight Amendment), etc.

But perhaps the most famous example of legislating morality came in the form of a constitutional amendment that was adopted seventy-five years after ratification of the Bill of Rights. It pertained to an extremely divisive issue that partially fueled the War Between the States. The issue, of course, was slavery, which was outlawed, or—to put it bluntly—declared morally wrong by the Thirteenth Amendment on self-evident moral grounds. This is *the* classic example of legislating morality, and no reasonable person would declare that legislating against slavery was beyond the legitimate role of government.

A decade or so later, in declaring its opposition to polygamy, even the Supreme Court upheld the right of the government to legislate morality. In the *Reynolds v. United States* decision of 1878, the Supreme Court outlawed polygamy, which was being practiced by Mormons in Utah, by appealing to the fact that Americans were a "Christian people" in the moral sense of the term. Here, the court used acknowledged moral principles to override a religious practice to the contrary. In a similar situation, the Court recently ruled that Native Americans could not use illegal drugs (such as peyote) in their religious ceremonies. These cases illustrate that the Court has considered the accepted national morality so important that even some religious practices had to give way to it.

To bring things closer to home, the civil rights legislation of the '50s and '60s provides another example of morality being legislated. Once our country finally had the courage to admit that it is clearly wrong to discriminate against people simply because of their race, we rightly legislated against it. Of course, we didn't immediately stamp out racism in the hearts of people by passing a law, but we clearly legislated morality by criminalizing racist behavior. In other words, *we legislated and thus imposed one set of values on everyone in society, in order to protect the "unalienable Rights" of one segment of our society. According to the* Declaration of Independence, *that is exactly what government is designed to do: "That to secure these rights, Governments are instituted among Men."* Martin Luther King Jr. put it best when he said, "It may be true that the law cannot make a man love me. But it can keep him from lynching me, and I think that's pretty important."[6]

Of course, we didn't only legislate morality in the 1860s and the 1960s. The issues gripping our country today—rights of the unborn, women's rights, gay rights, minority rights, religious rights—have people on all sides trying to legislate their particular morality. To take the most volatile example: conservatives claim that abortion is morally wrong because they believe it ends the life of an innocent human being; liberals claim that since a woman has a moral right to control her own body, she should also have the right to choose an abortion. Notice that each side in this ongoing debate believes it has a moral justification for its position, and each side continually seeks to legislate that position (the "pro-choice" morality has been legislated—or, more correctly, judicially implemented—since 1973). The same can be said for any of the other issues mentioned above because anyone who says, "There oughta be a law that . . ." is trying to legislate morality.

A MORAL COMMON SENSE

We also legislate morality on much less controversial issues such as murder, rape, theft, child abuse, etc. These have all been prohibited by legislation since the founding of our country. But some people don't believe these issues actually constitute "legislating morality" because they say that they aren't really moral issues—they're common sense issues. To which we respond: "Exactly! You've just discovered the Moral Law, which, by definition, is a moral kind of common sense." In fact, most moral issues would not be controversial if everyone obeyed the Moral Law.

Still, some may be thinking: "If everyone knows this Moral Law intuitively, why isn't it more apparent to everyone? And why do we have disagreements over what's right and wrong?"

We'll address the right and wrong issue fully in chapter 3, but right now we want to reemphasize that the Moral Law actually *is* clear to everyone. It is evident by a person's *reactions* rather than by his or her *actions*. For example, you may not be conscious of the Moral Law when you lie to someone (your action); but when someone lies to you, the Moral Law becomes bright as the sun, because being lied to upsets you as soon as you realize it (your reaction). In this same way, the Moral Law came clearly to Thomas Jefferson and the other Founding Fathers because they believed that they were recipients of unjust treatment by the king. Their reaction is emphatically expressed in the *Declaration of Independence*.

So what we're saying is that *the Moral Law is not always the standard by which we treat others, but it is nearly always the standard by which we expect others to treat us.* It does not describe how we behave, but how we expect others to behave. In other words, it is not the way people *do* behave but the way people *ought to* behave. And that's exactly what good laws are supposed to do—legislate "oughts" and "ought nots."

CONCLUSION

When you think about it, all laws declare directly, or by implication, that one behavior is right and its opposite is wrong. In other words, all good laws are just laws, and to legislate justice is to legislate morality. Since securing justice is, in fact, the primary function of our government, *legislating morality is not only constitutional but unavoidable and necessary. The only question is "Whose morality should be legislated?"*

The Founding Fathers employed the morality based on the Moral Law and codified it in our Constitution and civil laws. We should use the same objective standard when writing laws today. We'll talk about how we can do this in chapters 9, 10, and 11.

But before we do that, we must first deal with the question "Even though legislating morality is constitutional, is it enforceable?" That's the subject we'll discuss in chapter 2.

CAN WE LEGISLATE MORALITY?

2. IS IT ENFORCEABLE?

"Nothing that is morally wrong can ever be politically right."
—Anonymous

When people say, "You can't legislate morality," they usually mean either one of two things: (1) that it's impossible to *enact* moral laws, or (2) that it's impossible to *enforce* moral laws. We've already shown in chapter 1 why the first objection is not valid: Laws normally have moral implications because they declare explicitly one behavior to be "right" and another to be "wrong." (Even traffic and seat belt laws are based on the fact that we believe that it's morally right to prevent death and injury.) As we have seen, it's impossible to legislate without legislating morality.

The second objection—the problem of enforceability—is the one we'll address here. Those who cite this objection claim that morals should not be legislated because they cannot be enforced. You've heard their reasoning:

- "They're going to do it anyway!"
- "You can't make people be good!"

- "Laws can't change hearts!"

We'll address each one of these claims below. But first, let's tackle the trump card typically played to prove that morality can't be legislated and enforced: Prohibition.

"WHAT ABOUT PROHIBITION?"

Those who object to "legislating morality" usually cite the aborted attempt at prohibition to prove their point. Prohibition (1920–1933), the law prohibiting the manufacture and sale of intoxicating alcoholic beverages, was clearly an attempt to legislate morality, which was overturned, partly due to problems with enforcement. However, Prohibition did not prove that morality cannot be legislated or enforced. Those who assert that it did make a number of erroneous assumptions.

Erroneous Assumption #1: Prohibition was a complete failure.

When people say that "Prohibition failed," they usually mean that it could not keep people from drinking. This is, of course, true, but no law is 100 percent successful. We need to take a closer look at Prohibition before judging its success or failure.

To understand the objective behind Prohibition, it is important to understand the history leading up to the Amendment. The Eighteenth Amendment, which was ratified in 1919, came about only after a long process of activism against alcohol (led largely by sober women fed up with drunk men). This anti-alcohol movement wasn't as much motivated by a moral objection to drinking as it was by the immorality, family dysfunction, and criminal activity that drinking spawned.

In the 1830s, with whiskey considered legal tender, annual per capita consumption of hard alcohol (i.e., 80-proof whiskey) reached a staggering 7.1 gallons.[1] In some cases, even preachers were "paid" with whiskey! Alcoholism and its related problems—crime, family violence, incompetence in shops and factories, gambling, etc.—became so troublesome between 1820 and 1850 that some began to refer to our country as the "Alcoholic Republic." This prompted politicians such as Thomas Jefferson, James Madison, and, later, Abraham Lincoln to urge abstinence for the good of family and country.

Jefferson thought it best to urge voluntary abstinence. But

twenty-five years after his death, with little sobriety achieved by voluntary means, the states began to legislate against alcohol. In 1851 Maine became the first state to go "dry," and by 1855 thirteen of thirty-one states had such laws. By 1916, twenty-one states had banned saloons, and dry members of Congress outnumbered their "wet" colleagues two to one, setting the stage for the Amendment in 1919.

Prohibition on a national scale went into effect in 1920, and was repealed in 1933 by the Twenty-First Amendment. Despite its legal reversal, a good argument can be made that Prohibition did not fail in its intended purpose of sobering the country up. Alcohol consumption dropped dramatically during Prohibition. Norman H. Clark writes, "Although determining the extent of drinking by any group at that time is difficult, Prohibition was at least partly effective. Records show that annual per capita consumption stood at 2.60 gallons for the period 1906 to 1910, before state dry laws had much impact. In 1934, when accurate statistics were again available, the figure was less than a gallon, and even as late as 1945, it was only two gallons."[2] While consumption slowly began to rise during the latter 1920s as contempt for the law grew, it wasn't until 1975 that per capita consumption rose to what it had been before Prohibition![3] In other words, upon repeal of Prohibition, Americans didn't immediately resume their old pre–1920 drinking habits. Prohibition seems to have had a long-lasting effect on the attitude of the nation toward alcohol.

Moreover, by significantly reducing alcohol consumption, Prohibition also cut down the physical, psychological, and social abuse connected with it. Former U.S. Health and Welfare Secretary Joseph Califano writes, "During Prohibition, admission to mental health institutions for alcohol psychosis dropped 60 percent; arrests for drunk and disorderly conduct went down 50 percent; welfare agencies reported significant declines in cases due to alcohol-related family problems, and the death rate from impure alcohol did not rise. Nor did Prohibition generate a crime wave. Homicide increased at a higher rate between 1900 and 1910 than during Prohibition, and organized crime was well established in the cities before 1920."[4] Thus, those who cite Prohibition as a failure overlook these significant beneficial aspects.

Erroneous Assumption #2: Laws with enforcement problems should be repealed.

Most opponents of prohibition cite problems with enforcement in their argument against having such a law. However, the moral rightness or wrongness of a law is not determined by whether its enforcement is successful or unsuccessful. Enforcement against murder is less than completely effective, but that doesn't mean laws against murder should be repealed. If enforcement were the standard, then we should repeal laws against car theft. After all, car theft is getting very difficult to enforce in the United States. In fact, we've always found it difficult to enforce a number of our laws, including laws against murder, spouse and child abuse, rape, and theft, yet no sane person would ever suggest that these laws should be repealed because they're difficult to enforce. Enforceability isn't the issue. The issue is whether a particular activity is right or wrong. We should legislate against what is objectively wrong regardless of whether or not it's difficult to enforce.

Police enforcement of Prohibition was a problem for three major reasons: (1) people could make booze themselves with legal ingredients; (2) the vast land areas, borders, and sea lanes that needed to be patrolled made it virtually impossible for the police to stop rum-runners; and (3) in many cases the police didn't want to stop them because the police had a piece of the action themselves!

But the fact that there was a widespread breakdown in law enforcement of Prohibition does not necessarily mean the law was wrong. First, even though ingredients for fertilizer bombs, like ingredients for moonshine, are easy to get (as Oklahoma City bomber Timothy McVeigh showed), we don't argue that laws against fertilizer bombs should be repealed. Second, our vast land areas, borders, and sea lanes make nearly *all* laws difficult to enforce, not only prohibition. For example, we have a hard time keeping illegal aliens from entering the U.S., yet even most liberals do not want to repeal all immigration laws and allow anyone and everyone to walk across unopposed. This would certainly threaten both the viability and security of the nation. Finally, when law enforcement is corrupt, the solution is to correct the bad enforcement, not discard the good law—if, in fact, the law is a good one. (Indeed, that is exactly what the

Wickersham Commission recommended in 1931, after completing its research on the successes and failures of Prohibition.[5]) In other words, instead of claiming that the laws need to change, maybe the enforcement efforts need to change. If something really should be illegal, it's better to improve enforcement than repeal the law.

Erroneous Assumption #3: Repeal of Prohibition didn't legislate morality.

Those who oppose Prohibition overlook the fact that their view also legislates morality. It says that it is morally right to make strong alcoholic beverages available to any adult who wants them. It believes it is morally wrong to pass laws that forbid alcohol purchase and consumption, even knowing the abuses that may result from it. In other words, the opponents of Prohibition also want a morality—*their morality*—put into law.

The alleged failure of Prohibition acts as a smoke-screen to hide the real issue. The real issue is that everyone's opinion on alcohol legislation is based on some kind of moral belief. Those who use Prohibition as an example of why we cannot legislate morality simply wish to legislate a different morality. In fact, as we have shown, legislating morality is inescapable. The only question is, whose morality will be legislated? In 1920 the morality of the Prohibitionists was legislated; in 1933 the morality of the anti-Prohibitionists was legislated.

Erroneous Assumption #4: Over-legislating morality proves morality can't be legislated.

Let's assume for the sake of argument that Prohibition was not a wise law. Does this mean that no legislation concerning any addictive drugs, including alcohol, should be made? By no means. Even most people who favor the repeal of Prohibition are glad for laws against drunk drivers that make the roads safer for them and their families. The alleged failure of Prohibition does not prove that we cannot legislate morality, but that we should not over-legislate morality. That is, Prohibition did not negate the possibility of enforceable, moral legislation. At best, Prohibition only provided us with an example of what can happen when morality is over-legislated.

Today we're still legislating morality with regard to alcohol. The morality imposed today no longer prohibits the manufacture and sale of intoxicating alcoholic beverages, but allows use only as long as that use stays within the boundaries of reasonable protection for all. For example, since there's a great potential for harm to the drinker and to others, we've set limits and conditions on alcoholic consumption: You must be at least twenty-one years of age, and you must not use it irresponsibly. Certainly groups like Mother's Against Drunk Driving (MADD) and Students Against Drunk Driving (SADD) are not over-legislating morality by pushing for stronger laws against drunk driving.[6] Laws that prohibit minors from buying alcoholic beverages and laws that limit the alcohol content of such beverages do not constitute cases of over-legislating morality.

Present laws allow people to drink, but they also punish those who get behind the wheel and put themselves and others at risk. And despite the fact that enforcing drunk driving or underage drinking laws is difficult, few are suggesting we do away with these laws. What the anti-Prohibitionist overlooks is that such restrictions on drinking are also cases of legislating morality—the very thing they insist we should not be doing. The fact is that laws that save lives—whether they are fastening our seat belts or putting less alcohol under our belts—are good laws.

While the debate continues about whether we have gone far enough to protect society from alcohol abuse, there should be no debate about whether or not it is right to legislate against such abuse. As with virtually any liberty, America recognizes that the liberty to drink is not absolute. A person's liberty to drink ends where the exercise of his liberty threatens his life or the life of others. Individual liberties are one thing, but self-destruction or the destruction of others is another. There is no true liberty to destroy one's own life or that of another. And that's exactly why legislating morality is necessary—moral laws are needed to recognize where a person's fist ends and your nose begins.

"THEY'RE GOING TO DO IT ANYWAY!"

At a time when many Americans want to reverse the steady moral decline in our country through tougher laws and more severe punishments for criminals, there are a few prominent liberals and conservatives (and, of course, libertarians) who believe that we can alleviate the crime problem altogether by simply legalizing what is now considered illegal.

The legalization of illegal drugs is one example. That's what William Buckley argues from the Right, and what former Surgeon General Joycelyn Elders asks us to consider from the Left. Underlying their position is the admission that our government finds it very difficult to enforce anti-drug laws (the same trouble we had with Prohibition). Many who agree with legalization figure, "Since *they're going to do it anyway* and we can't do much to stop them, we might as well get something out of it." After all, think of the tax revenue that legalized drugs could generate, and the savings in law enforcement costs, not to mention the complete elimination of a black market that draws our inner city youth into a life of violence and crime. Eleanor Clift, panelist on the weekly TV talk show *The McLaughlin Group*, made a similar case for prostitution on a recent program. Ms. Clift argued for legalization by asserting that "[prostitution] is the oldest profession in the world. We're not going to stop it."[7]

Ms. Clift is correct in saying that we're not going to stop prostitution completely by having laws against it. And, as Buckley and Elders assert, laws aren't going to end drug use either. However, there are two serious problems with this type of argument. First, while laws may not stop prostitution or drug use completely, they certainly reduce the frequency of such activities. (More on this later in the chapter.)

Second, to see the fallacy of the argument, apply that logic to any of the crime problems we are experiencing in this country. Take murder, for example. Even though we have a law against it, there will always be some people out there who are going to kill other people. Should we legalize murder in order to save law enforcement costs because "people are going to do it anyway?" What about child abuse, spouse abuse, and racism? People have always abused children, spouses, and those of other races, and laws against those crimes have always been difficult to enforce. Should we do away with those laws as well?

Of course, no one would suggest that we do away with such laws. But some people may be thinking, "The comparison of drug use and prostitution to murder and child abuse is invalid because the first affects only consenting adults while the latter harms innocent people." They may believe that drug use and prostitution are "victimless" crimes, and, therefore, shouldn't be outlawed; in other words, whatever consenting adults do should not be outlawed. But allowing consenting adults to do as they please actually imposes negative effects on others. We'll discuss how this happens in chapters 3 and 9.

For now, our point is this: Laws in the United States, as we discussed in chapter 1, should be designed to protect the "unalienable Rights" of the people. They should not be based on what people do, but on what is right as defined by the Moral Law. In other words, by definition, laws are prescriptive—they *prescribe* what *ought* to be done, while behaviors are descriptive—they *describe* what *is* being done. If everyone were to commit murder, that wouldn't make murder right. And it certainly wouldn't be wise to discard all laws against murder because enforcement is difficult.

In other words, we have (and should have) laws against activities that are clear violations of the Moral Law. If the behavior is objectively evil, the question of enforceability is irrelevant. We must get back to evaluating laws based upon the rightness or wrongness of the activity in question, not on the issue of cost, enforceability, or how many people in the country are "doing it."

"YOU CAN'T MAKE PEOPLE BE GOOD!"

You've no doubt heard this objection to legislating morality: "You can't make people be good!" In a certain sense, this objection is valid. Most effective laws are designed to restrain evil rather than to compel good. However, some laws in our country actually go beyond simply restraining evil and enter the realm of compelling good.

For example, laws that *compel you to do* something rather than *prohibit you from doing* something include: (1) Taxes. You are compelled to pay taxes, which go toward maintaining a compassionate, safe, and livable society (*supposedly* accomplished through government expenditures on welfare, police, national defense, environmental protection, roads, etc.); (2) Military Service. Upon reaching the age of eighteen years, men are compelled to register with the Selective Service so the nation will be prepared to defend itself in time of war; (3) Education. Parents are compelled to educate their children in either a public, private, or home school because education is a "good" thing; (4) Justice. We are compelled to serve on jury duty when called in order to keep the wheels of justice turning; (5) Safety. When traveling in a car, we are compelled to secure our children in a child restraint seat.

So even if laws can't make people *be* good morally, they can compel us to *do* good socially.

This "You can't make people be good!" objection is closely related to another criticism of legislating morality: the belief that "laws can't change hearts." The logic behind this view (held by both conservatives and liberals) says that "laws can't fix the problem; the only true way to change behavior is to change the attitudes or the hearts of people." Conservatives (particularly religious conservatives) often say that hearts and attitudes are changed by God as a result of a religious commitment. Liberals (particularly humanists) say that such changes occur solely through the personal willpower of the individual or by behavioral modification. Both methods may do so, but conservatives and liberals both fail to acknowledge the power of law to change hearts and attitudes. Let's take a closer look.

"LAWS CAN'T CHANGE HEARTS!"

My (Frank's) seven-year-old son is quite strong willed (much like his father). Although he usually obeys the rules, sometimes he can become outright defiant. One day, not long ago, my wife—frustrated after dealing with three whiny little boys all day—asked him to stop complaining every time she asked him to do something. After he made some smart-aleck remark back to her (exactly what she was asking him to *stop* doing), I glared at him sternly and commanded, "Don't you argue with your mother!" He immediately shot back, "Why not? You always do!" (You know, I've found that I really don't like dealing with someone who is like me, even if he is only seven years old!)

Of course, many of you know exactly what we mean by strong-willed children. Keeping them within set boundaries can be difficult, especially if you don't like constant warfare (my son has an answer for everything). And even when you do get them to comply, you've got to repeat yourself two minutes later because they're doing it again. It seems they comply on the outside, but on the inside they remain intent on rebelling.

This illustrates the objection that "laws can't change hearts." After I lay down the law, my son may sit down on the outside (his behavior), but he's no doubt still yelling and jumping on the inside (his attitude). And as soon as I—the authority figure—turn my head, his attitude emerges again. So the logic of the objection goes like this: Since laws really can't change people, and the police can't always be there to enforce compliance, why bother trying to enact moral laws at all? This objection ignores at least three very important facts.

The first is that even if laws do not change hearts, they are necessary to restrain evil. Their primary intent is not to *change hearts* but to *restrain actions*. Even libertarians acknowledge that some limits must be put on human behavior to protect life, liberty, and property. Restraining evil is necessary because letting people do whatever they want, whenever they want is harmful to all. Liberty is not absolute. We saw what absolute liberty—rampant freedom—did to South Central Los Angeles during the riots following the Rodney King verdict in 1992. Within a few hours the community was torn apart. The fact is, moral laws are essential to the survival of a functioning society. A lawless society is self-destructive.

We acknowledge this reality in our homes. Despite the difficulty in getting strong-willed children to comply with proper rules, few believe that scrapping all rules and allowing kids to do whatever they want would be in the best interest of all concerned. (Most five-year-olds would play video games all day and dine on candy every night if we let them.) Parents recognize that children are human beings, and since human beings are not indestructible, reasonable limits on behavior are necessary to secure the continued well-being of everyone. These limits must be established despite the fact that parents can't always be there to enforce them. As parents, it's our goal to ensure that—given enough instruction, repetition, and discipline—our children will obey our rules even when we're not there.

The second fact ignored by the objection is that the vast majority of people will obey the vast majority of laws even in the absence of visible law enforcement (just like we hope our kids will do). Despite the fact that a larger percentage of people are committing crimes today than they were thirty-five years ago (again, violent crime is up 550 percent since 1960), studies show that less than 10 percent of all *criminals* commit about two-thirds of all crimes.[8]

Most people are law-abiding citizens who don't require someone constantly looking over their shoulder to keep them in line. In other words, the law, aside from law enforcement, has a certain restraining effect in itself. So when immoral behavior is legalized (the restraining effect of the law is removed), that behavior eventually loses its stigma of immorality. This is because many believe that whatever is legal is moral. That's why legalization only results in more immoral behavior.[9]

The third missed fact—and the most important of all—is this: *Even though laws don't change hearts overnight, they often help change attitudes over the long term.* Both conservatives and liberals miss this reality when they claim that "laws can't change hearts." Let's take three of the most divisive issues in the history of our nation to prove our point.

We'll start with slavery. One hundred and forty years ago, there was so much controversy over the question of slavery that many people thought it better to divide the nation and kill their own relatives rather than agree on a legislative solution. Today, apart from the tiny fraction of racist extremists in this country, everybody believes that slavery is morally wrong. Did hearts and attitudes change overnight because we outlawed slavery? No. Behavior changed because slave owners didn't want to go to jail, but the law did help change pro-slavery attitudes over the long term. Legislating against slavery helped change attitudes because the majority of people have always believed that whatever is illegal must also be immoral (and vice versa). Before the Civil War, slave owners could rationalize the obvious immorality of slavery under the cover of "it's legal." Afterward, the law didn't provide that convenient excuse, and attitudes slowly changed.

Believe it or not, Prohibition is also an example of how laws affect attitudes. Even though 73 percent of the delegates at the state constitutional conventions voted to repeal Prohibition in 1933, Americans didn't immediately resume their old pre–1920 drinking habits. As we mentioned earlier, it wasn't until 1975 that per capita consumption rose to what it had been before Prohibition. There might have been other factors that kept people from drinking as much in the '30s and '40s (e.g., the Depression, WWII, and the fact that some states remained dry). But given the advances in manufacturing, distributing, communication, and advertising (i.e., TV) in the '50s and '60s, one would think per capita drinking would have surpassed pre-Prohibition levels much earlier than 1975 if Prohibition truly had no long-lasting effect on personal attitudes. The illegality hangover from Prohibition in the minds of the nation's older population seems to be the most plausible reason why per capita drinking remained at a lower level for quite some time.

Finally, abortion, the most divisive issue in our nation today, also provides an example of the power of law on attitudes. For nearly the first two hundred years of our nation's history, abortion was outlawed in all cases unless the mother's life was in danger. (In 1967, a few states such as New York began to include rape and incest as other legal exceptions, but abortion on demand remained illegal.) So when the Supreme Court decided *Roe v. Wade* in 1973 by a vote of seven to two, they overturned two hundred years of judicial and legislative precedent as well as the laws of every state—all fifty—which prohibited abortion. In effect, seven unelected judges reversed the expressed will of the majority by judicial fiat. And when all fifty states have outlawed something, the prevailing attitude of the country is not hard to figure out: In 1973 the vast majority of Americans believed that abortion was immoral.

Today the country is about evenly split. What happened? Why has there been such a change in attitude about abortion since 1973? Simple: The law was changed. In a situation the reverse of slavery, what was once considered illegal (and thus immoral) became sanctioned by the federal government. Couple the impact of the law change with the fact that abortion has since been advertised as a "safe" procedure performed by respected and trusted medical doctors to "terminate a pregnancy," and we can understand why more people now believe that abortion is morally acceptable (or at least morally neutral) than twenty-five years ago. The history of abortion, like that of slavery and Prohibition, shows that laws can change hearts and attitudes when given enough time.

CONCLUSION

We have seen that the objections against the enforceability of moral legislation are either wrong or miss the point:

- A good case can be made for legislating against all addictive drugs, including alcohol. And, in fact, we do legislate against them. Even if it is argued that Prohibition was a case of over-legislating morality, this certainly doesn't nullify the possibility of proper legislation. Indeed, even people *opposed* to

Prohibition want their moral view legislated. And although enforcing Prohibition was difficult, the law significantly reduced drinking and drinking-related problems from 1920 to 1933 and for some time after.

- "They're going to do it anyway" avoids the true issue of whether the activity is right or wrong. We outlaw many things (e.g., murder and child abuse) because they are clearly wrong, even though they're difficult to enforce. If ease of enforcement is the measure by which we impose laws against an immoral activity, our standards will continue to erode and evil will not be restrained.

- Even though many laws are difficult to enforce, most people obey them without the continuous presence of law enforcement. But since many believe that whatever is legal is moral, legalization of immorality will only result in more immoral behavior.

- Some laws actually do "make people be good," and, over the long term, laws have a demonstrated ability to change attitudes. Since laws can change attitudes, if we don't stand firm against legalizing immorality, we might eventually start calling evil "good"!

So legislating morality is constitutional (chapter 1) and must be done despite enforceability problems (chapter 2). However, another question remains: "Is it ethical? Should someone be able to 'cram *their* values down *your* throat'?" That's the issue we'll address in chapter 3.

3. IS IT ETHICAL?

"DON'T CRAM YOUR MORALS DOWN MY THROAT!"

Perhaps the most popular objection raised in the debate over legislating morality goes something like this: "You shouldn't try to impose your morals on other people, so stop trying to cram your religion or morals down my throat!"

Most Americans agree with this sentiment, especially as it pertains to religion. Few believe that it's right to impose one set of religious beliefs on the people of our nation. After all, we are not like Iran, where the government forces its citizens to live under the religious regulations of a particular faith (Islam). Our Founding Fathers valued religious freedom so much that they made it illegal for our government to establish one religion for the whole country. So in America, we believe it's unethical to cram religion down someone's throat.

But as we discussed in chapter 1, there is a critical difference between legislating *religion* and legislating *morality*. We can avoid legislating a particular religion, but we can't avoid legislating morality. All laws, by their very nature, declare one behavior to be right and another to be wrong. We need laws to maintain a safe and functioning society. So the only question is, "Whose morality do we legislate?"

As shown in chapter 1, there is really only one morality all people inherently understand. It is not the morality written *only* in religious books—it is the Moral Law written on our hearts. While none of us practices this self-evident Moral Law consistently, we all expect others to do so, especially when it comes to how they treat us. The principles of this Moral Law should be the principles we put into the laws of our land.

In later chapters, we'll discuss how we can apply this moral standard to specific issues in our country without "cramming" anyone's personal morality down our throats. But first, we need to deal with two issues in this chapter: (1) Is it ethical to impose moral values on others? and (2) Are moral values absolute or relative?

IMPOSING MORAL STANDARDS ON OTHERS IS UNAVOIDABLE

Ironically, those who most loudly protest legislating morality believe it is *morally wrong* for others to legislate morality. But therein lies the inconsistency. They are in effect saying, "You ought not to impose ought nots." That's merely another way of saying, "It's not moral to impose morals." The people who are supposedly against "legislating morality" are trying to impose on everyone else the moral position that moral positions should not be imposed on everyone! Obviously, this reasoning is self-defeating.

These people are inconsistent because they are not opposed to legislating *all* moral standards—only the standards that are not of their choosing. They do not wish to do away with moral standards completely (that would be impossible). They simply want to replace the existing moral standards with their own. A few examples relating to some controversial moral issues will illustrate what we mean.

Let's look first at capital punishment. Laws favoring capital punishment definitely impose a moral standard on others, namely, that those who intentionally kill the innocent should die for their crime. But opponents of capital punishment seek to impose their moral standard on both the victim and society. By opposing capital punishment, they are saying, in effect, the murder victim does not merit capital justice, and society need not be *forever* protected from repeat murderers. So whether you're for capital punishment or against it, your position imposes a form of morality on others. Again, the only question is, "Whose morality is the 'right' one to impose?"

Of course, you can't talk about "cramming morals down someone's throat" without the subject of abortion coming up. And it's widely believed that the "religious right" (read "pro-life") are the ones in this ongoing debate who want to do just that, while the "pro-choice" (read "pro-abortion") folks are the reasonable ones who don't want to impose anything on anyone. Nothing could be further from the truth. The fact is that both sides in the abortion debate are actively seeking to impose their own moral standards on the rest.

Everyone realizes what "pro-life" people want to impose: They want to protect the baby and thus impose on the mother the duty of carrying her child to term. But what is so often missed in this debate is that "pro-choice" activists want to impose their morals on others, as well: They want to impose the morals of the mother on the baby and, in some cases, on the father. When abortion is the choice, the morals imposed on the baby come in the form of a knife, a vacuum, or scalding chemicals. Such a choice also imposes on the biological father by depriving him of fatherhood and the right to protect his child.

In short, while the "pro-life" side wants to impose on the mother, the "pro-choice" side wants to impose on the baby and the father. In other words, both sides wish to impose their own morality on others. The question remains, which morality is the "right" morality to impose? We'll discuss this and the abortion issue in more detail in chapters 8 and 10.

But wait. What about libertarians? They want to allow consenting adults to do just about anything they want to do. They're not trying to impose their morality on others, are they? Actually, libertarians are no different than all the other folks on the political landscape in that they seek to impose their morality on others through the political process. They claim that liberty or freedom is virtually absolute, so consenting adults should be free to choose, express, or engage in virtually any activity, be it illicit sex, illegal drugs, abortion, etc. Libertarians seek to impose this morality by fighting for laws that allow unlimited free expression and personal liberty (or by trying to overturn laws that restrict such liberty).

The problem with the strong libertarian position is that total freedom for one individual cannot exist safely in a world where there are other people. Many individual freedoms must be limited or restricted to some degree because others may be harmed by them. Even the cherished freedoms in the First Amendment must be limited. For example, as strong as the right to free speech is, the Supreme Court has ruled that there is no right to enter a crowded building and scream "Fire!" when there is no fire. The truth of the matter is that *granting people too much freedom can be equally as harmful as restricting freedom too much because the negative effects of that freedom may be imposed on innocent people.*

Think about it this way: Imagine what would happen if we gave people the absolute freedom to do whatever they wanted to do—if we simply did away with all laws. Suppose someone could steal your car, for example, and kill you if you tried to take it back, only then to go on their merry way without punishment. Would there be *any* order or security? Clearly some moral standards need to be imposed in order to prevent anarchy and protect the innocent. We don't allow "consenting adults" to steal, rape, or murder because innocent people would be hurt. The fact is, if we didn't impose moral laws on everyone, people who would otherwise be criminals would impose their moral (rather, immoral) standards on innocent people.

"As long as you don't hurt someone else..."

Of course, even libertarians would agree that we need laws against rape, murder, theft, and child abuse regardless of whether or not "consenting adults" are involved. But what about the issues that seem to affect only the consenting adults themselves, such as prostitution or drug use? After all, aren't the libertarians and liberals right when they claim that "you should be able to do whatever you want to do as long as you don't hurt someone else?"

That argument sounds reasonable but it's a lot more complicated than it sounds. First of all, what does "hurt" mean? Does it only pertain to physical harm? Should someone be allowed to bring psychological or emotional harm against you without punishment? Apparently our courts don't think so: many people in our nation sue for such nonphysical damages and win huge monetary paybacks in court.

Second, many of the private acts libertarians claim are "victimless" actually can and do "hurt" other people. For example, legalizing prostitution would grant more freedom to some sexually consenting adults, but it would also impose an environment of immorality on you and your children if a "legal" house of prostitution set up shop next to your house. Such activity would further spread venereal diseases in the community, diseases which often infect innocent spouses. Likewise, decriminalizing drugs would give people more choices, but it would also legitimize activities that impose addiction, sickness, injury, and even death on individuals and their families.

The fact is, people don't live in a vacuum—no person is an island. Granting more freedom to everyone can negatively affect those who don't directly exercise that freedom. So the key point is this: *When libertarians or liberals seek to give people more freedom (i.e., by passing a law that legalizes a formerly illegal activity), they do exactly what they condemn conservatives for doing. They impose their morals (and thereby the associated effects) on people who do not agree with those morals.*

In the final analysis, those who say they want no morals imposed on others really want their own morals imposed on everyone. The truth is, all laws impose morals on others, good or bad. Good laws don't allow "anything goes"—they protect innocent people by limiting the freedom of others to do harm. And that means a good morality must be imposed. In other words—getting back to the subject of this chapter—legislating morality is not only ethical, it is also unavoidable and necessary for a functioning society. It is impossible *not* to legislate morality.

MORALITY: IS IT ABSOLUTE OR RELATIVE?

We've spoken much about the Moral Law in this book and how it helps every person distinguish right from wrong. The existence of the Moral Law has far-reaching implications. For when we say that the Moral Law impresses upon all people a fundamental sense of right and wrong, we are really saying that there are absolute moral values. *An absolute moral value is something that is binding on all people, at all times, in all places.*

But this goes completely against the prevailing wisdom of

our culture today. Many in our country, particularly the younger generation, believe that values are relative, not absolute. However, just because something is popular doesn't mean it's true. The fact is, relativism has some fatal problems.

Problem #1—Relativism is self-defeating.

Relativists usually make two primary truth claims: (1) There is no absolute truth, and (2) There are no absolute values. You can probably already see the problem with their first claim: If there really is no absolute truth, then the claim that "there is no absolute truth" can't be absolutely true. This is called a "self-defeating" statement. It's like saying, "I can't express myself in words." (What do you mean, "you can't express yourself in words"? You just did!) Or, you may hear a relativist say it this way: "That's true for you, but not for me!" Or this way: "There's no such thing as truth." When someone makes either of these claims, just ask, "Is *that* true?" You can see that the relativist's statements are irrational because they affirm exactly what they are trying to deny.

Even Joseph Fletcher, the father of modern situation ethics, falls into this trap. In his book *Situation Ethics,* Fletcher insists that "the situationist avoids words like 'never' and 'perfect' and 'always' . . . as he avoids the plague, as he avoids 'absolutely.' "[1] Of course, this is tantamount to claiming "One should never say 'never' " or "We should always avoid using the word 'always.' " But these very statements do not avoid what they say we must avoid. Relativists are *absolutely* sure there are no absolutes.

Like absolute truth, absolute values are also undeniable. To see our point, imagine you are having an intense discussion with a friend of yours who disagrees with your position. Suppose your friend is arguing that there are no absolute moral values; that people have different values, so there is no way you can say that you are right and the other people are wrong. How do you think your friend would react if you said, "Shut up! You have no right to express your opinion"? Of course your friend would vehemently object because you failed to respect what everyone knows to be true—the fact that she *does* have a right to express her opinion.

This little scenario happened to me (Norm) many years ago while I was speaking to a group of affluent, well-educated Chicago suburbanites. After suggesting there are such things as objective moral values to which we all have an obligation, one woman stood and protested loudly: "There are no real values. It's all a matter of taste or opinion!" I resisted the temptation to make my point by shouting, "Sit down and shut up, you egghead! Who wants to hear your opinion?" Of course, if I had been so rude and discourteous she would have rightly complained that I had violated her right to her opinion and her right to express it. To which I could have replied, "You have no such right—you just told me those rights do not exist!"

The point is this: Her complaint would prove that she actually did believe in a real absolute value—she valued her right to say that there are no absolute values. In other words, even those who deny all *values*, nevertheless *value* their right to do so. And therein lies the inconsistency. Moral values are literally undeniable and therefore exist.

Indeed, it is impossible to deny all absolutes without setting up some of one's own. The late Allan Bloom, who was a professor at the University of Chicago, used to confront his relativistic students with an ethical dilemma. In India, the cultural custom was to burn the widow of a deceased husband at the husband's funeral. So Bloom, trying to get his students to admit that such a practice was *absolutely* wrong, asked them this question: "If you had been a British administrator in India, would you have let the natives under your governance burn the widow at the funeral of a man [her husband] who had died?"[2]

Of course, it's obvious that burning living people with their deceased relatives is absolutely wrong, and it would be the duty of the British administrator to outlaw such a practice. However, this left Bloom's students in a dilemma. If they said they would *not* have stopped it, they would have been an accomplice to murder. But if they said that they *would* have stopped it, then they would be admitting that relativism is false. What did Bloom's relativistic students do? Instead of dealing with the dilemma, they skirted the issue. The typical student response was a diversionary statement such as "The British should not have been there to begin with," or else stunned silence.

Problem #2—We wouldn't know injustice unless there was an objective standard of justice.

Several years ago a professor, who was teaching a class in ethics at a university in Indiana, assigned a term paper to his students. He allowed the students to write on any topic of their choice, only requiring them to properly back up their thesis with documented sources. One student, a relativist, wrote convincingly on the merits of moral relativism. He argued, "All morals are relative; it's all a matter of opinion; I like chocolate, you like vanilla," etc. His paper was well written, properly documented, the right length, on time, and stylishly presented in a handsome blue folder. The professor read the entire paper and then wrote on the front cover, "F. I don't like blue folders!"

When the student got the paper back he was enraged. He stormed into the professor's office and declared, " 'F. I don't like blue folders!' That's not fair, that's not right, that's not just! You didn't grade the paper on its merits!"

Raising his hand to quiet the bombastic student, the professor calmly retorted, "Wait a minute. Hold on. What's this you say about being *fair, right,* and *just?* Didn't your paper argue that it's all a matter of taste? You like chocolate, I like vanilla?"

The student replied, "Yes, that's my view."

The professor responded, "Fine, then. I don't like blue. You get an F!"

Suddenly the light bulb went on in the student's head as he finally got the message. He really *did* believe in moral absolutes: at least he believed in fairness, rightness, and justice. He realized that he was charging his professor with injustice by appealing to an objective standard of justice. That simple fact defeated his entire case for relativism.

The moral of the story is that there are absolute morals. And if you really want to get relativists to admit it, all you have to do is treat them unfairly. Their reactions will reveal the Moral Law written on their hearts and minds. The student illustrated here realized there *is* an objective standard of right and wrong by how he *reacted* to the professor's treatment of him. As we pointed out earlier, this is the typical way the Moral Law becomes as bright as the sun. It's not always apparent from our actions (as evidenced by the terrible things human beings do to one another), but it's brightly revealed in our reactions—what we do when we personally are treated unfairly.

Problem #3—Measurement is only possible with an objective standard.

Another way to detect a problem with the all-truth-is-relative reasoning is to simply ask the question "Relative to what?"

Suppose you're sitting in your car at a traffic light and the car next to you appears to be moving. Is it you moving or the other car? Is there any way to tell who is moving if both you and the other car are actually in motion? You say, "Look at a tree." Suppose the trees are moving too, as well as the buildings, light posts, telephone poles, the road, and everything else? The fact is, with everything moving, there's no way to measure change. Something must be a stationary, absolute reference point in order to figure out who is moving and who isn't.

Like motion, morality makes no sense if there isn't an unchanging reference point. As we discussed in chapter 1, if there is no absolute moral reference point, statements like "Hitler was evil," "Racism is wrong," or "You shouldn't abuse children" have no objective meaning. They're merely someone's opinion on par with "Chocolate tastes better than vanilla." But we know Hitler was wrong, as is racism and child abuse, because we have an absolute reference point called the Moral Law.

In fact, without the absolute reference point provided by the Moral Law, simple value-laden terms such as "good," "bad," "better," and "worse" would have no objective meaning. But they *do* have meaning. For example, when we say, "Society is getting worse," we are comparing society to some external standard. Likewise, when we say Mother Teresa was "good" and Hitler was "bad," we are implicitly comparing each one of them to some standard beyond both of them. We recognize Mother Teresa was "good" because by helping the poor she more closely followed the Moral Law we all intuitively understand. On the other hand, it's obvious to us that Hitler was "bad" because his actions were contrary to the Moral Law—he didn't treat people as he would want them to treat him.

Problem #4—Without absolutes, moral disagreements are impossible.

Think about the last time you had an argument with someone. Why were you arguing? Because you believed that your position was "right" and the other person's was "wrong." Of course! But "right" and "wrong" only make sense if there is a standard that defines "right" and "wrong." Anytime you argue with someone, you are implicitly admitting that there is such a standard. In fact, your argument is based on your belief that you are closer to that objective standard of rightness than your opponent.

But real moral arguments are not possible without moral absolutes. Without absolutes, all disagreements would be nothing more than differences of opinion. For example, one person would be "right" in asserting Hitler was "better" than Mother Teresa. Another person would also be "right" in declaring that murder is the "best" thing anyone could do; there's nothing wrong with child abuse or slavery; rape should be encouraged; kindness to others should be outlawed; there's no moral difference between the ideals of the Ku-Klux Klan and those of Martin Luther King, etc. Our morally informed consciences tell us that these conclusions are nonsense—they're *absolutely* wrong. And if they are wrong, then so is relativism.

In other words, we know through the Moral Law that there are things that are absolutely wrong (e.g., murder, rape, child abuse, etc.). So relativism must be false. To believe in relativism is to argue that there are no real moral differences between Mother Teresa and Hitler, freedom and slavery, equality and racism, care and abuse, love and hate, or life and murder.

This issue really hinges on whether human beings *determine* right and wrong or *discover* right and wrong. If human beings determine right and wrong, then anyone would be "right" in asserting any of the absurd conclusions we just listed above. But people don't *create* truth, they *find* it. Newton didn't *determine* the law of gravity, he *discovered* it. Likewise, human beings haven't determined that murder is wrong. We've discovered it's wrong through our consciences, which reflect the Moral Law.

As we noted in chapter 1, this Moral Law must have a source higher than ourselves. For the moral prescription that is on the hearts of all people must have been put there by a Moral Prescriber. So what is manifested through the Moral Law is God's definition of right and wrong. And we need God's definition because without an absolute authority to adjudicate between the opinions of people, we're left with just that—opinions. In other words, absolutes are absolutes because they are the final standard by which everything is measured.

For those of you who are not religiously minded, don't shut down because we have said that God is the source of right and wrong. While this may logically be the case, it does not follow that someone's religion must be legislated to achieve moral laws.

We can legislate the Moral Law without legislating religion, as we'll discuss later. In fact, one can believe in the Moral Law without *acknowledging* a Moral Lawgiver. There just doesn't seem to be any adequate way to *justify* such a belief.

ABSOLUTE VS. RELATIVE: WHY THE CONFUSION?

If there really are absolute moral values, as we have argued, then why do so many believe that morality is relative? Rationally, the reason lies with the failure to make proper distinctions. Let's take a look at those distinctions and clear up the areas of confusion:

Confusion #1—Absolute values vs. changing behavior

A common mistake of relativists is to confuse behavior and value, what *is* and what *ought* to be. What people *do* is subject to change, but what they *ought* to do is not. This is the difference between sociology and morality. The former is *descriptive;* the latter is *prescriptive.*

In other words, relativists often confuse the changing behavioral situation with the unchanging moral duty. For example, when discussing a moral topic like premarital sex or cohabitation, you often hear people in support of it say something like "Get with it, this is the modern world!" as if current behaviors dictate what's right and wrong. To illustrate the absurdity of the relativist's reasoning, you only need to turn the discussion to a more serious moral issue like murder, which also occurs much more frequently in this generation. How many relativists would speak in support of murder by asking us to "Get with it, this is the modern world!"? That's where their reasoning takes them when they confuse what people do with what they ought to do.

Confusion #2—Absolute values vs. changing perceptions of the facts

Another confusion exists between an absolute moral value and the understanding of the facts used in applying that value. For example, a couple of hundred years ago witches used to be sentenced as murderers, but now they are not. A relativist might argue, "See! Our moral values have changed because we no longer seek to kill witches. Morality is relative to time and cul-

51

ture." But the relativist's claim is incorrect. What has changed is not the moral principle that murder is wrong, but the perception or factual understanding of whether "witches" can really murder people by their curses. People no longer believe they can. Hence, people no longer consider them murderers. In other words, *the perception of a moral situation is relative* (whether witches are really murderers), *but the moral values involved in the situation are not* (murder always has been and always will be wrong).

Failure to make this distinction also leads people to believe that cultural differences reflect essential differences in core moral values. For example, some believe that since Hindus revere cows and Americans eat them, there's an essential difference between the moral values of Americans and Hindus. But the reason people in India consider cows sacred has nothing to do with a core moral value—it has to do with their belief in reincarnation. Indians believe that cows may possess the souls of deceased human beings, so they don't eat cows. In the United States, we do not believe that the soul of our deceased relative may be in a cow, so we freely eat cows.

In the final analysis, what appears to be a difference is actually an agreement. The core moral value that it's wrong to eat "Grandma" is considered absolute by people in both cultures. They only disagree on where "Grandma's" soul resides. This is a difference that's based on *perception of the facts* pertaining to the moral value. But there is a fundamental agreement that the moral value must be upheld.

This also answers the objection that we can't legislate a common morality because there are no core values we can agree upon. Some say America is a melting pot of people from many different cultures who have many different moral values, so legislating a common morality is impossible. But, as we have seen, this isn't true—core moral values actually transcend cultures just as simple math equations do. A common morality can and must be legislated for the society to survive. More on this in later chapters.

Confusion #3—An absolute value (what) vs. a relative cultural practice (how)

Another important difference, often overlooked by moral relativists, is between the absolute nature of the moral value and the relative way in which that value is manifested in different cultures. For example, all cultures have some form of greeting, but many cultures differ widely on just what that greeting should be. In some cultures it is a kiss; in others, a hug; and in still others, a handshake or bow. *What* should be done is common, but *how* it should be done differs. Failure to make this distinction misleads many to believe that because people have different practices they have different values. The moral value is absolute, but how it is manifested is relative.

Confusion #4—*Which absolute value applies vs. relative values*

Relativists often point to the issue of abortion to demonstrate that people have different moral values. Some think abortion is acceptable while others think it's murder. But this is actually very similar to our above example about cows. The confusion often results from a differing perception of the facts.

Contrary to the relativist's view, most of those who believe abortion is acceptable do not reject the absolute moral principle that innocent human life should be protected; they simply do not believe that an unborn baby is a human being. (As we saw in chapter 2, *Roe v. Wade* has helped further this perception that the unborn are not human.) People on the pro-abortion side believe that a different moral principle applies to the issue—the moral right to privacy that a woman has to control her own body.

In fact, instead of providing an example of relative moral values, the entire abortion controversy exists not because either side denies the moral value of preserving human life. It exists because each side defends a different moral value—protecting life vs. individual liberty. The question is over *which* value applies (or takes precedence) in the issue of abortion.[3] If the unborn are human beings, then the pro-life value should be applied in legislation (since a person's right to life supersedes another person's right to individual liberty). If the unborn are not human beings, then the pro-choice value should be applied in legislation. Pro-lifers argue that if there's doubt as to when life beings, then prudence demands the benefit of the doubt be given to protecting life (since it is more serious to end life than to restrict freedom). We'll say more on this in chapter 10.

Confusion #5—*Absolute ends (values) vs. relative means*

Often moral relativists confuse the end (the value itself) with the means to attaining that value. Several political disputes are of this sort. On some issues (not all), liberals and conservatives want the same things—the same ends. They simply disagree on how to get there.

Nearly all politicians agree that justice should be done (the end), but they disagree as to whose program is the best means to attain that justice. For example, regarding the poor, most liberals believe the best way to help is through government welfare programs. But since most conservatives think handouts create dependency, they would rather stimulate economic opportunity so the poor can help themselves. Notice that the end is the same (assist the poor), but the means are different. Likewise, both the militarist and the pacifist desire peace (the end); they simply disagree as to whether a strong military force is the best means to attain this peace. They both agree on the absolute end, but disagree on the relative means.

CONCLUSION

First, with regard to the question of whether or not legislating morality is ethical, we have seen that those who protest the loudest against legislating morality are merely trying to legislate their own particular brand of morality. Those who say, "It is morally wrong to cram your morals down my throat," are arguing from a moral position. Since all laws declare one behavior right and another behavior wrong, legislating morality is not only ethical, it is unavoidable.

Second, although it is widely believed that all morality is relative, core moral values are absolute and transcend cultures. The Moral Law is real and moral absolutes are unavoidable. Even those who deny them, use them. The reasons for rejecting them are often based on a misunderstanding or misapplication of the moral absolutes, not on a real rejection of them. That is, moral values are absolute, even if our understanding of them or the circumstances in which they should be applied are not.

So we have seen that legislating morality is constitutional (chapter 1), enforceable (chapter 2), and ethical (chapter 3). The question now is, "Whose morality is being legislated?" That's the question we'll begin to tackle in chapter 4.

PART II

HOW HAS MORALITY BEEN LEGISLATED?

HOW HAS MORALITY BEEN LEGISLATED?

4. "WE THE PEOPLE..."

"We the People..." These words begin the preamble to the Constitution of the United States. As Lincoln observed many years later, they indicate that our country was founded *by* the people and *for* the people, and was thus designed to be responsive *to* the people. Recall from chapter 1 that alleged abuse of government power was the chief reason the colonists split from England in the first place. As a result, the Founders wrote into the Constitution checks and balances in an attempt to ensure that no governing body would wield too much power. Realizing that power corrupts, and absolute power tends to corrupt absolutely, the Founders intended for the people and the states to have most of the control. The Tenth Amendment to the Constitution, reserving most rights for the states, makes that perfectly clear.

Unfortunately, in the last half of this century, the federal government has generally ignored the Constitution and taken power from the states and from the people. The primary culprit has been the Supreme Court, which has assumed a legislative role, often overruling the expressed will of the people. In effect, the Court has forced its own brand of morality on the country.

In the next two chapters, we'll show how the Court has injected into the bloodstream of American society a relativistic morality without a single vote from a citizen or member of Congress. The Court's actions have had fatal consequences for the nation's moral health. But before we look at what the Supreme Court has done in terms of legislating morality, we must first investigate where the Court's morality has come from. As we shall see, their morality has had far-reaching effects, not only on the United States but on the rest of the world as well.

IDEAS MATTER

As we stated in chapter 1, the moral philosophy upon which our nation was founded was presented explicitly in our *Declaration of Independence*. It reads: "We hold these truths to be self-evident, that all men are created equal, that they are endowed by their Creator with certain unalienable Rights, that among these are Life, Liberty and the pursuit of Happiness." Notice that our Founding Fathers, in accordance with the Moral Law, affirmed their belief in (1) a Creator (God), (2) Creation (that man was created), and (3) God-given moral absolutes (that man has God-given "unalienable Rights").

Tragically, since the late 1940s, our government has often governed as if it no longer believes in these truths declared in the *Declaration of Independence*. The People's Republic of China, established in 1949, never believed them. China's track record since 1949 provides us with an important lesson for our discussion on morality. Columnist Charley Reese began a recent editorial with this vivid illustration:

> Let's suppose someone murdered every man, woman, and child in the states of Vermont, New Hampshire, Maine, Massachusetts, Connecticut, Rhode Island, New York, New Jersey, Pennsylvania, and Ohio. Imagine that vast stretch of land lying empty of all living human beings. As if in a Stephen King novel, you could drive from New Jersey to Maine, from New York to the western border of Ohio, and not once ever see a living human being—only gigantic stacks of millions of rotting corpses. Well, that's how many people the communist thug government of China has murdered since 1949. It has murdered the equivalent of the combined populations of those states, around 60 million.[1]

Not only has the Chinese government killed 60 million of its own people since 1949 (that's an average of more than 1.2 million *per year*), its forced abortion policy kills countless unborn children, terrorizes women, and further upsets the gender balance of Chinese society. The policy is a brutal attempt to control population growth, which allows Chinese couples only one child. To enforce this, the government monitors menstruation cycles, and drags women off to abortion clinics if they are found pregnant with their second child.

In addition to these forced abortions, sex-selection abortions in China have also soared. Since a majority of couples desire their only child to be a boy, Chinese women often abort their first pregnancy when they discover it's a girl. This bias against the feminine gender has left the sex-ratio in large regions of China favoring males 64 percent to 36 percent![2] (If for no other reason, all feminists should be pro-life.)

Consider also the horrifying story that came out of China in 1995. Reported by Hong Kong's *Eastern Express* newspaper, and also carried in major newspapers in Japan and the Philippines, this story maintains that human fetuses are being sold and consumed as health remedies in the southern town of Shenzhen. If this story is true, it represents the ultimate depths to which godlessness can sink.

According to the account, an *Eastern Express* reporter, who feigned an illness in order to investigate widespread rumors of this practice, was given a jar of ten thumb-sized fetuses to eat, on March 2, 1995, by a doctor at the Shenzhen Health Center for Women. The doctor said, "They can make your skin smoother, your body stronger, and are good for the kidneys." The doctor added that she personally liked her fetuses with pork soup.[3] She said the best fetuses were firstborn males from young women. "I wash them with clear water until they look transparent and white and then stew them. Making soup is best.... They are wasted if we don't eat them."[4]

Dr. Warren Lee, who heads the Hong Kong Nutrition Association, said that eating fetuses is "a kind of traditional Chinese medicine."[5] And a recent book by a respected Chinese dissident confirms tales of cannibalism in that country.[6] Whether these incidents are true or not, they can be the logical outworking of a philosophy that has no absolute standard of morality.

Why are we talking about horrific abuses of the Chinese government? Because the ideology behind the Chinese government has been creeping into the American system since the late '40s, and especially since 1961. And bad ideas left uncorrected yield equally bad results.

The foundations of the American government and the Chinese government could hardly be more different. The American government, as mentioned above, was established upon the Moral Law affirmed in our *Declaration of Independence* (Jefferson called it "Nature's Law"). It declared that human rights are given by the Creator, so they can't be taken away by government (in fact, according to the *Declaration*, it is government's duty to protect those rights). As a result, in the American system, justice is discovered by appeal to the Moral Law—the objective standard that transcends the ideas of those in power.

Nearly two centuries later, China's government was established upon the assumptions of atheism—there is no God and thus no God-given Rights. The state gives rights and the state takes them away. In the Chinese system, justice is decided by the arbitrary will of those in power. Indeed, it was Mao Tse-Tung who said that justice is decided by the one standing on the right side of a gun.

Where did this stark difference in government philosophy originate? China's ideology—and the one that's been creeping into the American system since 1961—was given a strong impetus from the teachings of Charles Darwin. Now some of you may be wondering what on earth Charles Darwin and his theory of evolution has to do with governments and morality. As we shall see, there is a very important connection.

The 1800s: "God is dead."

In 1859 Darwin released his famous book *On the Origin of Species*, which theorized that all animals evolved from common primitive ancestors through purposeless forces over millions of years. Twelve years later, Darwin released *The Descent of Man*, in which he asserted that humans arose from the same common ancestors as well. Prior to Darwin, some believed in evolution, but they had no scientific theory to support their view. In fact, virtually every founder of modern science believed in Creation, including Kepler (physical astronomy), Pascal (hydrostatics), Boyle (chemistry), Newton (calculus), Mendel (genetics), and Kelvin (thermodynamics). In other words, for the first 240 years of modern science (1620–1860), the belief in the Creation of the world was the dominant view in the scientific community. Sir Isaac Newton's statement serves to illustrate this belief: "This most beautiful system of the sun, planets, and comets could only proceed from the counsel and dominion of an intelligent and powerful Being."[7]

But when Darwin unveiled his theory of evolution, which included a process he called "Natural Selection," evolution gained scientific legitimacy, and the world experienced a turning point in history. Darwin and his followers made evolution into a surrogate for the Creator. Although Darwin grew increasingly agnostic about the existence of a Creator, he referred to "Natural Selection" as "my deity," and defended his characterization this way: "I speak of Natural Selection as an active power or deity; but who objects to an author speaking of the attraction of gravity as ruling the movements of the planets? . . . It is difficult to avoid personifying nature."[8]

The co-founder of Natural Selection, Alfred Wallace, went even further in replacing God with evolution. He said, "Natural Selection is Supreme" and went on to explain, "[There is a power] not only adequate to direct and regulate all the forces at work in living organisms but also the more fundamental forces of the whole material universe."[9]

Thomas Huxley, known as "Darwin's Bulldog" because of his strong defense of Darwin, showed to what extent evolution had replaced God when he wrote, "I can see no reason for doubting that all are coordinate terms of nature's great progression, from formless to formed, from the inorganic to the organic, from blind force to conscious intellect and will."[10]

In other words, Huxley believed that a blind force directed the evolutionary process from the nonliving to the living and from the non-intelligent to intelligent beings. Or, to put it more simply, Huxley believed that through evolution an effect could receive from its cause something the cause didn't have to give in the first place![11]

Herbert Spencer went even further. Called "our great philosopher" by Darwin, Spencer asserted that evolution was a cosmic process that explained not only biology but also astronomy, geology, and psychology. According to Spencer, everything is evolving. This universal process of evolution led German biologist and philosopher Ernst Haeckel to conclude, "With this simple argument the mystery of the universe is explained, the deity annulled, and a new era of infinite knowledge ushered in."[12] No longer did finite man need an infinite God. Science could bring man infinite knowledge!

Karl Marx, who was already a convinced atheist, rejoiced in the nail he believed evolution placed in the theistic casket. He proudly announced, "But nowadays, in our evolutionary conception of the universe, there is absolutely no room for either a Creator or a ruler."[13] Marx's writings are, of course, at the foundation of the modern view popularly called communism.

In 1878, Charles Hodge, a noted Princeton scholar, summed up the heart of the evolutionary ideology well. Only seven years after Darwin had announced that man descended from one ancient primitive ancestor, Hodge wrote, "What is Darwinism? It is atheism. This does not mean as before said that Mr. Darwin himself and all who adopt his views are atheists; but it means that his theory is atheistic; that the exclusion of design from nature is ... tantamount to atheism."[14] In other words, there may be those who believe in some kind of God and evolution, but they no longer believe in a Creator of all living things. According to the Darwinists, evolution had eliminated the need for the Creator.

Not only had scientists drawn the implication that evolution had replaced the need for a Creator, but German philosopher Friedrich Nietzsche drew the conclusion that without God there were no absolute moral principles either. He declared, "God is dead. God remains dead. And we have killed Him. How shall we, the murderers of all murderers, comfort ourselves?" Nietzsche answered, "Must not we ourselves become gods simply to seem worthy of it?"[15]

In effect, Nietzsche understood that when God "died," all absolutes died with him. Therefore, with no Moral Lawgiver to prescribe right and wrong, he claimed we must create our own morality. After all, if values do not originate in heaven, then we must make them up on earth. This is why the great Russian novelist Fyodor Dostoevsky wrote in *The Brothers Karamazov*, "If God does not exist, then everything is permitted."

Despite his militant atheism, Nietzsche also realized that a world without a belief in God and moral absolutes would lead to unprecedented bloodshed. Nietzsche died in 1900, but before his death he predicted that the twentieth century would be the most murderous in human history. His insights were prophetic. For when man killed belief in God in the 1800s, he also killed moral restraint in the 1900s.

The 1900s: "Man is dead."

As the atheistic evolutionists buried God, they buried with Him traditional morals that protect human life as well. Consequently, more people have been killed in wars and by genocide in the twentieth century than in all the previous centuries combined. Only a small part of this can be attributed to more lethal weaponry; the contribution of evolutionary philosophy to the holocausts of the 1900s cannot be overstated.

In 1924 Adolf Hitler, in his book *Mein Kampf* (My Struggle), made it clear that Darwin's theory of Natural Selection was the basis for his belief in Arian superiority and a justification for what would be his mass-murder of the Jews. He wrote:

> If nature does not wish that weaker individuals should mate with the stronger, she wishes even less that a superior race should intermingle with an inferior one; because in such cases all her efforts, throughout hundreds of thousands of years, to establish an evolutionary higher stage of being, may thus be rendered futile.
>
> But such a preservation goes hand-in-hand with the inexorable law that it is the strongest and the best who must triumph and that they have the right to endure. He who would live must fight. He who does not wish to fight in this world, where permanent struggle is the law of life, has not the right to exist.[16]

As his writings and actions prove, Hitler was indeed a racist who used evolution as the philosophical basis for his treachery. He believed the survival of the fittest was the "law of life" and, therefore, the Jews had no right to exist if they didn't want to fight.

Of course, reasonable people condemn Hitler's views by appealing to the Moral Law. But those who embrace the view of the hard-core Darwinists—that there is no God—have no Moral Law, or absolute "good" or "bad," to appeal to. As we've already discussed, without God to provide an objective standard of right and wrong, people set the rules. And if people set the rules, there is no objective moral standard by which to evaluate Hitler's actions against those of, say, Mother Teresa.

Hitler eventually killed some twelve million people: six million Jews and six million non-Jews. Hitler's ally, the Italian Benito Mussolini, justified war on his belief that it sped up the evolutionary process. His ally and then enemy, Josef Stalin, also atheistic in his beliefs, killed some tens of millions of people, most of them innocent Russian citizens. And as already noted, the godless communist regime in China has killed sixty million with no end in sight! It is literally true that when belief in God dies, man dies.

As the history of the twentieth century proves, the implications of believing in evolution at the exclusion of the Creator have been devastating (and they remain so today). Large-scale evolution is not only a theory that affects how one looks at things in the biology lab; it has a dramatic impact on government, philosophy, law, and ethics, as well. Darwin's purely naturalistic theory of origin gives people apparent intellectual justification for denying the existence of God and for setting their own standards of right and wrong. If God does not exist, ultimately man has no one to whom he must answer—there is no authority higher than himself. And if man is the ultimate authority, then human beings are perfectly justified in defining morals and ethics that fit their own desires, even if those ethics are the ones espoused by Hitler, Mussolini, Stalin, and the Chinese government—murder, torture, and abuse.

At this point you may object to this reasoning. Perhaps you're thinking, "Look, regardless of whether evolution is true or not, there's no way that murdering millions of innocent people can ever be considered anything other than absolutely wrong." Most atheists would agree, but they simply could not *justify* their belief. The Moral Law tells them intuitively that genocide is wrong. But they can't appeal to the Moral Law to justify their belief because acknowledging the Moral Law would logically mean acknowledging the existence of the Moral Lawgiver . In fact, one atheist I (Norm) debated, admitted that he had no objective standard by which he opposed evil. He said his opposition was simply based on his own "benign moral feeling."

Well, feelings come and feelings go, and they are, therefore, a poor foundation upon which to build a society or government. Governments that respect human rights are those that base that respect on the eternal nature of the Creator. Once a government adopts the beliefs associated with atheistic Darwinian evolution—that there is no Creator or Creation—that government will inevitably deny the existence of unalienable rights. That process has been occurring in the United States since World War II. While unalienable rights remain inscribed in our founding documents, many of those rights have been eroded by widespread acceptance of the Darwinist philosophy. Two famous trials, fifty-six years apart, point out the extent to which the Darwinist philosophy has taken hold despite its unreasonable claims about reality.

THE SCOPES I TRIAL

As noted earlier, many Germans, including Hitler, bought into social Darwinism, which had devastating effects on ethics. But even before Hitler's regime, the German atrocities of World War I were reported to Americans by leaders who had traveled abroad after the war. The abuse of teaching evolution to justify anti-Christian and even inhumane activity had Americans concerned, and there was a strong political movement in the United States to exclude the teaching of evolution in the public (government) schools. Many states passed laws against teaching evolution, including Tennessee. This set the stage for the famous Scopes Trial in the summer of 1925.

The American Civil Liberties Union (ACLU) persuaded John Scopes, a high school biology teacher, to claim that he had taught evolution to his students in direct violation of the Tennessee law. The ACLU financed Scopes' defense in order to challenge the law. During the trial, many religious people rallied around their champion, William Jennings Bryan (a lawyer and former presidential candidate), who spoke against what they perceived to be the godless teaching of evolution. The champion of the liberal and humanistic cause was the famous criminal lawyer, Clarence Darrow. (Today, many people have heard of this trial through the popular, but historically inaccurate, movie and theater production titled *Inherit the Wind*.[17])

Darrow argued persuasively that public schools should teach both theories of origins. His chief witness, John Scopes, stated that position in convincing terms. He said, "Education, you know, means broadening, advancing, and if you limit a teacher to only one side of anything the whole country will eventually have only one thought, be one individual. I believe in teaching every aspect of every problem or theory."[18]

Darrow argued in summation this way: "For God's sake, let the children have their minds kept open—close no doors to their knowledge; shut no door from them. Make a distinction between theology and science. Let them have both. *Let them both be taught. Let them both live."* (emphasis added).[19]

Despite the efforts of Darrow and Scopes, a hollow legal victory was won by Bryan and the Creationists—John Scopes was found guilty of teaching evolution and fined $100 (This was later overturned on a technicality). However, the moral and social victory was won by the evolutionists. With strong media support, public opinion shifted in favor of a more pluralistic approach— evolutionists, too, should have the freedom to present their theory in government schools. As secular humanists made advances, gradually the laws against teaching evolution were discarded. In fact, in 1968 the Supreme Court declared that such laws were unconstitutional (*Epperson v. Arkansas*).

THE SCOPES II TRIAL

In November 1981 an NBC news poll showed that 76 percent of all Americans believed that both evolution and Creation should be taught in government schools. Since most schools at the time were teaching only evolution, Arkansas legislators deemed it wise to pass a law to ensure that Creation would also be taught.

Earlier that year (March 1981), Arkansas legislators passed Act 590 by wide margins: the Arkansas Senate voted 22 to 2, the House voted 69 to 18, and the Act was quickly signed by Governor Frank White. The Act required a "balanced treatment" (not necessarily equal time) of both evolution and Creation in government schools. It forbid any reference to religious books (such as the Bible) and demanded that only scientific evidences (and inferences) be allowed. The Act also provided that the teacher could opt not to teach origins at all, thus sticking to science in the strictly observable sense and avoiding speculations about origins.

Act 590 seemed to be an eminently fair law, one which the ACLU should have been glad to champion. After all, it was the ACLU who had argued (through Clarence Darrow) in 1925 that public schools should teach both theories of origin. Surely they would support Act 590. But instead of supporting the act, the ACLU chose to attack it! On May 27, 1981, they filed suit charging that the law would lead to an unconstitutional establishment of religion. But, since the Act forbid any reference to religious books, the establishment position was an ACLU smokescreen to prevent the other theory of origin from entering the debate. In effect, this time the ACLU argued that it is wrong to teach *two* theories of origin! This was an obvious bias. Otherwise, why would the American Civil *Liberties* Union have been against a teacher having the *liberty* to teach both sides of an issue?

The case officially became known as *Mclean v. Arkansas*, and unofficially as "The Scopes II Trial." The trial took place from December 7 to December 17, 1981, in Little Rock, Arkansas, and I (Norm) took the stand on December 11 as a witness for the state. There were a number of points I made, but three in particular speak to the heart of the issue and show why teaching Creation is not an establishment of religion.[20]

First Cause vs. Object of Devotion

First, teaching a theory that there may be a creator/first-cause of the universe is not the same as asking students to make a religious commitment to Him. Students can believe *that* there is a Creator but still not believe *in* Him. There's a huge difference between intellectually theorizing about a first cause and coercing students to worship Him. I offered numerous actual illustrations to prove this point at the trial. For example, I mentioned that Aristotle believed in an "unmoved mover" of the universe because the principle of causality demanded it. (Since every effect must have a cause, Aristotle concluded that there must be some unmoved mover who started the universe into motion.) However, this first cause was not an object of religious commitment for Aristotle. He didn't worship it; he simply viewed the unmoved mover as a purely scientific explanation without any religious significance. I also mentioned Plato, who, like Aristotle, believed in a creator ("Demiurgos") that had no religious significance.

I further made the point that students can study historical figures such as Jesus Christ or Muhammad without making religious commitments to them. We can't throw out of our schools everyone and everything that could possibly evoke a religious commitment in people. If we did, we would have to remove rocks from geology class because some people worship them! Although some people do make religious commitments to Jesus, Mohammed, and ordinary rocks, that doesn't mean we cannot study those figures in a historical and detached manner. The historical first cause of the universe can be studied in the same way.

My assertion to the court was this: Since the evidence for a Creator of the universe and life can be presented without indoctrinating students into a particular religious system, why shouldn't the evidence be presented? After all, there are only two ways to explain the origin of the universe: either there was an intelligent creator or there wasn't. Why should only one of the two possibilities be allowed in our government schools? To borrow the words of Clarence Darrow: "Let them both live!"

Source of a Theory vs. Evidence for It

The second major point I made refuted the ACLU claim that Creation should not be taught in the schools because the idea came from a religious source, the Bible. I showed that the ACLU position is based on a genetic fallacy, which says that something is false or should be rejected because of its source. I testified that true science distinguishes between the *source* of a theory and the *evidence* for it. For example, Kekule, discoverer of the model for the complex benzene molecule, got the idea while dreaming about a snake biting its tail. And Tesla, inventor of the alternating current motor, got the idea from a vision he had while reading the German mystical poet Goethe. (I was going to give more examples, but the judge interrupted me by saying, "I have your point.") My point was that none of those theories were rejected because of their source. To the contrary, they were accepted because they withstood the test of scientific investigation and had scientific justification.

The theory of Creation has ample scientific justification from a forensic perspective (see below) and should not be ruled out simply because it has a religious source. Besides, it would be absurd to disallow something from being taught in government schools merely because it came from the Bible. The Bible speaks against murder and for love—should those teachings be disallowed in our government school classrooms because they are taught in the Bible?[21]

Macroevolution Is Not Empirical Science

My third main point challenged the ACLU's claim that evolution is scientific but Creation is not—their implication being that whatever isn't "scientific" should not be taught in a science class. However, it turns out that neither the theory of evolution nor the theory of Creation fits the evolutionists' own definition of science.

Darwinists dogmatically assert that only evolution is science. But by their own definition—which says that nothing is scientific unless it is observable, testable, repeatable, and governed only by natural laws—evolution itself does not qualify! Scientists have observed small changes in a given form of life as it adapts to its environment (microevolution), but no one has ever observed one type of life becoming another (macroevolution).[22] In fact, with all their intellectual capacity, scientists themselves can't make one life form evolve into another. Breeding attempts always reveal a limit to genetic change—a dog always remains a dog, a cat is always a cat, etc. Yet Darwinists believe that natural selection—which they define as a random process *with no intellectual capacity* (Darwinist Richard Dawkins calls this mysterious process "the blind watchmaker")—can accomplish what they themselves (intelligent beings) cannot!

Furthermore, evolution does not fit their definition of science because no one has ever observed or can repeat another foundational element of their theory—the spontaneous generation of life from nonliving matter. Darwinists know life doesn't come spontaneously from nonlife, but by faith they believe otherwise. Friends, macroevolution is philosophy or religion, not empirical science! In fact, some scientists admit that the evolutionary view is based on faith without concrete evidence to support it. Harold C. Urey, a Nobel laureate, said:

> All of us who study the origin of life find that the more we look into it, the more we feel that it is too complex to have evolved anywhere. *We all believe as an article of faith* that life evolved from dead matter on this planet. It is just that its complexity is so great it is hard for us to imagine that it did (emphasis added).[23]

Science of Orgins: Forensic Not Empirical

To divert attention from my testimony, the ACLU blew smoke in the eyes of the court and public by bringing up irrelevant matters such as my religious beliefs concerning demons. And the judge, despite seeing my points, was intent on ignoring them. On January 5, 1982, he declared Act 590 unconstitutional. In the decision, he wrote that an essential characteristic of science is that science is guided by natural law and must be explanatory by reference to natural law. In effect, the judge accepted the evolutionists' presupposition that science must only seek causes that are natural rather than supernatural. He also accepted the presupposition that the entire history of the universe can be explained by the natural forces that describe how things operate now. This is also known as operation science or empirical science. But by this narrow definition of "science," the judge and the evolutionists ignored an entire field of accepted science that does not necessarily seek natural or repeatable causes. That field of science is known as forensic or origin science and is used every day, particularly by our law enforcement authorities.

The O. J. Simpson trial hinged on forensic science. The murders only happened once (they could not be recreated in the laboratory), and the cause of the murders could not be explained by natural law (based on past experience, we know that Ron and Nicole could not have been stabbed by lightning, an earthquake, or a tornado). The murders were clearly the work of an "intelligent" being and could thus be best explained by utilizing forensic science. It would be a mistake to apply the assumptions of operation science to a situation that demanded forensic science such as the O. J. trial. Someone using operation science would assume some natural force like lightning killed them, while someone using forensic science would properly seek a murderer.

Forensic science depends on the principle of uniformity— that similar events in the present had similar causes in the past. For example, using the principle of uniformity, we can conclude that natural laws eroded the Grand Canyon over thousands or millions of years, even though we were not there to observe it. We can do this because we can observe natural laws eroding similar land masses today. However, we would never assume that the faces on Mount Rushmore were the result of erosion brought on by natural laws. The principle of uniformity tells us that something as specified and as complex as the faces on Mount Rushmore can only come to be through the hands of an intelligent being—in this case an intelligent sculptor.

Likewise, the principle of uniformity tells us that the cause for the universe, and for the specified complexity we call life, must be an intelligent being like the one who sculpted the faces on Mount Rushmore. These events have similar characteristics: they each happened only once so they can't be repeated in the laboratory, and they are events whose uniqueness, complexity, and specific design could only have been caused by an intelligent being. We *never* see random natural laws chiseling a highly detailed sculpture of a president's head into stone. So why should we assume such laws could be responsible for something vastly more specific and complex such as life?

Nevertheless, the Darwinists, the ACLU, and the judge insisted that the origin of the universe must be explained by the assumptions of operation science instead of the study of origins—that everything has been caused by natural laws. But this assumption—that the universe has always been governed by natural laws without interference from a creator—is a philosophical not scientific claim (if science is understood in the empirical, operational sense). With this assumption, they've philosophically locked God out of the universe and ignored the entire discipline of forensic scientific inquiry. Moreover, their claim that there is an unintelligent "blind watchmaker" with the creative power to bring complex things into existence cannot be observed in the laboratory nor can it be found plausible through the principle of uniformity. We simply *never* see specified and complex systems arise without intelligent intervention. This is why, after investigating the incredible irreducible complexity of the cell, microbiologist Michael Behe (author of *Darwin's Black Box: The Biochemical Challenge to Evolution*) concluded that "life on earth at its most fundamental level, in its most critical components, is the product of intelligent activity."[24] Thus the entire Darwinian macroevolutionary model, being devoid of significant empirical or forensic evidence, is built on philosophical hopes rather than scientific observations.

Law professor Phillip Johnson, author of the block-busting book *Darwin on Trial* (a book that remains a thorn in the side of dogmatic Darwinists), exposes the fact that Darwinism is more philosophy than science. He wrote:

> As a general theory of biological creation, Darwinism is not empirical at all. Rather, it is a necessary implication of a philosophical doctrine called scientific naturalism, which is

based on the a priori assumption that God was always absent from the realm of nature.[25]

Years earlier, physicist Robert Jastrow, an evolutionist, observed:

> Either life was created on the earth by the will of a being outside the group of scientific understanding; or it evolved on our planet spontaneously through chemical reactions occurring in nonliving matter lying on the surface of the planet. The first theory is a statement of faith in the power of a Supreme Being not subject to the laws of science. The second theory is also an act of faith. *The act of faith consists in assuming that the scientific view is correct, without having concrete evidence to support that belief* (emphasis added).[26]

Jastrow is right. Darwinism requires faith. Faith not only that the "blind watchmaker" can create complex biological systems but faith in the origin of life from nonliving matter and faith in the origin of the matter itself. And there's no real evidence to support that faith.

The truth is that Creation and macroevolution each demand a certain degree of faith. And neither theory fits the Darwinists' own definition of "science" because neither theory is repeatable nor observable. That is, neither is "science" in the empirical sense, but both are "science" in a forensic sense. As a result, both theories should be tested by the rigors of forensic science and judged by the forensic evidence. When studying the origin of the universe and the origin of life, we must use the proper tools and make the necessary distinctions.

Unfortunately, the Darwinists will have none of this. They see themselves as locked in a battle with religious fundamentalists who, according to Johnson, Darwinists see as "a threat to liberal freedom, and especially as a threat to public support for scientific research."[27] As a result, Darwinists endeavor to blur these distinctions of scientific inquiry and equate anything termed "evolution" with fact, and anything termed "Creation" with fantasy. In doing so, they dogmatically demand that our children learn only their view. Yet, as Johnson somewhat sarcastically points out, their view doesn't fit the evidence:

> Maybe Darwinism really is false in principle, and not only in detail. Maybe mindless material processes can't cre-

ate information-rich biological systems. That is a real possibility, no matter how offensive it is to scientific naturalists. How do Darwinists know that the blind watchmaker created the animal phyla, for example, since the process can't be demonstrated and all the historical evidence is missing? Darwinists may have the cultural power to suppress questions like that for a time, but eventually they are going to have to come to grips with them.[28]

The fact is, using the principles of forensic science (the law of causality and the principle of uniformity), the evidence for the origin of the universe and of life strongly points away from the Darwinian view and to an intelligent being (a creator).[29] Why should we forbid our school children from studying that evidence? Besides, if the evidence for evolution is so compelling (as many evolutionists and the ACLU uncritically maintain it is), then the theory of evolution should be able to withstand a fair hearing from its only alternative—Creation. Why not let the students utilize their own intellectual capacities by allowing them to decide for themselves which theory is more reasonable? After all, free inquiry is what the ACLU claims to support. That's what the ACLU Academic Freedom Committee advanced in 1976, when they declared, "One of the objectives of universal free education is to develop in children the intellectual capacities required for the effective exercise of the rights and duties of citizenship. *Experience demonstrates that this is best accomplished in an atmosphere of free inquiry and discussion*" (emphasis added).

As we have seen, when it comes to education about origins, the ACLU abandons "free inquiry and discussion" for classroom censorship and a one-sided indoctrination into the theory of macroevolution—a theory that is not seen in rocks, but is found only in the imaginative reconstructions of naturalistic scientists.

CONCLUSION

Abraham Lincoln once said, "The philosophy of the schoolroom in one generation will be the philosophy of the government in the next." One reason our society is in a moral crisis is due to the fact that over the last half-century we have been indoctrinating our children with an evolutionary (i.e., atheistic) philosophy that presupposes no moral absolutes. Is it any wonder why our moral standards are going the way of the Chinese?

The battle over what we teach our children is crucial to the moral health of our nation, and the Scopes II trial was not the final word on the Creation/evolution debate. In 1987, a similar case went to the Supreme Court, which resulted in a startling conclusion. In the next two chapters we will show how this and numerous other Supreme Court decisions have deeply upset the moral health of our country, and how our national governing power has been transferred from "We the People" to "We the Supreme Court."

5. ROOTS OF THE POWER SHIFT

We began the last chapter by pointing out the moral differences between a country founded on the Moral Law (the United States), and one founded on atheism (China). Unfortunately, the rights spoken of in the *Declaration of Independence* hold very little meaning to our youth. In our TV-dominated culture, most teenagers are more familiar with the content of beer commercials than the *Declaration of Independence*. "It doesn't get any better than this!" is better known among our youth than "We hold these truths to be self-evident."

But don't place all the blame on the kids—they're not likely to learn what we don't teach them. We no longer teach the moral absolutes proclaimed in the *Declaration of Independence*; we now teach moral relativism, the natural outgrowth of evolutionary theory. The ideals of our *Declaration* were thrown out of our government schools (and virtually out of public life) in the early '60s, and since then our cultural indicators have taken a nose dive. Sadly, when it comes to the moral health of our country, it couldn't get much *worse* than this:

FROM 1960–1992, THE U.S. POPULATION INCREASED 41%. YET OVER THE SAME PERIOD:[1]	
Violent Crime	Up 550%
Expected Prison Sentence	Down 60% (Average time served for murder in 1992: 5 years)
Births to Unwed Mothers	Up 400% (They now account for 30% of all births.)
Abortion	1 of every 4 pregnancies; 28 million from 1972–1992 (nearly 40 million by 1998); More than 99% of all abortions have nothing to do with rape, incest, or the life of the mother.
Divorce	Up 125%
Teenage Suicide	Up 200%
Education	SAT scores fell 73 points, even though inflation-adjusted expenditures rose more than 200%.
Hours of TV per Household	Up 40% (50 hrs./week)
Federal Tax Burden on Families	Doubled to 24% of income
Federal Social Spending	Up 550% (14.4% of GDP in 1992)

How and why has this happened? Much of the blame can be traced back to the social outworking of Charles Darwin's theory of evolution. Beliefs have consequences in behavior. We've already seen how belief in evolution spawned an atheistic philosophy that helped justify the immoral behavior of dictators such as Hitler, Stalin, and Mao Tse-Tung. But how has this atheistic philosophy altered the moral direction of a republic such as the United States? The answer lies with a different kind of dictator—one that works much more slowly but still manages to legislate laws that encourage immoral behavior. That dictator has been our own Supreme Court.

We will show later how a series of Supreme Court decisions trumpeted the start of the moral decline we've been experiencing since 1961. But first, let's take a look at the roots of those decisions. These roots go back about thirty years earlier to when secular humanists began a concerted effort to spread their influence in our society.

THE SPREAD OF SECULAR HUMANISM

As we saw in chapter 4, naturalistic evolution began to grow rapidly in intellectual circles after Darwin first published his theory in 1859. By 1933 some evolutionists were ready to write a doctrinal statement. That's when a group of prominent American Darwinists got together—including the father of modern American education, John Dewey—and called themselves "religious humanists," and wrote "Humanist Manifesto I." In it they declared (among other things):

> To establish such a religion of humanism is a major necessity of the present. It is a responsibility that rests upon this generation. We therefore affirm the following:
>
> First: Religious humanists regard the universe as self-existing and not created.
>
> Second: Humanism believes that man is a part of nature and that he has emerged as the result of a continuous process. . . .
>
> Fifth: Humanism asserts that the nature of the universe depicted by modern science makes unacceptable any supernatural or cosmic guarantee of human values.[2]

The first and most obvious claim of these humanists is that they consider humanism to be a religion despite the fact that humanism denies the existence of God. The term "religion" or its equivalent occurs twenty-nine times in the short document. Second, the document contains many tenets of this self-proclaimed religion of humanism. Among them are at least three basic beliefs which are still believed by most secular humanists today. They are:

(1) no Creator of the universe (there is no supernatural);

(2) no creation of man (man evolved);

(3) no moral absolutes.

Does this ring a bell—a liberty bell? Humanist beliefs are exactly opposite to the beliefs that our *Declaration of Independence* claims are "self-evident." If these beliefs could permeate our culture, they would have a profound effect on behavior in our nation. And that is exactly what has happened.

Following Humanist Manifesto I, humanist beliefs began to permeate our education establishments, particularly through the efforts of Dewey. Humanist teachings influenced our teachers, our politicians, our lawyers, and ultimately our Supreme Court justices. Their success was not the result of some sinister left-wing conspiracy, but rather an open call to militantly spread the "common faith" of Humanism. Dewey's 1934 book *A Common Faith* made this prefectly clear. Here's how the book ended: "Here are all the arguments for a religious faith that shall not be confined to sect, class, or race. Such a faith has always been the common faith of mankind. It remains to make it explicit and militant."[3]

Like Dewey, other humanists asserted that they were part of an atheistic religion with evolution (anti-creation) as its central belief. In fact, one humanist, Julian Huxley (grandson of T. H. Huxley, mentioned in chapter 4), wrote a book entitled *Religion Without Revelation*,[4] in which he urged the establishment of a "religion of evolutionary humanism." Another humanist, K. Kolenda, wrote *Religion Without God*[5] and there is even a journal called the *Religious Humanist*. So there is no question that humanists, especially since 1933, have claimed that their views, while atheistic or agnostic, are also religious. (Humanists officially reaffirmed their beliefs in 1973 with "Humanist Manifesto II.")

By the early '60s, the influence of these religious humanists had reached the highest levels of our judiciary. In 1961 the United States Supreme Court agreed with the humanists' claim that Secular Humanism is a religion. The Court noted in *Torcaso v. Watkins* that "among religions in this country which do not teach what would generally be considered a belief in the existence of God are Buddhism, Taoism, ethical culture, Secular Humanism, and others."

The *Torcaso* decision was much more significant than it

might appear. We'll fully elaborate on its significance in the next chapter. But first, we need to point out that *Torcaso* marked the beginning of a series of Supreme Court decisions that contributed to our moral decline by outlawing virtually every reference to God in American public life. In many of those decisions, the Court used the "Separation of Church and State" doctrine—supposedly found in the First Amendment—as the rationale for its decisions. So before we discuss the implications of *Torcaso* and the decisions that followed it, we need to take a close look at the First Amendment and the so-called "Separation" doctrine. When the true meaning of the First Amendment is understood, one can clearly see how our country has gotten off track morally, and why we believe our present governing situation is better described by "We the Supreme Court" than by "We the People."

THE SEPARATION OF CHURCH AND STATE?

Perhaps the best way to present how the Supreme Court has been affecting the moral health of the nation is to investigate its most used (and abused) doctrinal tool—the "Separation of Church and State." Whenever people talk about morality and government you always hear them saying, "What about the separation of church and state?" After all, that's what the First Amendment is all about, isn't it?

This is what the First Amendment says: "Congress shall make no law respecting an establishment of religion, or prohibiting the free exercise thereof; or abridging the freedom of speech, or of the press; or the right of the people peaceably to assemble, and to petition the Government for a redress of grievances." Notice that the words "separation," "church," and "state" do not appear in it. (Ironically, those words do appear in the old Soviet Constitution.)

Before we go any further, we need to calm any fears you may be having. Perhaps you're suspecting that we are trying to debunk "the separation of church and state" so we can advocate some sort of religious government for the United States. Rest assured that we are not. Let's simply say right up front that, in our view, no one should want the church running the government or vice versa. (Some on the "far right" do want this, and we'll explain why we believe they're wrong in chapter 7.) Nevertheless, this myth that the First Amendment separates church and state

79

has grown to such ridiculous proportions that it must be debunked before it contributes further to the moral breakdown of our country.

What the First Amendment Really Means

Of course, the obvious question is, "If the First Amendment doesn't mean the separation of church and state, then what does it mean?" Clearly, the Amendment prohibits Congress from establishing a national religion or denomination, but, as we have seen, it logically cannot prohibit Congress from establishing a national morality. The real question is, does the Amendment require absolute separation between government and religion to the point that everything in public must be sanitized of any reference to God? That's what the courts have led most people to believe over the past fifty years, but history doesn't support this now popular view.

When you look even casually at the historical situation surrounding our country's founding, it's not hard to identify the intent of the First Amendment. As we mentioned before, our Founding Fathers—having just come from a country with a government-run church—simply didn't want the same problems associated with church and government entanglement to beset their new nation. James Madison, who has been called the "Architect of the Constitution," said that the intent of the First Amendment was "that Congress should not establish a national religion, and enforce the legal observation of it by law."[6] The last thing he intended was the interpretation held by many today that seeks to exorcise religion from public life as if it were some kind of demon.

In fact, through the "free exercise clause," Madison and his colleagues wanted to ensure that citizens *would not be prevented* from practicing their religion or discriminated against for their religious beliefs. The Founders wanted to guarantee freedom *of* religion, not freedom *from* religion. If the First Amendment guaranteed freedom *from* religion, it would also require freedom *from* speech, *from* assembly, and *from* the press. That would mean you'd have to shut up when someone walked by; your group would have to disperse when someone walked through; and reporters and people carrying newspapers could not come into your presence. Absurd!

The modern interpretation of the First Amendment has so

prejudiced our way of thinking that many people don't realize how much the Founders actually wanted the government to *encourage* religion, not separate it completely from the government. In fact, the Founding Fathers intended the government to be free to support all religions. Their only rule in supporting religion was that the federal government could not prefer one particular sect or denomination over another. Being predominately Christian in their beliefs (twenty-seven of them had even attended seminary), the Founding Fathers wanted to support all Christian denominations without establishing any one in particular. How do we know?

First, because the neglected other half of the First Amendment, known as the "free exercise" clause, actually encourages religion by adding "nor prohibiting the free exercise thereof." In short, the federal government could neither establish one religion in particular nor forbid religion in general. The Founding Fathers knew that encouraging and supporting religion would help ensure a strong national morality, which was necessary for the success of the nation. On September 19, 1796, President George Washington said in his farewell speech: "Of all the dispositions and habits which lead to political prosperity, Religion and Morality are indispensable supports. . . . Reason and experience both forbid us to expect that *national morality* can prevail in exclusion of religious principle" (emphasis added).[7]

In short, Washington favored a "national morality," which only religion could foster. Benjamin Franklin declared, "Only a virtuous people are capable of freedom."[8] And John Adams, our second president, asserted, "We have no government armed with power capable of contending with human passions unbridled by morality and religion. Avarice, ambition, revenge, or gallantry, would break the strongest cords of our Constitution as a whale goes through a net. Our Constitution was made only for a moral and religious people. It is wholly inadequate to the government of any other."[9]

Second, the actions of the founders and our early presidents speak louder than their words. Many of them supported giving *federal* money and *federal* land to a number of different Christian denominations so that those groups could encourage religion among the Indians. The evidence is telling:

- In 1795, President Washington approved a grant of $1000 to build a church for the Oneida Indians.

- In 1796, an act was passed by Congress under President Washington regulating the land given to the Society of United Brethren for "propagating the gospel among the heathen." The act was extended under Presidents Adams and Jefferson.
- In 1803, Congress and President Jefferson approved a grant of $100 for seven years to a Roman Catholic priest to evangelize the Kaskaskia Indians, and $300 to help build them a church. Jefferson also approved similar treaties with the Wyandotte Indians in 1806 and the Cherokee Indians in 1807.
- In 1819, President Monroe, along with Congress, approved the grant of 640 acres to the rector of a Roman Catholic church in Detroit.
- In 1825, President John Quincy Adams, in a treaty with the Osage Indians, dedicated federal lands to a "missionary establishment" engaged in "teaching, civilizing, and improving said Indians."
- In 1833, Congress and President Jackson approved a grant of $3700 to build a church and a mill for the Kickapoo Indians.
- In 1838, President Van Buren, along with Congress, approved funds to help build a church for the Oneida Indians.[10]

Can you imagine even suggesting that the government do these things today? Recent Supreme Court rulings claim that saying a simple prayer at a graduation ceremony or displaying a nativity scene on public property violates the First Amendment. Today's Court comes to these untenable conclusions while the men who wrote the First Amendment didn't see any constitutional problem in subsidizing religious groups with federal tax dollars![11]

Further evidence that the Founders wanted to encourage religion lies with the fact that between 1789 and 1814 there were no fewer than seven presidential proclamations for the national observance of a Thanksgiving religious holiday. In wishing to encourage the Christian religion in general but not one sect in particular, these proclamations were generally free of denominational language, yet they were clearly religious in nature. President George Washington's 1789 National Day of Thanksgiving Proclamation reads as follows:

Whereas it is the duty of all nations to acknowledge the

providence of Almighty God, to obey His will, to be grateful for His benefits, and humbly to implore His protection and favor.... Now, therefore, I do recommend ... [that we] unite in most humbly offering our prayers and supplications to the great Lord and Ruler of Nations, and beseech Him to pardon our national and other transgressions...."[12]

Washington obviously was urging the people to engage in a fervent religious practice because he knew it was good for the moral state of the country. Other presidents made similar proclamations and they were *never* challenged as violations of the First Amendment.

How the First Amendment Was Redefined

As we have seen, there's irrefutable evidence that the Founders intended to support religion in general without promoting any denomination in particular. They supported many different denominations through direct financial subsidies, and religion in general through presidential proclamations. But since those early days, there have been a number of Supreme Court decisions that have given the First Amendment a different meaning than that intended by the Founding Fathers. One of the first cases to ignore the Founders and create a new meaning for the First Amendment was *Everson v. Board of Education* in 1947. This was the first case to cite the "separation of church and state" interpretation of the First Amendment that is now so predominant in our popular culture.

The separation language in *Everson* was taken from an old Thomas Jefferson letter. In 1802 Jefferson responded to the Danbury, Connecticut Baptists, who were concerned about a rumor that Jefferson was going to establish a national denomination. In his letter to assure them that this was not the case, Jefferson borrowed the words "the wall of separation between church and state" from one of the Baptists' own preachers, Roger Williams (a signer of the *Declaration of Independence* and the Constitution). Jefferson echoed Williams' sentiments that the church should be protected from interference by the government through a one-way "wall" (membrane) of protection. Jefferson wanted to protect the church from the government, not the other way around! He certainly didn't mean that the mere mention of anything religious by the government was unconstitutional.[13]

Nevertheless, nearly 150 years later, justices on the *Everson*

Court pulled Jefferson's letter out of context to support their view that the First Amendment requires "an impregnable wall" of separation between church and state. Their conclusion was seriously flawed for a number of reasons.

First, this is the same Jefferson who, within a year of writing the Danbury letter, gave federal money to evangelize the Indians. How could Thomas Jefferson have meant that the First Amendment required an "impregnable wall" of separation between church and state when he, as president of the United States, approved the federal funding of religious missionary groups on numerous occasions?

Second, this is the same Jefferson who, with state funds, set up a University of Virginia that included a department of Divinity, proposed laws that forbade swearing, and declared that students "would be expected to attend religious services."

Finally, this is the same Thomas Jefferson *who wasn't at the constitutional convention!* Thomas Jefferson had nothing to do with the writing of the First Amendment—he was in France as ambassador to that country during the constitutional convention. Jefferson wrote the *Declaration of Independence*, not the Constitution. So looking at old letters from Jefferson for insights into what the framers intended by the First Amendment doesn't make sense in the light of history. Instead, looking at Jefferson's actions (i.e., subsidizing religious groups with government money) proves that he believed the First Amendment did *not* separate church and state the way it is thought of today. In fact, two of our current Supreme Court justices, Chief Justice William Rehnquist and Justice Antonin Scalia, recently pointed this out when they called *Everson*'s separation doctrine "bad history [that] should be frankly and explicitly abandoned."[14]

The *Everson* Court not only used bad history to interpret the meaning of the First Amendment, they also used bad history to broaden its scope. The Court ruled that the First Amendment applied to the states through the Fourteenth Amendment. In other words, the *Everson* Court changed the First Amendment's meaning from "*Congress* shall make no law. . . ." to "Congress, the states, the counties, the cities, the school board, etc. shall make no law. . . ."

This was a huge stretch for the Court to make. The Fourteenth Amendment was ratified in 1868 to guarantee that no state would violate the civil rights of recently emancipated slaves. In the nearly eighty years between 1868 and 1947, the Fourteenth Amendment was *never* used to prohibit religious practices in individual states. But the *Everson* Court changed all that by beginning a judicial practice that is running out of control today—the illegitimate use of the Fourteenth Amendment to apply an incorrect interpretation of the First Amendment to all levels of government and every organization in this country that receives government funds. Because of *Everson*, the wording "Congress shall make no law" has been expanded to mean, among other things, "Remove that nativity scene from the firehouse lawn!"

The Founders—champions of state's rights (see the Tenth Amendment, and ponder the name United *States*)—never intended the First Amendment to apply to state governments. There are two very simple facts to prove this. First, many of the constitutions of the thirteen original states *required* their government officials to declare a personal faith in orthodox Christianity (although any one of numerous denominations were acceptable).[15]

Second, in 1791, upon ratifying the First Amendment, *five of the thirteen states had official state churches,* and the state representatives didn't run out and disestablish their churches after passing the First Amendment. The states certainly didn't ratify a law that they immediately would be in violation of! They knew that the First Amendment did not apply to them; it only applied to the federal government (state officials could read; the amendment said: "*Congress [i.e., the federal government]* shall make no law. . . ."). True, those five states with official churches gradually disestablished them over the years, but they did so *voluntarily.* Massachusetts was the last state to do so and that was in 1833, more than forty years later! Of course, one could cite a number of good reasons why states should not establish their own churches, but claiming that the First Amendment prohibits the practice is not one of them. That is, one may question the wisdom of a state religion, but no one should challenge its constitutionality.

The important point, however, is that the First Amendment—whatever its statements about religion are taken to mean—cannot be construed to forbid the establishment of a national morality. Indeed, the promotion of the God-given natural laws in the *Declaration*, in later legislation by Congress and presidents, and in the early pronouncements of the Supreme Court reveal that our nation was established on a national, God-given morality.

CONCLUSION

The writings and actions of the Founding Fathers make it clear that the First Amendment was never intended to be interpreted and applied as it is today. The *Everson* decision was obviously just plain wrong, and its effect on the moral health of our country has been devastating. As we mentioned earlier, *Everson* set the stage for a flurry of Supreme Court rulings that began in the early '60s and have since exorcised religion—and, by association, our founding morality—from public life, all in the name of the groundless "separation of church and state" doctrine.

In the next chapter, we will survey these cases and their perverse implications. We will also show why the intent of the Founding Fathers should be our guiding light when we interpret and apply the Constitution today.

6. "WE THE SUPREME COURT..."

In 1976 humanist Paul Blanshard wrote, "My Primary hero (in helping 'substantially to make the nation into a secular society') is the United States Supreme Court."[1] While the Supreme Court is only one of many factors that have contributed to the secularization of America, the court's impact has been significant. In this chapter we will see what the Court has done to merit Blanshard's praise and the scorn of many others.

We concluded chapter 5 by pointing out the enormous impact that the 1947 *Everson* decision had on the reigning interpretation of the First Amendment. *Everson* gave birth to the now ingrained "separation of church and state" dogma that was in no way the intent of the Founders. But *Everson*'s effect was not immediate. It wasn't until 1961 that the use of the *Everson* decision really began to alter the moral direction of the country. That year the floodgates of judicial restraint broke down completely, and an onslaught of Court decisions against religion in the public square got underway.

THE COURT RULES

It began with *Torcaso v. Watkins.* As you remember from the beginning of the last chapter, *Torcaso* noted that Secular Humanism is a religion and therefore has First Amendment protection, even though Humanism claims that there is no God. This 1961 Court ruling to recognize Secular Humanism as a religion has led to a perverse outcome in this country. We'll discuss that outcome later in this chapter.

The very next year, 1962, the Court declared in *Engel v. Vitale* that state-formulated school prayer from a New York school district was an unconstitutional violation of the First Amendment—this despite the fact that prayer had been part of our schools for 340 years. The prayer the New York schools were using at the beginning of each day was brief and nondenominational: "Almighty God, we acknowledge our dependence upon Thee, and we beg Thy blessings upon us, our parents, our teachers and our country."[2] The schools did not compel students who objected to join in the prayer, yet the Court deemed it an unconstitutional establishment of religion. Ironically, there is more theological content in the *Declaration of Independence* than in that prayer!

Now let's stop and think about the *Engel* decision for a minute. If state-formulated school prayer really does violate the First Amendment, how did prayer and the country survive from 1791 to 1962? Why didn't the Founding Fathers, or someone in government during the next 171 years, declare school prayer illegal? The answer is very simple—because school prayer is not a violation of the First Amendment (and it never was). To the contrary—anything that expressly *restricts* school prayer is a violation of the First Amendment (recall from chapter 5 that, not only did the states have their own prayers, *five of the original thirteen had their own churches!*). Hence, by any reasonable reading of the First Amendment, the *Engel* decision itself is actually unconstitutional! Unfortunately, the 1962 *Engel* Court believed it knew more about the intent and application of the First Amendment than the men who wrote it.

The Supreme Court's onslaught against the Constitution continued in 1963 with *Abington v. Schempp*. There the Court again used *Everson's* First Amendment interpretation to strike any mention of God from government school classrooms—this time, devotional class Bible readings were declared unconstitutional. The Court said that reading portions of the New Testament could be "psychologically harmful" to the children. In doing so, this 1963 Supreme Court ignored the 1844 Supreme

Court, which had then opined in *Vidal v. Girard's Executors*: "Why may not the Bible, and especially the New Testament ... be read and taught as a divine revelation in the school? ... Where can the purest principles of morality be learned so clearly or so perfectly as from the New Testament?" Moreover, it was particularly ironic for the Court to censor devotional Bible-reading from schools in light of the fact that American schools were established to teach children to read the Bible.[3]

In addition to First Amendment issues, the Court's decisions affected morality in other areas. In the 1965 *Griswold v. Connecticut* decision, the Court created the right to privacy even though the word "privacy" does not exist in the Constitution. That led to the infamous 1973 *Roe v. Wade* case, which concluded that the right to privacy identified in *Griswold* includes the private right to abort children.

Even many advocates of abortion admit *Roe v. Wade* had little supporting precedent and was thus decided improperly. *Roe* was nothing more than judicial activism—judges making law rather than interpreting the Constitution. The effect of this activism was the obliteration of fifty state laws that prohibited or restricted abortion: laws that took over a century to develop. In other words, the *Roe* decision struck down the will of the majority in all fifty states and replaced it with the will of seven unelected judges—exactly the kind of tyrannical abuse of power that the Founding Fathers had fled from and wanted to prevent in this country!

What's worse, the *Roe* Court failed to address the central issue in the abortion debate, which is, of course, the question of whether or not an unborn child is a human being. The Court attempted to sidestep that question. Justice Harry Blackmun wrote: "We need not resolve the difficult question of when life begins."[4] In other words, *in ruling on the legality of abortion, the Supreme Court incredibly denied that it was necessary to discover when life begins!* Of course, by allowing abortion at virtually any time during pregnancy, the Court had by implication declared that life does not begin until birth. Such a conclusion obviously flies in the face of the medical evidence that individual human life begins at conception,[5] and the conscience of a nation that witnesses thousands of babies (not tissue blobs) born prematurely each year (more on this in chapter 10).

The 1980 Court was almost as reckless as the *Roe* Court.

Again using *Everson*'s separation interpretation to further secularize the schools, the Court decided in *Stone v. Graham* that posting the Ten Commandments in public schools was unconstitutional. (This despite the fact that the Ten Commandments are engraved in marble over the Chief Justice's head, and their giver, Moses, is the chief figure on the wall in the chamber of the House of Representatives.) Here's what the Court said: "If the posted copies of the Ten Commandments are to have any effect at all, it will be to induce the schoolchildren to read, meditate upon, perhaps to venerate and obey, the Commandments. . . . This . . . is not a permissible state objective under the Establishment Clause of the First Amendment." Friends, we have a lot of problems in our public schools today; but children obeying the Ten Commandments is not one of them!

When you look at the words of the man who wrote the First Amendment, James Madison, the blatant error of the 1980 Court is even more clear. Madison said, "We have staked the whole future of American Civilization, not upon the power of government, far from it. We have staked the future of all of our political institutions . . . upon the capacity of each and all of us *to govern ourselves, to control ourselves, to sustain ourselves, according to the Ten Commandments of God.*"[6] The 1980 Court obviously ignored Madison, the man who wrote the amendment that they had taken an oath to uphold.

Late the following year, the Scopes II trial began in Little Rock, Arkansas. We've already seen what happened in that trial (chapter 4), but Scopes II was still only a state trial. It wasn't until five years later that the same Creation-evolution controversy reached the Supreme Court of the United States. This time a Louisiana Creation-evolution law was challenged, and the case, *Edwards v. Aguillard*, made it to the Supreme Court in 1987.

The result was virtually a repeat of Scopes II. The Louisiana law that required balanced treatment for Creation when evolution was taught was struck down. The Court reasoned that the law was an unconstitutional "establishment of religion" because its purpose "was clearly to advance the religious viewpoint that a supernatural being created mankind." In effect, the Court declared that any reference to (or implication of) Creation, Creator, or a supernatural cause is religious and therefore unconstitutional. The implications of this decision show that the Court's reasoning was inherently flawed.

IMPLICATIONS OF THE *EDWARDS* DECISION

Implication #1—The Declaration of Independence is unconstitutional.

As shown in chapter 4, positing a supernatural cause of the universe does not mean that students will be coerced to worship that cause. In other words, theorizing about supernatural causes is not an establishment of religion, so the Court's reasoning in *Edwards* was clearly fallacious. But more problematic than their reasoning is the implication of their reasoning. By ruling that Creator and Creation are unconstitutional in our government schools, *in effect, the Supreme Court has ruled that the Declaration of Independence is unconstitutional in our government schools!* Our country was founded on Creator and Creation. Should our children be prohibited from reading and believing the *Declaration of Independence?*

If Thomas Jefferson were to come back to America today— the one who said, "taxation without representation is tyranny"—do you know what he'd find? He'd find his tax dollars going to pay government schoolteachers to teach his children that the *Declaration of Independence* is unconstitutional! It doesn't take a lot of imagination to know what Jefferson would do: Not that we would agree with such a reaction, but he'd undoubtedly start the second American Revolution! He'd say we failed in the first one.

Implication #2—Secular Humanism is the de facto established religion of the land.

The second serious implication from this decision is that, in its effort to prevent the establishment of theism, the Court established atheism (Secular Humanism) as the religion of the land. According to *Edwards*, the only point of view that can be taught by public schools is that which corresponds exactly to the religion of Secular Humanism. This is because on the issue of origins there are only two possible points of view:

DECLARATION OF INDEPENDENCE	OR	SECULAR HUMANISM
Creator		No Creator
Creation		No Creation (evolution)
Unalienable Moral Rights		No Unalienable Moral Rights

Now, by simple logic, if there are only two possible "relig-ious" positions, and if the Court has ruled that it is unconstitu-tional to teach one of them, then the Court has thereby estab-lished the other as the official religion of the land and the schools. The beliefs of Washington, Jefferson, and Madison have been censored, while the beliefs of Darwin, Dewey, and Marx take the protected center stage!

Like a child who traps himself by telling one lie to cover up another, the Court's own decisions contradict each other. In *Everson* the Court ruled that the First Amendment prohibits the es-tablishment of religion. In *Torcaso* they declared that Secular Hu-manism is a religion. Then in *Edwards*, they established one religion—Secular Humanism—over all others and rejected the foundational beliefs of the country in the process. If our judges would have stuck to the intended meaning of the Constitution, this whole mess never would have happened.

Implication #3—The Creator is off limits when studying the origin of the universe.

In declaring Creation off limits the Court has not only estab-lished Secular Humanism but also adopted an anti-supernatural bias into law. Instead of leaving the question of origins open to debate—and open debate should be the rule under which our ed-ucational system operates—our public system now flatly ex-cludes the possibility of considering or teaching supernatural Creation.

In other words, they have ruled the *possibility* of God out of existence. Taking His place, the evolutionists and the Supreme Court have been acting as if they are God by ordering our chil-dren to learn only one theory of origin: evolution (which they refer to as a "fact"). The implication to our children is that sci-ence has disproved God and any possibility of supernatural Cre-ation. They have insisted that our children may not see the evi-dence that points to a creator lest they draw the natural conclusion that the amazing design in nature implies an amazing Designer of nature.

Ruling out God is the goal of many of the Darwinists. One atheist, G. Richard Bozarth, has written:

> And how does a god die? Quite simply because all his re-ligionists have been converted to another religion, and there

is no one left to make children believe they need him. Finally, it is irresistible—we must ask how we can kill the god of Christianity. We need only insure that our schools teach only secular knowledge.... If we could achieve this, God would indeed be shortly due for a funeral service.[7]

Through the dictates of the Court on our educational system, the Darwinists have been effective in killing the "god of Christianity" and replacing Him with a belief in atheism. But since the Supreme Court killed "the god of Christianity" in our government schools, God is not the only one who has experienced a "funeral service." Unfortunately, funeral services have been on the rise for many of our school children as well. As we mentioned at the beginning of chapter 5, violence and suicide has risen dramatically among our youth. Just look at the top disciplinary problems experienced by our public school teachers only a couple of generations apart:

TOP DISCIPLINARY PROBLEMS ACCORDING TO PUBLIC SCHOOL TEACHERS[8]	
1940s	1990s
talking	drug abuse
chewing gum	alcohol abuse
making noise	pregnancy
running in the halls	suicide
cutting in line	rape
improper clothing	robbery
littering	assault

The connection is very simple: the Supreme Court ruled God out of existence and took Him out of the public square and out of our government schools. Since the Court took God out of our schools, we've gotten exactly what we should expect: godless schools.

Implication #4—The Supreme Court was wrong for almost the first two centuries of its existence.

The Court's rejection of the Creator directly contradicts scores of its earlier rulings, which specifically affirm the existence of God and uphold traditional moral principles. Here are just a few of the cases that cite God, Christianity, or traditional moral principles as rationale in their opinions: *Commonwealth v. Abner Kneeland*, 1838 (First Amendment religious protection extends only to believers in God, not atheists); *Vidal v. Girard's Executors*, 1848 (Bible reading is good for schoolchildren); *City of Charleston v. S. A. Benjamin*, 1846 (We should rest on Sundays because it is "the day of the Resurrection"); *Reynolds v. United States*, 1878, *Murphy v. Ramsey*, 1885, and *Davis v. Beason*, 1889 (Polygamy and bigamy are illegal because we are a "Christian people" and the family and "holy matrimony" are foundations of civilization); *United States v. Macintosh*, 1931 (noted that "we are a Christian people"); *Zorach v. Clauson*, 1952 (The First Amendment does not require government hostility to religion; our people and institutions "presuppose a Supreme Being").[9]

The relevant sections of the Constitution have not changed between these decisions—which affirm Moral Law principles—and all those we mentioned earlier (including *Edwards*), which deny them. If the Constitution hasn't changed, why have Court opinions changed? Why do they conflict? How can the Court rightly have it both ways? Simple. They argue that the Constitution is an evolving document.

IS THE CONSTITUTION AN EVOLVING DOCUMENT?

Some on the Left rightly point out that our society is more pluralistic today than it was when our Constitution was written over two hundred years ago. After all, 99 percent claimed to be Christians in the late 1700s, but today we have a much more diverse mix of religions and cultures in this country. Don't these changes necessitate that the Supreme Court interpret the Constitution differently in order to fit our ever-changing society? Shouldn't we consider the Constitution to be an "evolving" document?

This argument goes back to Herbert Spencer, whom Charles Darwin called "our great philosopher." Remember, it was Spencer who theorized that everything is evolving, including laws and morals (everything, of course, but his theory—that, apparently, is not evolving). Many on the Supreme Court have adopted Spencer's view. Unfortunately, applying his view to the Constitution destroys the integrity of the law and disconnects the people from the law-making process. For if an unelected tribunal of judges can pour any interpretation they desire into a law, then the intentions of the people expressed in that law can be frustrated and usurped. The law ultimately means nothing if its original intent is not honored. Stop signs are useless if drivers are free to interpret them as "Go!"

In the cases we've discussed thus far, the Supreme Court justices—instead of being guardians of the Constitution—have twisted it to their own liking, which is exactly what Thomas Jefferson said we should not do. Jefferson declared: "On every question of construction [we should] carry ourselves back to the time when the Constitution was adopted; recollect the spirit manifested in the debates; and instead of trying [to find] what meaning may be squeezed out of the text, or invented against it, conform to the probable one, in which it was passed."[10]

In light of this, the only proper way to keep our laws "up with the times" (if that is desirable) is to use the established procedure to amend the Constitution. In other words, if excessive pluralism means that it's no longer practical for government to fund or even casually acknowledge religious causes and organizations, then we should urge our representatives to pass an amendment stating as much. But that's a decision for "We the People," not the Supreme Court. *Allowing the Court to read their own meaning into the Constitution defeats the whole purpose of a government of the people, by the people, and for the people.*

CONCLUSION

We began chapter 5 by citing the dismal state of our cultural indicators. Crime is up and test scores are down. Such changes in behavior don't happen in a vacuum. Behavior can ultimately be traced back to beliefs, and beliefs to education. When the elite in education and government begin to promote new beliefs, eventually the citizens learning those new beliefs will exhibit new behaviors. Our citizens have now learned godless Secular Humanism, and so they now exhibit godless behavior.

The sad fact is that we have learned this new "religion" not because it is supported by superior reasoning or new revelation, but because the Supreme Court has ruled the old religion off limits. By nothing other than their personal philosophical prejudices, the justices have legislated their own views while censoring the views upon which this country was founded. In fact, judging from the Supreme Court decisions we have reviewed in these last two chapters, one thing is for sure: We are absolutely certain that at least one branch of government believes in legislating morality. Unfortunately, that branch is the only branch that should not be involved in legislating anything!

Judicial activism has turned our nation's moral sensibility on its head. Instead of a coherent system of rational decisions based on the intent of the people as expressed in the laws of Congress, we are left with a fractured and contradictory set of decisions that have helped to destroy our educational establishments, undermine the moral foundations of our country, and fuel the dramatic rise in crime and disrespect for life.

The start of the long road back to a civil society begins by reintroducing the Moral Law back into the public debate. That's the task for the remainder of this book.

PART III

WHOSE MORALITY SHOULD WE LEGISLATE?

7. YOURS OR MINE?

8. OURS!

7. YOURS OR MINE?

After reviewing the avalanche of Supreme Court "legislation" in the previous two chapters—legislation that has established Secular Humanism as the religion (and morality) of the land—we believe that the country has good reasons to get back to the Moral Law upon which our nation was founded. Unfortunately, there are some on the extreme right and the extreme left who do not agree with us. Those on the extreme right are the theonomists. They want the Bible to be established as the law of the land. Those on the extreme left are the secular humanists. They want to continue in the direction of the Court and eradicate from public life any and all references to God, religion, or traditional morality. In effect, both groups are saying, "Establish *my* morality!" Yet both groups represent separatist moralities that could destroy our great nation, if adopted.

We have already seen the dismal results we've experienced from trying out the secular humanist morality. But before we take a closer look at that position, let's address those who want to establish the Bible as the divine law of the land.

SHOULD THE BIBLE BE LEGISLATED?

In the face of an increasingly secularized culture and government, many religious people are crying, "Back to our Christian roots; back to a Bible-based government!" Some of these folks are theonomists, who wish to turn the United States into a theonomy such as ancient Israel. That is, theonomists want biblical law, particularly the rules and regulations of the Old Testament, to be binding on every citizen of the nation. There are a number of problems with this view.

First, contrary to what the theonomists claim, *the United States has never had a government based on biblical law.* Our government is based on the Moral Law, which *is consistent with biblical principles*, but is not based on the written code of the Bible itself. Remember that our national birth certificate, the *Declaration of Independence*, is not a distinctively Christian document. It was written by Thomas Jefferson, who wasn't even a Christian. As a deist, Jefferson rejected miracles. He believed that God created the world but then left it alone, so that miracles are not possible. In fact, Jefferson took a pair of scissors to his New Testament and cut out all of its miracles—including the resurrection of Jesus Christ (which is the central historical fact in the Christian faith). His own abbreviated Bible ends with these words: "There laid they Jesus, and rolled a great stone to the door of the sepulchre, and departed."[1]

Despite Jefferson's deism, it *is* true that many of our Founding Fathers were Christians who put biblical principles into our Constitution (1787). However, the Constitution itself makes no reference to the Bible or any binding Christian basis for it. It doesn't even begin with God, but with "We the people..." Although the courts have referred to America as "Christian" in a moral sense, Christianity was never the established religion of the nation. Given these facts, while we cannot deny that there was a strong Christian influence in the founding of our country, there is no reason to claim that the United States has ever had a Christian government. Therefore, our nation cannot "return" to something it never had.

The only time there was any form of Christian government on this land mass was in the Pilgrim settlements in New England, but that was over one hundred years before our nation was born. It must not be forgotten that under the Puritans in

Massachusetts there was no religious freedom. They persecuted those who did not believe their way. Many of those calling for a return to "Christian America" have forgotten what this so-called "Christian" state was like. Ironically, some of them are Baptists, who have forgotten that Roger Williams—a Baptist preacher and signer of the *Declaration of Independence* and the Constitution—founded the state of Rhode Island to serve as a refuge from religious persecution by the Puritans!

The second problem with the theonomists' position is that it would violate the First Amendment by ending religious freedom in our nation. Theonomists want the same Law of Moses that was binding on the people of Israel to be binding on all the people of America. But there was no freedom of religion in Israel before the coming of Christ because God himself was the ruler of the nation. Moreover, there was no separation of religion and politics as we know it because God ruled in their political lives as well as their religious lives. However, once Christ came, even the theonomy of Israel was superseded.[2] Yet even though Israel is no longer ruled directly by God, theonomists want to establish divine law in the United States! If the theonomists ever get their way, there will be only one religion (Reformed Protestant theonomy) and one religious code in this country, and that religious code will include capital punishment for idolatry, witchcraft, adultery, rape, apostasy, sorcery, and blasphemy.[3] This certainly wouldn't jibe with the First Amendment or even the intent of the Bible itself for our nation.

The third problem with the theonomists' position is that their own Bible doesn't support their view! The Bible claims that the Law of Moses was only given to the nation of Israel. Psalm 147:19–20 reads, "He has revealed his word to Jacob, his laws and decrees to Israel. He has done this for no other nation; they do not know his laws."[4] God did not give this law to the non-Jews (the Gentiles). The Bible says explicitly that "Gentiles ... do not have the law."[5] The Jews were given an "advantage" over Gentiles, said the apostle Paul, in that "they have been entrusted with the very words of God."[6] He added, "Theirs is the adoption as sons; theirs the divine glory, the covenants, the receiving of the law, the temple worship and the promises."[7] As Moses said to Israel, "What other nation is so great as to have such righteous decrees and laws as this body of laws I am setting before you today?"[8] None of those laws were given to the Gentiles. In fact, in the entire history of the world, ancient Israel is the only nation ever established by God to live under divine law. (Of course, Gentiles who lived in Israel had to abide by Israel's civil laws,[9] just as Christians today who live in Islamic nations are compelled to live by Quranic law.) But nowhere does the Bible teach that the divine law for Israel is the divinely prescribed basis for the civil laws of Gentile countries. Although the Bible claims that numerous Gentile countries were condemned for a multitude of sins, never once does the Bible say that a Gentile nation was condemned for not worshiping on the Sabbath or for not bringing a lamb to the Jerusalem temple. Instead, they were condemned for violating the law they had—the Moral Law, "written on their hearts."[10]

You may be thinking, "If God hasn't given the other nations the Bible to run their governments, then from what source should they draw their moral principles and laws? Should they simply make them up?" Absolutely not! God gave people in every nation the Moral Law. The apostle Paul states very clearly in Romans 1 and 2 that the standard by which the other nations know right from wrong is the Moral Law, not the Bible. It is not the Law of Moses, but the law "written on their hearts."[11] This Moral Law is "clearly seen . . . so that men are without excuse."[12] It is so plainly visible to all people that those who do not live according to it "perish," and are "held accountable to God."[13]

At the very birth of our country, our Founding Fathers recognized this. They understood the utility of the Moral Law for governments. First they condemned King George III by the Moral Law, and then they explicitly founded their new government on it. As we have seen, the *Declaration of Independence* spoke of "Nature's Law," which provides "unalienable Rights" for all citizens.

What the theonomists fail to see is that the Bible and the Moral Law perform different functions. Since they both have the same source (God), they have similar moral principles. But that doesn't mean they should be used interchangeably in a functional sense. The Bible was not designed by God to be the normative basis for civil government. For that, He gave the Moral Law.

The fourth problem with the theonomists' position also entails a misinterpretation of the Bible. It confuses the future political reign of Christ with the present nonpolitical, spiritual reign. Theonomist Rousas Rushdooney asserts that "saints must prepare to take over the world's courts and its governments."[14] But the kingdom at present is not a political one. Jesus said, "My kingdom is not of this world. If it were, my servants would fight.... But now my kingdom is from another place."[15]

In short, according to their own Bible, the theonomists are wrong. The Bible's message for the entire world is not political but spiritual. It offers the free gift of spiritual and eternal forgiveness for violating the perfect standard of right behavior that we all have broken. Its central figure is Jesus Christ, the perfect God-man, who voluntarily took our deserved punishment on himself, and who will be our Substitute if we individually choose to accept Him. The Bible does not call us to reform society by political imposition of the Scriptures, but to live reformed lives through the Savior. Thus Jesus' Great Commission[16] is not a political or cultural mandate; it is a spiritual mandate. It is a command to make Christian disciples,[17] not to set up Christian dominions. As Charles Colson eloquently put it in his book *Kingdoms in Conflict*:

> The [theonomist's] mindset ... fails to make the crucial distinction between a Christian's function as a private citizen and as an officeholder. As private citizens, Christians are free to advocate their Christian view in any and every form.... But Christians elected to public office acquire a different set of responsibilities. Now they hold the power of the sword, which God has placed with government to preserve order and maintain justice. Now they act not for themselves but for all whom they serve. For this reason they cannot use their office to evangelistically "Christianize" their culture. Their duty is to ensure justice and religious liberty for all citizens of all beliefs.... If Christians today understood this distinction between the role of the private Christian citizen and the Christian in government, they might sound less like medieval crusaders. If secularists understood correctly the nature of Christian public duty they would not fear, but welcome responsible Christian political involvement.[18]

Conclusion Concerning Legislating the Bible

Should we legislate the Bible? No. The position of the far-right theonomists violates the Bible itself and the First Amendment. What we should legislate is the Moral Law—the self-evident truths that are in agreement with many biblical principles because of their common source (God). However, just because the Bible should not be legislated, doesn't mean that biblical principles or Bible-believing people are disqualified from the political realm. Here we need to make two critical distinctions concerning political involvement and the Bible.

First, while the Bible does not call for its political imposition on civil governments, it does call for those who believe in the Bible to be politically active. Christians are commanded to be "salt" and "light," and this includes getting involved in the political process, even running for office. The Bible does not command Christians to set up a *Christian* America; it simply commands them to help create a *moral* America. That is, Christians shouldn't try to set up a Christian government, but they should try to promote a Christianlike morality (i.e., the Moral Law) in government.

Second, the fact that the Bible is not normative for government does not mean it is not informative for Christians in government. There is no reason, for example, why a Christian politician cannot be enlightened by the social ethic of Scripture on the morally related issues before him or her. After all, the God of the Bible is the same God who inscribed His law on the hearts of all people. Indeed, the moral principles embodied in the second table of the Ten Commandments are similar to those of the Moral Law. In this sense—the sense that the Ten Commandments are consistent with Moral Law principles—it is right to legislate according to the Ten Commandments. However, it is wrong if we are talking about legislating the Ten Commandments as part of ancient Israel's divine law—divine law that included capital punishments for even noncapital crimes.

The divine law is for the church and the Moral Law is for the state. When sacred law is made the basis for civil law, non-Christians will reject it in favor of their human law. After all, history is replete with religious zealots, whether Constantine or Calvin, the Crusaders or the Pilgrims, who established their own divine rule over unbelievers.

We can be thankful in America that the divine law of the Puritan's theonomy was eventually replaced with the Moral Law of Jefferson's republic, and that the desire to establish one Christian denomination was replaced with the First Amendment prohibition against the establishment of any specific national religion.

"THE RELIGIOUS RIGHT" VS.
"THE RELIGIOUS LEFT"

As we look at both extremes, we need to be clear with our terminology. It would be very tempting to claim that the theonomists represent the views of what the liberal press calls "the religious right," but this would not be accurate. Most politically active, conservative religious people in this nation are not theonomists. In fact, leading theonomists have been critical of the Christian Coalition (the organization most thought to represent the "religious right") for being too moderate.[19] Most in the Christian Coalition simply want to halt our horrifying slide into moral decadence by returning moral decency and the respect for human life to society. They are not interested in replacing the Constitution with the Bible in our government. They are interested in restoring the Constitution *as* the bible *of* our government.

Conversely, there are folks on the other side of the political spectrum who *do* want to replace our Constitution with another document. Not literally through the legislative process, but effectively through the judiciary. That other group, with their Humanist Manifesto (see chapter 5), is a conglomeration of secular humanists, atheists, radical feminists, evolutionists, and other cultural elites whose views are perhaps best represented by the ACLU.

Although not usually thought of as religious, these people call themselves religious (i.e., "religious humanists") and have been recognized by the Court as religious. While the religious on the Right have faith in God and transcendent values, those on the Left have faith in materialism (there is no God, matter is all there is) and evolution (which they tend to deify). Both groups espouse beliefs that are beyond empirical verification and are thus philosophical or religious. (We bring these observations up simply to show that the Left's criticisms of the Right really boomerang back to hit their own position.) Since the press calls those religious folks on the Right the "Religious Right," we properly could call those on the Left the "Religious Left." However, we think both are pejorative terms and will thus refer to such political groups as the "Left" or "liberals" and the "Right" or "conservatives."

No one in recent times has critiqued the Left better than

Judge Robert Bork. The absolutes of the Left, as Bork astutely summed up in *Slouching Towards Gomorrah,* fall into one of two categories: radical individualism and radical egalitarianism.[20] Radical individualism expresses itself in the Left's hostility toward religion and traditional morality. Religion and traditional morality must be exorcised from society, they say, because they hinder individuals from expressing themselves and experiencing any possible pleasure (usually sexual) that crosses their minds. Radical egalitarianism, which Bork describes as the Left's insistence that outcomes rather than opportunities be equal, expresses itself in the Left's support for quotas, affirmative action, and extreme versions of feminism.

The Left's insistence on these twin absolutes has touched virtually every aspect of our culture. It starts in the schools. The media likes to paint only those on the far right as "extremists," but the Left also exhibits a moralizing religious fervor about their own absolutes. Humanist John Dunphy is not shy about spreading the humanist gospel:

> I am convinced that the battle for humankind's future must be waged and won in the public school classroom by teachers who correctly perceive their role as the proselytizers of a new faith: a religion of humanity that recognizes and respects the spark of what theologians call divinity in every human being. These teachers must embody the same selfless dedication as the most rabid fundamentalist preachers. For they will be ministers of another sort, utilizing a classroom instead of a pulpit to convey humanist values in whatever subject they teach, regardless of the educational level—preschool day care or large state university.[21]

Did you hear that? The Left has a "new faith" that they would like to spread. They call this new faith the religion of Secular Humanism; their pulpit is the public school lectern; their missionaries are public schoolteachers; their prospective converts are your children; and their missionary budget? Oh . . . you and I pay that—it's called "taxes."

As they proselytize *your* children with *your* money, they seek to replace the traditional morality with their own morality. They want to replace the old absolutes—sexual fidelity, the sanctity of life, and advancement through hard work—with their new absolutes—sexual license, the sanctity of convenience, and advancement through victimization.

To see this, we only need to look at one of the signatories of the second Humanist Manifesto, Joseph Fletcher, author of *Situation Ethics: The New Morality*. In his book, Fletcher argues that "only the end justifies the means: nothing else,"[22] and all "decisions are made situationally, not prescriptively."[23] He rejected all traditional ethical norms and insisted that we should avoid absolutes like the plague.[24]

Despite Fletcher's claim to avoid absolutes, he signed Humanist Manifesto II, which asserts the Left's own absolutes: total sexual freedom for consenting adults, abortion, euthanasia, and suicide.[25] Such assertions show that the Left is not only morally but intellectually bankrupt. How can they claim that there are no absolutes and then go on to assert some of their own? Thinking people understand that relativism is self-defeating. The Left claims that all values are relative, so that the individual is free to decide right and wrong for himself. But that is an absolute in itself! What the Left really means when it asserts relativism is that all *traditional* absolutes are relative—their new absolutes are the only true absolutes.[26] Reasonable people know better.

SHOULD HUMANISM BE LEGISLATED?

The word "should" usually implies one of two things: intrinsic morality or pragmatism. Either we "should" do something because it is morally right according to an objective standard of right and wrong (morality), or we "should" do something because it will bring the right outcome (pragmatism). (Of course, morality demands we do right regardless of the outcome, which is why we often wish morality didn't exist: it binds us to inconvenient outcomes.) When we address the question, "Should Humanism be legislated?" we are addressing it in both senses. Namely, is it morally right to legislate the absolutes of Humanism, and will Humanism "work" if it is legislated? The answer to both questions is an unequivocal *no*!

First, Humanism is literally an immoral philosophy because it denies any cosmic guarantee of human values. Without unalienable rights firmly rooted in the ultimate authority of the Creator, which Humanism vehemently denies, human rights are left entirely in the hands of those in power. As we saw in previous chapters, the history of the twentieth century has proven Humanism to be an absolute disaster, from Hitler to Stalin to Mao. Moreover, Humanist ideas are contrary to the succinct statement of the Moral Law found in the Golden Rule. Which of the leaders who signed the Manifesto in favor of abortion truly believes that his mother should have killed him in her womb? (As Ronald Reagan said, "I've noticed that all those in favor of abortion are already born.") In short, since humanistic laws can not guarantee unalienable human rights and are contrary to the simplest expression of the Moral Law, they provide an inadequate basis for a just civil government.

Second, not only is Humanism immoral, it doesn't work. Not only has Humanism failed in Germany, Russia, and China, it hasn't worked in this country either. The question "Should we legislate Humanism?" has already been answered because that's what the courts have been legislating in this country since 1961. And as we all know, it has failed miserably. Adding to the depressing statistics we quoted at the beginning of chapter 5, we note that illegitimate births in the United States constituted just 3 percent of all births in 1920 (the first year statistics were gathered) and rose to just over 5 percent in 1960. During Humanism's heyday, the figure shot up to 11 percent by 1970, over 18 percent by 1980, and 30 percent by 1991. Black illegitimacy stood at a shocking 68 percent in 1991 compared to 22 percent of white births. More depressing carnage from the morality of Humanism is the teenage murder rate: between 1985 and 1993, murders committed by eighteen- to twenty-four-year-olds increased by 65 percent and those committed by fourteen- to seventeen-year-olds skyrocketed by 165 percent.[27]

Now, we are well aware that correlation alone does not prove causation. These horrifying statistics during the dominance of Humanism also parallel a similar increase in automatic dishwashers in American homes. We posit no causal connection there. However, we have more than correlation here. The very morality of Humanism logically leads to the results we've seen in this country and the others we've mentioned. Humanists often argue that there have been terrible atrocities committed in the name of God and religion. No doubt they are correct. However, such acts were the *illogical* outworking of Christianity. They were not condoned by Christ, who commanded his disciples to love their enemies. But the important point here is that the evil acts committed in the name of atheism are the *logical* outworking of atheism. In other words, if there is no God, no standard of right and wrong, no ultimate judgment, then why not kill six million Jews to get what you want? Why not have sex and then kill the unborn baby or leave the mother if you can get away with it? Why not murder that kid for his Nikes? Why not?

Humanists who argue that Christianity, not Humanism, has been destructive leave three very important facts out of their argument. First, they ignore the incredible contributions of Christianity to humanity, from education to hospitals to charities to the general restraint of evil and furtherance of good will in our society. This country would not have been discovered, born, civilized, educated, or cared for if it weren't for Christianity. By contrast, Humanism has only taught people to pursue their own selfish desires.

Second, humanists forget that far more evil has been done in the name of atheism than in the name of Christianity. As we indicated in chapter 4, more blood has been spilled in the twentieth century as a result of atheism than has been spilled for all other causes in all other centuries combined.

Third, humanists seem to ignore the fact that behavior flows from beliefs. The behavior our nation is now experiencing—behavior without moral limits—has resulted quite naturally from the humanistic belief that there are no moral limits. By attacking every religious public expression and establishing Secular Humanism (atheism) as the religion of the schools, humanists have been successful in removing from society the belief in God and the Moral Law. As a result, we now have a society that behaves as if there is no God-given standard of behavior. Remove God from the culture and the culture will become godless. That's exactly what American culture has become, and that's why we posit a direct causal connection between Humanism and the moral shambles in which we now live.

CONCLUSION

The extremes of the far right theonomists and the far left humanists must be rejected. Neither the Bible nor radical secularism should be legislated by our government. But we need not choose between whose sectarian morality should be legislated—yours or mine. We simply should reaffirm the morality that birthed our great nation—our morality. Our morality—yours *and* mine—is the subject of the next chapter.

WHOSE MORALITY SHOULD WE LEGISLATE?

8. OURS!

"ANTI-INTELLECTUALISM" AND THE CASE FOR A COMMON MORALITY

In 1992, the Supreme Court decided *Planned Parenthood v. Casey*. By a five to four vote, the Court basically reaffirmed the abortion rights it granted to women in its 1973 verdict in *Roe v. Wade*. In refusing to overturn *Roe*, the Court reasoned this way:

> Some of us as individuals find abortion offensive to our most basic principles of morality, but that cannot control our decision. Our obligation is to define the liberty of all, not to mandate our own moral code. . . . At the heart of liberty is the right to define one's own concept of existence, of meaning, of the universe, and of the mystery of human life.[1]

There is so much wrong with this reasoning that one hardly knows where to begin. We will start by pointing out that underlying this statement is the philosophy of relativism. We have already seen why relativism is self-defeating. Notice the inconsistency here. In their definition of "liberty," the Court reveals that their concept of morality is relative to each individual. In effect, there is no objective "right" morality—it's up to the woman to decide what is "right" for her. Question: By what objective standard did the Court make *that* claim about morality? What was their absolute point of reference if everything is relative? In other words, if moralities are relative, as they claim, how could they imply it would be objectively wrong (i.e., *immoral*) to mandate their moral code on the entire country?

Despite claiming that they *should not* mandate their own personal moral code, that is exactly what the Court went on to do. By legislating from the bench, the Court, in effect, made a new law. They failed to acknowledge that all laws mandate a moral code because all laws declare one behavior right and another behavior wrong. In this very case, when the Court decided to uphold *Roe*, it mandated one morality on the entire country, namely, the morality of the radical Left: that abortion must remain legal; that state governments cannot prohibit it; that fathers have no right to stop it; and that unborn babies have no right to life.

To really grasp the folly of the Court's reasoning, simply ponder what is meant by "At the heart of liberty is the right to define one's own concept of existence, of meaning, of the universe, and of the mystery of human life." Commenting on this foolish claim, Judge Robert Bork writes, "One would think that grown men and women, purporting to practice an intellectual profession, would themselves choose to die with dignity, right in the courtroom, before writing sentences like those."[2] Bork goes on to point out that the Court's "grandiose rhetoric" appeals to the "radical autonomy" demanded by modern liberalism and displays the "anti-intellectualism" of that movement.

Bork is right. The Court's reasoning is anti-intellectual, contradictory, and nonsensical! First, against their own standard, the Court's decision does not allow the fathers or the babies the liberty to "define their own existence." Notice that by granting absolute liberty to the mother, the Court took away the liberty of all governments (i.e., the people), fathers, and babies. Absolute liberty cannot exist in a world where there are other people because it tramples the rights of those other people. Yet absolute liberty is what the Court granted. Second, because the *Casey* decision invalidated democratically decided laws, the Court's decision denies the people the liberty to govern themselves through their own state governments. Third, *shackled by the Court's monolithic definition of liberty, no court in the land would have grounds to convict anyone of any crime—even murder!* After all, by the Court's logic, thieves could be stealing because theft is simply an expression of "their own concept of existence." Racists could be discriminating because, as they "define the universe," only members of their own race should be treated fairly. And murderers could be killing because, by their own definition of "the mystery of human life," their victims are not human. With such conclusions afforded by the Court's contorted definition of liberty, the question must be asked, "If mothers can decide for themselves who lives and who dies, on what grounds do we refuse others in society that same privilege?" Why should Timothy McVeigh serve time for the Oklahoma City bombing? Why should Paul Hill go to jail for killing an abortion doctor? Why should anyone go to jail for anything?

Later, in the same opinion, the Court gave more unjustified reasons for their refusal to allow significant restrictions on a woman seeking an abortion. They opined,

> [The Mother's] suffering is too intimate and personal for the state to insist . . . upon its own version of the woman's role, however dominant that vision has been in the course of our history and our culture. The destiny of the woman must be shaped to a large extent on her own conception of her spiritual imperatives and her place in society.

They offer no intellectual support for this claim. It is simply an emotive declaration that expresses the Left's radical individualism. Of course, the Court would never apply such reasoning (and grant absolute liberty) in cases hostile to leftist causes. Case in point: Do you think the Court would agree with their own reasoning if it was applied to deadbeat dads?

> [The Father's] suffering is too intimate and personal for the state to insist . . . upon its own version of the man's role, however dominant that vision has been in the course of our history and our culture. The destiny of the man must be shaped to a large extent on his own conception of his spiritual imperatives and his place in society.

Never! They vehemently and rightly would ridicule such reasoning! And we vehemently and rightly should refute it when it is applied to abortion.

So what's the point? Besides the instructive benefit of showing the intellectual bankruptcy of the Supreme Court, why have we spent so much time reviewing the *Casey* decision? *Because the truth of the objective Moral Law is most clearly seen by analyzing the tangled rhetoric of those who ignore it.* Moreover, *Casey* shows the arrogance of those on the Left who set up their own baseless moral absolutes in place of the objective absolutes derived from the Moral Law.

As we have been asserting throughout this book, there is a *real* right and wrong, and that real right and wrong is external to ourselves. Consequently, contrary to what the Court implied, *we don't determine right and wrong, we discover it.* Those who choose to define right and wrong according to their "own concept of existence, of meaning, of the universe" endanger themselves and the rest of us around them.

People are not indestructible. Our existence and the universe is not altered by "our own concept" of them. Like the physical universe, the moral universe is governed by unforgiving laws that we do not have the power to alter. No one would claim, for example, that a child could become physically and emotionally healthy by eating literally anything he wanted to eat including battery acid, arsenic, and lead paint chips. There are natural *physical* limits on what one can and cannot eat. In the same way, there are natural *moral* limits to what one can and cannot do. Human beings have natural limits that, if ignored, lead to injury, disease, or death. Yet those on the Left naïvely assert that one morality is not better than another. How many more gruesome statistics spawned by their own morality do they need to see before they will concede that all moralities are not equal; that the Moral Law morality is correct and is meant for our own good? Indeed, the Moral Law recognizes nature's unforgiving moral limits and prevents us from destroying ourselves and others when we obey its precepts. It is truly the common morality of us all.

The Moral Law is self-evident to most people. However, as we have seen, people can choose to suppress its morality whenever it interferes with their personal lusts and desires. If we continue to let the Supreme Court and the Left suppress the Moral Law morality from our public life, our country is not likely to survive the evil that will continue to grow within it. We must have the intellectual fortitude to remind people that there is a real Right and Wrong. In fact, that real Right and Wrong is the foundation upon which our country was birthed.

OUR MORALITY:
"WE HOLD THESE TRUTHS
TO BE SELF-EVIDENT . . ."

As we saw in chapter 1, Thomas Jefferson incorporated the Moral Law into the *Declaration of Independence*, the founding document of our country (1776). Jefferson's wording in the *Declaration* reflected that of the English philosopher John Locke, who spoke of the "Law of Nature," which teaches us that "being all equal and independent, no one ought to harm another in his life, health, liberty, or possessions; for men being all the workmanship of one omnipotent and infinitely wise Maker. . . ."[3] Jefferson phrased it this way: "We hold these Truths to be self-evident, that all Men are created equal, that they are endowed by their Creator with certain unalienable Rights, that among these are Life, Liberty and the pursuit of Happiness."

Notice that Jefferson believed that these unalienable rights are rooted in the "Laws of Nature," which derive from "Nature's God." In fact, inscribed on the Jefferson Memorial in Washington, D.C., are these words Jefferson wrote:

> God who gave us life gave us liberty. Can the liberties of
> a nation be secure when we have removed a conviction that
> these liberties are the gift of God?

Here again, it is clear that Jefferson's America was based on the concept of God-given rights grounded in God-given moral rules called "Nature's Laws."

In basing this country on the Moral Law, Jefferson and his co-founders avoided the problems we discussed in the last chapter. Namely, a Moral Law government avoids the intolerance of a purely religious government and the moral relativism of a purely secular government. Instead, it secures the unalienable rights of individuals and thereby places moral restraints on the government itself. That is, if it is adhered to.

Unfortunately, the takeover by the Left of our Court, media, and education systems has led to the virtual expulsion of the Moral Law from our government and its rulings. The power brokers on the Left have distorted the rights guaranteed by the *Declaration*. Sadly, they have succeeded in reversing the natural hierarchy of rights. They have literally ignored the right to life while driving the right to liberty to obnoxious extremes. *The right to life is the right to all other rights; if you don't have life you don't have anything (including liberty).*

This reversal of the rights hierarchy has been devastating. Not only has it destroyed the respect for life, thus leading to over 35 million (mostly convenience) abortions and a growing demand for euthanasia, it has also helped fragment our society into a smattering of whining special interest groups all demanding absolute liberty to do their own thing. But as we have observed, absolute liberty cannot exist in a world where there is more than one person. Your right to liberty must end where it infringes on the life, liberty, or property of someone else. The signers of the *Declaration of Independence* knew this. They understood that "liberty" and "happiness" had limits, but, as Judge Bork pointed out, "It would have spoiled the effect to have added 'up to a point' or 'within reason' to Jefferson's resounding generalities."[4] As we discussed in chapter 1, the Founders more than a decade later codified some limits on those rights in the Constitution. However, since that time, many of those limits have been redefined or completely annihilated by an activist Supreme Court.

"OUR" MORALITY IS TRULY MULTICULTURAL

Multiculturalism today—the "politically correct" version—tends to teach that Western cultures are evil and minority cultures are good. But the ironic fact about cultures is that virtually all of them throughout history *fundamentally agree* on what is good and what is evil. Contrary to popular belief, the great moral writings of the world do not manifest a total diversity of perspectives. Indeed, there is a striking similarity among them.

The great Oxford scholar C. S. Lewis challenged his readers to cite a culture where the opposite of Moral Law principles were extolled: "Think of a country where people were admired for running away in battle, or where a man felt proud of double-crossing all the people who had been kindest to him. You might just as well try to imagine a country where two and two made five."[5] Lewis admitted diversity of customs across cultures, but rightly affirmed common values underlying those customs. He wrote, "Men have differed as regards what people you ought to be unselfish to—whether it was only your own family, or your fellow countrymen or everyone. But they have always agreed that you ought not to put yourself first. Selfishness has never been admired."[6] Indeed, there is no land where murder is virtue and gratitude is vice.[7]

Lewis wrote an entire book (*The Abolition of Man*)[8] in defense of the Moral Law and the transcultural consistency of moral values. Appendix III in this book is adapted from the appendix in *The Abolition of Man*, which shows that ethics have been consistent across cultures. In other words, as Lewis' research points out, *it doesn't matter if we're talking about the cultures of the ancient Egyptians, medieval Norsemen, or modern-day Aborigines, all have agreed on the basic concept of right and wrong.* The Moral Law is found in ancient Hindu, Chinese, and Greek writings. Even before Socrates, the Greek philosopher Heraclitus believed in an unchanging Logos (Reason) behind the changing flux of human experience.[9] Plato held to moral absolutes.[10] The Stoics developed moral law theories well before the time of Christ.[11] And, of course, Christ summarized a central principle of the Moral Law with the Golden Rule: "Do to others what you would have them do to you."[12]

Lewis points out that the Moral Law is literally undeniable because it is the implicit standard by which all value judgments are made. In other words, moral judgments would be impossible without the unchanging standard we call the Moral Law. Lewis writes:

> This thing which I have called for convenience the Tao, and which others may call Natural Law . . . is not one among a series of possible systems of value. It is the sole source of all value judgments. If it is rejected, all value is rejected. If any value is retained, it is retained. The effort to refute it and raise a new system of value in its place is self-contradictory. There never has been, and never will be, a radically new judgment of value in the history of the world. What purport to be new systems or (as they now call them) 'ideologies,' all consist of fragments of the Tao itself, arbitrarily wrenched from their context in the whole and then swollen to madness in their isolation, yet still owing to the Tao and to it alone such validity as they possess.[13]

Lewis is right. Even those who deny the Moral Law value their *right* to do so. But this *right* is given by the Moral Law itself. So in their effort to reject the Moral Law they affirm it. And so it is with the Left. In their efforts to destroy traditional values, they seek to replace traditional values with some of their own. But their own values are nothing but fragments of the Moral Law "swollen to madness in their isolation."

William Watkins shows this clearly in his insightful book *The New Absolutes.* Watkins writes, for example, that the "old" absolute concerning religion is that "religion is the backbone of American culture, providing the moral and spiritual light needed for public and private life." The "new" absolute concerning religion, courtesy of the Left, goes something like this: "Religion is the bane of public life, so for the public good it should be banned from the public square." The Left would like to leave us with what Richard Neuhaus insightfully exposed in his book *The Naked Public Square.* Concerning life, Watkins informs us that the "old" absolute is "Human life from conception to natural death is sacred and worthy of protection." The "new" absolute of the Left reads, "Human life, which begins and ends when certain individuals or groups decide it does, is valuable as long as it is wanted."[14]

As Watkins shows, the Left is asserting that their "new" absolutes are better than the old ones. But in doing so they unwittingly affirm the Moral Law. C. S. Lewis again:

> The moment you say that one set of moral ideas can be better than another, you are, in fact, measuring them both by a standard, saying that one of them conforms to that standard more nearly than the other. But the standard that measures two things is something different from either. You are, in fact, comparing them both with some Real Morality, admitting that there is such a thing as a real Right, independent of what people think, and that some people's ideas get nearer to that real Right than others. Or put it this way: If your moral ideas can be truer, and those of the Nazis less true, there must be something—some Real Morality—for them to be true about.[15]

Watkins goes on to point out eight additional "new" absolutes of the Left. But why should these "new" absolutes be blindly accepted? Our questions are these: "Why should our country accept and advance these 'new' absolutes? Why are the 'new' absolutes 'good' and 'right'? By what standard—by what authority—does the Left judge them 'good' and 'right'?"

As we have seen from the ramblings of the Supreme Court,

the Left cannot provide sound answers to these questions. To do so they would need to admit to the existence of the Moral Law and the Moral Lawgiver. But if they were to do that, their "new" absolutes would not measure up against the "old." Hence, they refuse to admit to the Moral Law and argue emotively rather than reasonably.

IF THE MORAL LAW IS UNIVERSAL, WHY DO SOME PEOPLE DENY IT EXISTS?

Any case for the Moral Law must deal with this objection: If the Moral Law is universal, why do some people deny that it exists? Let's briefly review from chapter 3 the five confusions people make when they deny the Moral Law. Then we will provide two more answers to this question:

1. *They confuse absolute values with changing behavior.* How people behave doesn't change how they should behave. A wrong doesn't become a right because more people are doing it.

2. *They confuse absolute values with changing perceptions of the facts.* Values stay the same but our factual understanding of moral situations change. For example, people used to seek capital punishment for witches because they thought their incantations could kill people. In other words, they thought witches were murderers. The reason people no longer seek to punish witches is not because their values have changed, but because their factual understanding about witches has changed. The absolute value against murder remains, but people no longer believe that witches are murderers.

3. *They confuse absolute values with how those values are expressed.* Different customs from different cultures do not necessarily signify different values. For example, the value of greeting others is absolute; the expression of it—be it a handshake, a hug, or a kiss—is not.

4. *They confuse which absolute value applies with relative values.* Values are not relative because there are people on both sides of an issue (e.g., abortion). The argument is over which absolute value applies (takes precedence), liberty or life.

5. *They confuse absolute ends (values) with relative means.* We often agree on the value (the ends), we merely disagree on how to secure it (the means). For example, liberals want to give the poor a handout, conservatives want to help the poor help them-

selves—same ends (help the poor), different means.

These five confusions all result from an honest failure to make proper distinctions. However, in addition to these intellectual mistakes, there are volitional reasons why people deny the Moral Law (point 6, below). And, sadly, many people deny the Moral Law because they've been taught it doesn't exist (point 7, below).

6. *People* choose *to deny the Moral Law because they don't* want *to live by Moral Law principles.* The Moral Law is real, but quite often we refuse to acknowledge it. Everyone knows the experience of suppressing the conscience and rationalizing actions contrary to it. "I know I shouldn't steal this . . . but . . . but, they owe me!" "I know I shouldn't have said that . . . but . . . but, she was asking for it!" "I know we should wait . . . but . . . but, everyone is doing it and no one else will know." As history has proven again and again, human beings have a unfailing propensity to suppress the Moral Law when that law gets in the way of their desire for pleasure, power, or property. In other words, because we don't want to do right, many of us reject that there *is* a right. And this sums up a fundamental flaw of humankind: Our problem is not that we don't *know* what's right—our problem is that we don't have the will to *do* what's right.

7. *People deny the Moral Law because they've been taught by those who have made one or all of the six mistakes listed above.* This work—the dumbing-down of America—is the ongoing project of our liberal education establishment, reinforced by its willing accomplices in the media and entertainment industries. Now please don't blow a circuit breaker here. We are not saying that there are no good teachers, media, or entertainment out there. We are simply pointing out that the Left has been successful in moving the philosophy of these influential institutions toward moral relativism. This is important because that which is promoted by the institutions of education and entertainment in our culture tends to be believed. And beliefs lead to behavior.

We see the behavior deduced from relativism expressed every day in our country. Despite the fact that our government schools teach our children that there is no absolute right and wrong, we are somehow surprised when an eleven-year-old guns down his classmates or a teenage mother leaves her baby in a trash can. Why are we surprised? Why should our children act "right" when we teach them that there is no "right?" C. S. Lewis put it more articulately, this way: "In a sort of ghastly simplicity we remove the organ and demand the function. We make men without chests and expect of them virtue and enterprise. We laugh at honor and are shocked to find traitors in our midst. We castrate and bid the geldings be fruitful."[16]

So people deny the Moral Law for a number of reasons, including the failure to make proper distinctions, the refusal to live by its implications, and the dumbing influence of our educational, media, and entertainment establishments. The bottom line is that none of these reasons are valid. The Moral Law stands.

HOW DO WE DISCOVER RIGHT AND WRONG FOR SPECIFIC CASES?

Attempts to find *one* test by which we might discover whether given activities are right or wrong according to the Moral Law have met with failure. Philosophers and ethicists have proposed many tests throughout the centuries, but all have inherent weaknesses. Ironically, the Supreme Court may have come closest. In a case that included a controversy over what was art and what was pornography, the Court's test for identifying pornography was tantamount to "I know it when I see it."[17]

Moral law philosopher J. Budziszewski attributes this ability to "know it when I see it" to the "factory-installed Baloney Meter" we all have.[18] When we see or hear something that just isn't right our "Baloney Meters" tell us, "Oh, that's baloney!" The Baloney Meter, of course, is the Moral Law at work through our consciences. As we have seen, propagandist education can knock our Baloney Meters out of calibration. Yet, when properly calibrated, our Baloney Meters tell us to do good and shun evil. They also help us identify what is good and what is evil.

Despite the fact that right and wrong for many issues are obvious (e.g., murder, rape, theft), not all moral questions have self-evident answers. To apply moral principles to specific issues often requires the exercise of practical wisdom, which cannot be categorized by an exhaustive set of rules. Nevertheless, while we cannot produce an exhaustive list, we want to point out a number of principles that we believe must be applied if morality is to be legislated properly.

First, increased incidence of disease and death is a good indi-

cator that moral principles are being violated. In other words, if a law—or the removal of one—dramatically damages health or reduces life-span, we are probably not legislating rightly. While the results don't determine the rule, bad results may indicate a bad rule. And when government edicts help destroy rather than protect the general welfare, then the government is legislating improperly. After all, what could be more basic to the government's mission than to protect and do no harm?

Second, lawmakers must legislate according to the natural hierarchy of absolutes.[19] When there is a conflict between two absolutes or rights, the lower must give way to the higher. For example, people should be valued more highly than things, and life more highly than liberty. Since the Supreme Court will not recognize that life is the right to all other rights, we stand on the slippery slope of—forgive the comparison—Hitler's Germany. Don't reject this point because of the emotional impact. The comparison is a valid one. Hitler's Germany treated people as means rather than ends. People were only considered valuable for what they could do for the people in power. They were not deemed valuable for their intrinsic worth as human beings. What is different about the rationale used for abortion or euthanasia in America today?

Third, a government must take great care to balance personal rights with personal responsibilities. Judge Bork writes, "One of the prices we pay for our Bill of Rights is an emphasis on personal freedom that is not balanced in the document by a Bill of Personal Responsibilities or a recognition, as in the constitutions of other countries, of limits set by community welfare."[20] Indeed, the Left has led many to believe that everyone has a right to virtually everything; that somehow there's a free lunch and, in many cases, the government is supposed to provide it. The Left claims that there is a right to abortion, a right to health care, a right to paid leave, a right to welfare, a right to a certain wage, a right to arts funding, a right to same-sex marriage, and—when it's all over—even a right to die (and they claim they don't believe in absolutes. . . . Who are they kidding?). If no one takes any responsibility, who will provide for all these rights? Our laws should not create rights without demanding responsibility.

Fourth, laws cannot be written solely with the extreme exception in mind. For example, just because tough cases may exist regarding abortion or euthanasia doesn't mean that laws prohibiting or limiting these practices should be overturned. "What ifs" can be leveled at virtually any law. Arguing from exceptions is like arguing that we should do away with all speed-limit laws because someone, somewhere, might someday need to rush his pregnant wife to the hospital. Extreme exceptions do not invalidate the greater beneficial aspects of good laws.

Fifth, ambiguity over "where you draw the line" is not an argument for drawing no line at all. There have been many suggestions over where to set the legal drinking age. But arguments over whether it should be 18, 19, 20, or 21 do not negate the wisdom of having a legal limit at all. While we might debate the relative merits of each age, surely any reasonable adult age is better than having no age at all. The same holds true for setting punishments. We may disagree on how severely to punish murderers—be it life in prison or capital punishment—but it would be disastrous to repeal all punishments because we can't figure out "where to draw the line." As we continue to search for the optimum, any common sense punishment is better than none.

Sixth, laws must be in accord with our reactions, not necessarily our desires. As we have pointed out earlier, the Moral Law is best revealed in our *reactions*, not our *actions*. Being selfish creatures, we do not always desire to do what is right, but we expect others to do right to us. (This is no doubt why Jesus summarized the Moral Law by declaring: "In everything, do to others what you would have them do to you."[21] Confucius recognized the same truth when he said, "Never do to others what you would not like them to do to you."[22]) While we may desire to do evil, we react against evil that is done to us. In other words, laws should be tested by our reactions. They should not permit evil even though some people may desire to do evil.

Seventh, lawmakers who believe and live by the Moral Law themselves will be better legislators of it than those who do not. The Left would have us believe that character doesn't matter in government; that a politician's private morals should not be used to judge how he or she will legislate. Why then did the Left attack former KKK member David Duke when he attempted to run for office in Louisiana? Because they rightly concluded that private beliefs *can and do* affect how someone will legislate. The truth is, those on the Left bring up character only when it suits their purpose. For example, they screamed that the character of Clarence Thomas—who allegedly *said something inappropriate*—

would affect his performance on the Supreme Court. But when there was far more evidence that Bill Clinton actually *did something illegal,* those same people argued that character didn't matter for the president. In truth, *part of a leader's job—especially the leader of our country—is to be a moral example for the nation and its children.* Moreover, everyone knows that good public leadership· requires high personal integrity. For if a leader deceives those closest to him, what will stop that leader from deceiving those he cares less about? Contemporary thinker and author Ravi Zacharias, in his book *Deliver Us From Evil,* astutely observes that "one can no more reconcile immorality in private with a call to public integrity than one can reconcile being a racist in private with being unprejudiced in public."[23] Personal beliefs and actions do matter in public life. Those who haven't suppressed the Moral Law in their own lives will be more likely to advance it in government. Unfortunately, the reverse is also true.

Eighth, laws with a long history in this country and across cultures must not be discarded lightly. The judicial activism we have seen, stripping the nation of laws with deep roots and long histories, has disconnected the people from the law-making process and unleashed a host of evils that were once restrained by the force of law. Our Founders thought they had separated the powers of our government to prevent such rash political moves. Little did they know that the branch intended to be weakest (the judiciary) would assume much more power than it was granted and legislate without the input of the other two branches. This must not be allowed to continue. Judge Bork has recommended a constitutional amendment to allow the Congress to overturn the decisions of a runaway court.[24] This seems like a good idea to us. In any event, laws must be changed only after careful study and consideration. Zacharias writes, "It has been rightly said that before any fence is removed, one should always pause long enough to find out why it was placed there in the first place."[25]

Finally, laws that promote traditional morality and religion can only be good for the country. If you doubt this, you only need to consider the challenge of Jewish talk radio host Dennis Prager: "Imagine it is midnight, and you are walking in a very bad area of the city. You are alone in a dark alley, and all of a sudden you notice that ten men are walking toward you. Would you or would you not be relieved to know that they had just attended a Bible class?"[26]

These principles, while not exhaustive, will help lawmakers come to the right conclusions regarding the moral issues facing our country. Of course, conclusions that murder, theft, and rape are wrong do not require the wisdom of Solomon. However, issues such as homosexuality, abortion, and euthanasia (which we will address in chapters 9, 10, and 11) appear much more complex to the modern mind. Granted, they are not quite as obvious as murder, theft, and rape. But we submit that one reason for their apparent complexity is due to our nation's recent inability to reason logically, not because the issues themselves are particularly perplexing from a moral point of view. The American mind is no longer honed by a careful study of the classics, but polluted by the mindless TV imagery and propaganda of the Left.[27] Today, our moral positions are more often fueled by feelings and emotions than by careful thought. Of course, our nation has certainly made moral misjudgments before (e.g., slavery), but the really "tough" issues of today were hardly moral mysteries earlier in our history or in the history of humanity, for that matter. While abortion, homosexuality, and euthanasia have always been practiced (just as murder, theft, and rape have), they have never been accepted as morally right in any culture that has stood the test of time. As history has shown, cultures that give way to such radical autonomy soon destroy themselves from the inside out.

CONCLUSION

The morality our country should be legislating is the one that is common to all cultures and all peoples. The Moral Law is not *mine* or *yours*, it is *ours*. It is the morality no one invented, but the one we all inherited. Those who deny it exists assume an absolute standard by which to do so and, thus, refute their own argument. Their emotive proclamations against the Moral Law often hide the real reason for their objection—they don't want to act the way the Moral Law tells them to, even though they want others to act that way toward them!

While it is impossible to present an exhaustive list of principles that properly apply the Moral Law, we have presented a handful of the more prominent ones that must be applied if morality is to be legislated properly. In the next three chapters we will use those principles to apply the Moral Law to three of the nation's most controversial issues—homosexuality, abortion, and euthanasia.

PART IV

HOW SHOULD WE LEGISLATE MORALITY ON THE TOUGH ISSUES?

9. HOMOSEXUALITY:
TOLERATING OURSELVES TO DEATH

10. ABORTION:
CHOOSING OURSELVES TO DEATH

11. EUTHANASIA:
EXTERMINATING OURSELVES TO DEATH

9. HOMOSEXUALITY: TOLERATING OURSELVES TO DEATH

MORALISTS ON THE LEFT

As Bill Bennett has documented in his *Index of Leading Cultural Indicators*,[1] the effects of the sexual revolution from the '60s and '70s are being felt now more than ever. Abortion, unwed mothers, absentee fathers, divorce, child abuse, and AIDS are at or near all-time highs. It's gotten so bad that even liberals are looking for legislative ways to reverse the trend.

For years liberals have proposed a government solution to just about every problem. We've got poor—we need government welfare. Kids aren't learning—we need to spend more money on public (government) schools. There's racial inequality in the workplace—we need to impose affirmative action through the EEOC. Companies are polluting—we need to strengthen the EPA.

In fact, the Left in the United States has believed that government should be and can be used to change every human behavior they don't like . . . *every human behavior but sexual behavior.* Liberals have long believed that sexual behavior is beyond the ability or mission of government to influence. They have claimed that whatever consenting adults do in their own bedroom is their own business. Government cannot and should not attempt to restrict that behavior in any way. When it comes to regulating sex, liberals have long demanded that the government remain impotent.

But it seems now that some who have been traditionally on the Left are starting to change their tune. After years of accusing conservatives of trying to legislate sexual morality, homosexuals are now seeking to harness the power of the state to, in a sense, regulate promiscuous behavior in their own community. Namely, homosexual activists are now lobbying for legalization of homosexual "marriage." They admit that the typical homosexual lifestyle entails unstable relationships characterized by anonymous liaisons and multiple partners. Since such behavior fosters social instability and the spread of disease, leaders of the homosexual community are now arguing that changing the law would encourage homosexuals to commit to one another in loving, monogamous relationships. Richard Tafel of the Log Cabin Republicans sums up the homosexual position well:

> As gays and lesbians continue to come out, they are looking to society's institutions for guidance on how to live their lives. The civilizing effect of marriage should not be denied to anyone willing to take the vows and live by them. Marriage would not only bring long-term stability and prosperity to the lives of millions of gays and lesbians, but it could seriously improve their health and deepen their personal fulfillment. If two gay people are willing to make a solemn pledge of love, honor, and commitment, and to uphold the virtues of fidelity and personal responsibility, what logical reason is there to deny them?[2]

In order to support their cause, homosexual activists like Tafel are admitting what conservatives have said all along—morality can be legislated; laws can, to a certain extent, encourage people to be good. As a result, they argue that a homosexual marriage law would help homosexuals ground themselves in monogamy, thus benefiting themselves and society.

Are these homosexual activists correct? Is homosexual marriage a good idea? Would it benefit homosexuals and society? In this chapter, we will address those questions by first looking at the empirical data regarding the healthfulness of homosexual acts and long-term homosexual relationships. We will then discuss arguments commonly used by homosexuals to defend their lifestyle, such as the argument from tolerance and the argument from genetics ("we were born this way"). Finally, we will conclude with an analysis of homosexuality from the perspective of the Moral Law, the standard we've been using throughout this book. Specifically, are homosexual acts congruent with or in violation of the Moral Law? Our intent is to conclude with an objectively supportable public policy position regarding homosexual acts and homosexual marriage.

THE HEALTHFULNESS OF THE HOMOSEXUAL LIFESTYLE

In today's pluralistic society, controversial public policy questions, such as homosexuality, must be decided on evidence rather than on sectarian religious belief. For what one person may find sinful according to his or her religious perspective, others may find perfectly appropriate according to theirs. However, our common morality—the Moral Law—tells us not to harm ourselves or others. So the best way of finding common ground and a sensible policy position is to investigate the objective data on the healthfulness of the homosexual lifestyle. Just what does the evidence show? Is it really harmless, or is it actually harmful?

One study of objective data regarding homosexuality was published in 1994 in the *Omega Journal of Death and Dying*.[3] The study compared 6,737 obituaries/death notices from eighteen U.S. homosexual journals with obituaries from two conventional newspapers. The intent was to discover what kind of effect the homosexual lifestyle had on life-span as compared to the life-span of heterosexuals.

The obituaries from the non-homosexual newspapers indicated longevity similar to U.S. averages: the median age of death for married men was seventy-five, and for married women, seventy-nine. But the median age of death for homosexuals, documented in the homosexual publications from 1980–1993, was absolutely alarming. Keep in mind that these obituaries were drawn from the gay community's own publications, so there is no anti-gay bias in the data that follows.[4] The median age of death for homosexual men *who did not have AIDS* was forty-two. For homosexual men who did have AIDS, the median age of death was thirty-nine. (See Table 1, and read note 4 for confirmation of this study.) Lesbians did not fare much better. The 163 lesbians in the study registered a median age of death at forty-four and exhibited high rates of violent death and cancer as compared to women in general.

TABLE 1: *OMEGA* STUDY RESULTS STUDY COMPARING OBITUARIES OF 6,737 HOMOSEXUALS TO A SAMPLE OF OBITUARIES OF HETEROSEXUALS		
Population	Median Age of Death	% living past 65 years old
Married Men	75	80%
Single or Divorced Men	57	32%
Homosexual Men Without AIDS	42	9%
Homosexual Men Without AIDS With an LTSP*	41	7%
Homosexual Men With AIDS	39	less than 2%
Homosexual Men With AIDS With an LTSP*	39	less than 2%

What is so alarming about these results is that—even without the AIDS epidemic—the homosexual lifestyle is so unhealthy that homosexuals are dying at nearly *half the age* of the general population! Compare this to the average age of death of cigarette smokers. According to the Center for Disease Control, smokers die, on average, nearly seven years earlier than non-smokers.[5] If we believe that it is right to *discourage and restrict* smoking in our society, how can we honestly believe it is right to *sanction and encourage* homosexual behavior?

Drawing on the findings of additional research studies that have been conducted over the years, the *Omega* study also inves-

*LTSP: Homosexuals with a long-term sexual partner ("married" homosexuals).

tigated homosexual deaths prior to 1980 (all the way back to 1858). It's conclusion? The homosexual lifestyle was significantly unhealthy even before the AIDS epidemic:

> Old homosexuals appear to have been proportionately less numerous than their non-homosexual counterparts in the scientific literature from 1858–1993. The pattern of early death evident in the homosexual obituaries is consistent with the pattern exhibited in the published surveys of homosexuals and intravenous drug abusers. Homosexuals may have experienced a short life-span for the last 140 years; AIDS has apparently reduced it about 10 percent. Such an abbreviated life-span puts the healthfulness of homosexuality in question.[6]

WHAT ABOUT HOMOSEXUAL MARRIAGE?

In his blockbuster book *Men and Marriage*,[7] George Gilder points out that a civilized society exists only when men are domesticated by heterosexual marriage. When the commitment to marriage breaks down, society breaks down.

In addition to its civilizing effect, heterosexual marriage also has a positive health effect on those who engage in it. The empirical evidence from the *Omega* study shows that married men live an average of eighteen years longer than those who are single or divorced, and married women tend to live about eight years longer than their single or divorced counterparts. Moreover, all heterosexual subgroups (single or married) live far longer than their homosexual counterparts (single or those with long-term sexual partners). Nature seems to reward with good health and long life those who practice traditional morality.

Is this life-span disparity an argument for homosexual marriage? Homosexuals now contend that "marriage" would also help them increase their drastically shortened life-spans. Are they correct? Evidence from the *Omega* study and others suggests an emphatic no![8]

Take a look at Table 1 again. Notice that the age of death for AIDS victims was not affected positively for those who had a "long-term sexual partner" (LTSP). The median age of death for those with an LTSP and those without was the same: thirty-nine. Surprisingly, for the non-AIDS deaths, those with an LTSP actually fared *worse* (median age, forty-one) than those without such a partner (median age, forty-three).

Why did the presence of a long-term partner have no effect or actually shorten the life-span of the homosexual? The *Omega* study gave no substantiated answer but only speculated that even long-term homosexual relationships usually lack fidelity. However, at least five other recent studies,[9] which also discovered a negative health benefit from long-term homosexual relationships, offered a more concrete explanation for this surprising find: Coupled homosexuals tend to practice more anal intercourse and more anal/oral sex than those without a steady partner. In other words, "married" homosexuals tend to engage in more intimate and risky sexual contact than their "single" counterparts.

Why is this so? According to Gamalier de Jesus, a counselor with the New York Blood Center's Project Achieve (which recruits people at risk of infection by HIV in preparation for future vaccine trials), many long-term homosexual couples deliberately plan to have unprotected sex.

"I call it a rite of passage," de Jesus told *New York Times* reporter David Dunlap. "If they can get to the point where they can exchange body fluids, they see that as the greatest commitment they can have with another man. They test negative once. They test negative twice. And then they say, 'It's time to stop using condoms.' What better way to show trust, in this day and age?"

"That act is such a powerful bond between two people," he said. "All your life is condensed in those few seconds. There's a belief that the magic of the act itself is going to protect you from harm. Unfortunately, that can be the very thing that is killing us: romanticizing the act to the point of thinking nothing can go wrong."[10]

Dr. Barbara Warren, a psychologist who directs the mental health and social services program at the Lesbian and Gay Community Services Center in New York, confirms de Jesus' observations. She has also noticed that many men in romantic relationships—younger men, especially—forgo safer practices.

"If they have anonymous sex, they will use a condom," Dr. Warren said, "but if they're in love, they think that will somehow magically protect them. There's also an assumed fidelity that's not always the case."[11]

Believing that AIDS is inevitable provides another reason

why homosexual couples choose to have unprotected sex. Andrew Sullivan, former editor of *The New Republic* in Washington, who has HIV, discerns a streak of fatalism among gay men, given the high proportion of those who are infected:

> Even within the safer-sex parameters, you add up all the odds over an entire lifetime and many gay men feel it's inevitable they'll contract HIV. That's a very hard psychological barrier to break through for prevention, education, and, indeed, just morale.[12]

"Gay men have built up a callousness because they've been in the epidemic for so long," echoed Jerry Calumn, the education manager at the Dallas AIDS Resource Center. "I'm the perfect example. Here I was—an expert on relapse. I knew what the risks were. I knew what the signs were. I knew it all."

Neither Calumn's knowledge nor vigilance were enough of a counterweight for the depression he was feeling in March 1994, when he had anal sex without a condom. Three months later, he tested positive for HIV.

"One night of being deeply depressed and one unprotected sex act, and that was it," said Calumn, twenty-nine. "Alarms were really going off in my head," he recalled. "I wasn't stoned. I wasn't drunk. Nothing like that. But I very clearly remember that when it happened, I said, 'I don't care, if life is full of so much pain.' "[13]

Regardless of the reasons for the fact that monogamous homosexual unions don't improve (and, in fact, seem to worsen) the health of homosexuals, two conclusions from the data we have just reviewed seem inescapable: (1) From a public health perspective, gay marriage is an incredibly bad idea, and (2) Homosexual sex is inherently dangerous. In other words, it's not just promiscuous sex in general that's unhealthy, as the gay community contends. Rather, *the act of homosexual sex itself is unhealthy, whether you do it once or repeatedly; whether you do it with one person or many.*

LOGIC OF THE LEFT: ARGUMENTS FOR HOMOSEXUAL ACTS

Given the evidence that homosexual relations are extremely unhealthy, the Moral Law urges us to form public policy that will discourage such behavior rather than encourage it. Never-theless, despite what the facts may be, those who wish to engage in homosexual acts demand that public policy support their life-style. Their arguments are based on consent, genetics, tolerance, and the contention that morality cannot be legislated. We shall now address each one of these arguments.

"We are consenting adults!"

As we mentioned earlier, the homosexual community has long argued that what consenting adults do in the privacy of their own homes is morally permissible and the government should stay out of it. Notice the moral positions contained in that argument. First, *who said* consent makes something moral? That's an appeal to an absolute moral standard. Second, keeping the government out of it is also a moral position. It's based on the principle that it would be morally wrong for the government to infringe on the autonomy of individuals.

But the government restricts the actions of individuals all the time. No one argues that there shouldn't be laws against murder, assault, or child abuse. We all agree that those acts are wrong regardless of the issue of consent because not every act can be reduced to the level of preference. In other words, there are some issues that are objectively right or wrong, and others that are simply a matter of taste or opinion. For example, murder is objectively wrong, but liking chocolate better than vanilla is simply a matter of preference.

To further drive home this distinction, let us ask these ques-tions: Would the holocaust have been morally permissible if the Jews had consented to it? Was the mass suicide at Jonestown simply a matter of consenting adults exercising their rights? Would there be nothing wrong with a father and his adult daughter consenting to have a sexual relationship? How about three adults and the family pet?

If there is no objective right and wrong, we could not con-clude that such activities were morally wrong. We recoil at this suggestion precisely because there *is* a Moral Law—also known as conscience—pressing on us, which helps us conclude that some acts are undeniably and absolutely wrong.

Later we'll discuss whether homosexuality is one such act or whether it is simply a matter of preference. For now the point is this: While consent very often is important to the morality of an act (e.g., intercourse vs. rape), we can't universally say that whatever consenting adults do is okay. Some things are objectively wrong whether adults consent to them or not.

"You can't legislate morality."

Those who support legalization of homosexual acts or homosexual marriage claim that the rest of society should not impose their morality on them. In effect, homosexuals are claiming that it's morally wrong to impose a code of behavior on them. But, as we have seen, all laws legislate morality. All laws impose a moral code. In fact, the homosexual activists are trying to do the same thing they say heterosexuals shouldn't be able to do— impose a morality (or an immorality). The difference is that homosexual activists want to impose *their* morality.

What is their morality? Look at what homosexual activists demanded at the 1993 March on Washington for Lesbian, Gay, and Bi-Equal Rights and Liberation:

- The implementation of homosexual, bisexual, and transgendered curriculum at all levels of education.
- The lowering of the age of consent for homosexual and heterosexual sex.
- The legalization of homosexual marriages.
- Custody, adoption, and foster-care rights for homosexuals, lesbians, and transgendered people.
- The redefinition of the family to include the full diversity of all family structures.
- The access to all programs of the Boy Scouts of America.
- Affirmative action for homosexuals.
- The inclusion of sex-change operations under a universal health-care plan.[14]

It is ironic that the homosexual activists who tell society to "stay out of the bedroom" are the very ones militantly bringing the bedroom to society. (Tragically, what should be discreet in public life—sex—is now discussed and displayed with impunity, while what should be encouraged and expressed in public life— religion—is shouted into the closet.) As you can see, homosexuals want much more than tolerance—they want *endorsement.* Clearly, a position of neutrality ("live and let live") cannot be taken here. Homosexuals aren't taking that position toward your children. They want to impose their morality on every child in this nation. After all, heterosexuals reproduce, but homosexuals can only recruit. They've even been successful in getting some public schools to teach homosexuality in kindergarten classes![15]

As we saw in chapter 2, the law provides a moral reference point for our citizens and functions as a great teacher. Unfortunately, the law will become a very harmful teacher if homosexual activists get their way. Since many people believe that whatever is legal is moral, legalizing homosexual acts or marriages could encourage such behavior among our children.

Moreover, it's not only the activists that present a problem for children. Even homosexuals who keep to themselves in monogamous relationships impose an unhealthy example for your children. Why? Because, as we've seen, monogamy doesn't diminish the dangers of homosexuality; in fact, it seems to increase them. Homosexual acts with one partner or with many partners are inherently dangerous. So legalizing homosexual marriage would be an incredibly unhealthy policy that would condone destructive behavior and set the wrong example for our children.

What community could survive economically, medically, or physically if all of its children grew up and adopted the homosexual lifestyle? What parents hope their children grow up to engage in homosexual acts? The moral and eventual medical, economic, and social conditions of the community are adversely affected by homosexuality. These forms of harm clearly constitute a case of "hurting someone else," a violation of the standard with which every rational person agrees.

As we have said before, people don't live in a vacuum; no person is an island. Granting more freedom to perform homosexual acts will impose negative effects on those who do and those who do not exercise this freedom. The key point is this: When homosexual activists seek to give people more freedom (i.e., by passing a law that legalizes a formerly illegal activity such as sodomy or homosexual marriage), they do exactly what they condemn conservatives for doing. They impose their morals (and the associated effects) on people who do not agree with those morals!

In other words, those who say they want no morals imposed want their own morals imposed. The truth is, all laws impose morals on others, whether they are good or bad. Good laws don't allow "anything goes," rather they protect innocent people by limiting the freedom of others to do harm. And that means a good morality must be imposed. In other words, legislating a morality is not only ethical, it is unavoidable and necessary for a functioning society.

The question is, "Whose morality should we legislate?" Should we legislate the morality that kills people around the age of forty, or the one that preserves them until seventy-five or eighty?

"We were born this way."

Perhaps the argument that has advanced the homosexual movement more than any other in recent times is the argument from genetics: "We were born this way! You must accept what we do." No doubt there are many people who sincerely believe that they have been born with a propensity to commit homosexual acts. People we know have struggled with this quite painfully, and we must be careful not to minimize the severity of their struggle.

Nevertheless, there are serious problems with the theory that such a propensity is genetic rather than learned. For example, if homosexuality is genetic, how have the responsible genes been passed from generation to generation? After all, homosexuals, by definition, can't pass on anything because they don't reproduce. Perhaps regressive genes are partly responsible. Who knows? If there is a genetic link, researchers are in the dark. They make "clear neither what is inherited nor how it influences sexual orientation."[16] Furthermore, if sexual orientation is fixed from birth, why do some homosexuals switch to heterosexuality or bisexuality?

While there are some definite problems with the genetic argument, our intention is not to resolve the debate here.[17] In fact, for public policy purposes the outcome of the debate doesn't matter. *The question of whether homosexuality is acquired or learned is irrelevant to the question of what the law should be.* Why? Because laws can't excuse conduct on the basis of genetic tendencies. It doesn't matter who has been "born" with what—the law must prohibit the negative behavior of everyone for the common good of all.

In other words, the law must hold all people accountable to the same standards of behavior regardless of their genetic makeup. For example, if I'm genetically predisposed toward being violent, I still must obey the laws against assault. Likewise, if I'm genetically predisposed toward alcoholism, I must still obey the laws against drunk driving. *An orientation toward homosexuality doesn't make homosexual acts morally right any more than an orientation toward violence makes assault morally right.*

We can't excuse criminals for committing acts that have been outlawed simply because they may have been more predisposed to commit a particular crime than other people. If certain conduct is harmful, it must be outlawed or restricted to discourage its incidence and to protect innocent people from its effects. In fact, good laws are designed not only to protect innocent people (e.g., other motorists) but also to protect the perpetrator from his own folly (e.g., the driver from killing himself).

Laws regarding homosexuality are no different. They are designed to discourage potentially harmful conduct in order to protect society—and those who may wish to engage in that conduct—from unwanted consequences. Such laws are not, as many in the homosexual community claim, forms of prejudice analogous to bigotry or racism. Racism wrongly discriminates against someone for *benign characteristics* they have—over which they have *no* control—such as skin color or gender. Laws governing sexual conduct rightly discriminate against someone for the *harmful acts* they perform—over which they *do* have control—such as rape, incest, pedophilia, etc. In fact, the comparison to race is completely invalid: *sexual behavior is always a choice; race never is.* You can meet many former "homosexuals"; you will never meet a former "African-American."

Laws, of course, cannot prevent someone from having a particular skin color or "orientation" (if, in fact, we assume one really can be "born that way"). They can only prohibit unwanted *behavior.* But that's the very purpose and scope of the law—to discriminate against behaviors, not persons. As a society, we rightfully discriminate against all kinds of harmful behaviors (e.g., drunk driving, theft, rape, etc.) regardless of the fact that some people may have been "born" with a propensity to commit those crimes.

At this point, you may be thinking, "Nevertheless, we shouldn't criminalize homosexual acts because many people feel those acts are natural for them, and sex is a very vital and personal activity." The problem with this objection is that feelings don't determine right from wrong. There are many behaviors that may seem personal, natural, and right to some people—such as pedophilia and incest—but they are still morally wrong acts that carry with them devastating consequences. Our society, if it is to survive, cannot condone such activities.

Furthermore, we're not talking about outlawing activities that are necessary for an individual to survive (like breathing or eating). While sex is an extremely strong desire for most people, it's not necessary to keep one alive. In fact, there is no case on record of someone having died for lack of sex! People can have fulfilling lives without ever having sex.

Let's think about it this way: Suppose I honestly believe that I've been "born" homosexual. Question: Am I required to engage in homosexual acts? Am I not capable of controlling my sexual desires and remaining celibate? If you claim that I am not, then you have also made the absurd contention that no one in the history of the world has ever been morally responsible for any sexual crime, including rape, incest, pedophilia, and even sexual harassment.

Of course I can remain celibate. People do it all the time. I may not *want* to control myself, but I certainly can. You say, "That's not realistic! People are going to do it anyway." Not so. Abstinence was so realistic in the '40s and '50s that we didn't have nearly the degree of sexual problems we have now. When abstinence is encouraged and expected, it works. Our problem today is that we've bought into the fatalistic notion that people, like animals, are unable to control their instincts or feelings. As a result, there's no sense telling them to stop their destructive behavior—just tell them to put a condom on it.

In light of that philosophy, no wonder we're having big problems. Because promiscuity is expected, that's exactly what we're getting along with its devastating consequences—emotional turmoil, disease, and death.[18] Responsible sexual behavior is hard enough to maintain in a wholesome environment, but it's made worse by a society that continually bombards you with sexual images, removes the moral constraint of the law by legalizing deviant behavior, and urges you to "come out of the closet."

Nevertheless, we are all personally responsible for own behavior—sexual and nonsexual. The key point is that even if we are "born" heterosexual or homosexual, we are not required to engage in any particular form of sexual conduct. While we may have strong desires, our conduct is not mandatory. *A choice must still be made.*

When you think about it, homosexuals are really no different from heterosexuals when it comes to making choices. We all sometimes make wrong moral choices. Some of us are stronger than others, but all of us are tempted to make wrong choices because we've all been born with imperfections. In other words, we all have an inborn propensity toward selfishness that many of our Founding Fathers called "depravity."

This propensity manifests itself in different ways, so each of us have our own problems, our own struggles. For some of us it may be homosexuality; for others it maybe a propensity to engage in immoral heterosexual behavior; for still others it may be a bad temper, or an addiction to work, drugs, or alcohol. We all know what we should do, but often we give in to our imperfections and make wrong choices. *In fact, the fundamental problem in our world is that people willingly choose to do things that deep down they know they shouldn't do.*

This reality—the fact that we're all flawed to some extent—is precisely the reason we need a system of laws in our society. The father of our Constitution and the fourth president of the United States, James Madison, put it best when he said, "If men were angels, no government would be necessary."

Government is necessary because in its absence evil will prevail. One of government's chief responsibilities is to encourage the morality of the people and protect against those who do evil. The worst thing government could do is to excuse or—heaven forbid—encourage immoral and unhealthy behavior for any reason (including genetics). Unfortunately, that's exactly what the homosexual community demands our nation to do.

"What about tolerance?"

"Tolerance!" Like a broken record, that's about all we hear from the Left. They want our society to "tolerate" everyone and everything. The fact is, we are "tolerating" ourselves to death!

Here again the Left is inconsistent. First, they tell us to tolerate everyone, yet they themselves don't tolerate those whom they believe are intolerant. Second, they tell us to tolerate everything, yet they themselves don't tolerate racism, pollution, homophobia, murder, rape, or theft. Why do our friends on the Left demand that we write laws intolerant of harmful behavior like racism, but expect us to adopt laws that *encourage* harmful behavior like homosexual acts? Furthermore, we don't tolerate good, we only tolerate evil. So, the "tolerance" argument is an implicit admission that homosexual practices are evil. After all, whoever heard of tolerating good behavior? We only need to be asked to put up with homosexual acts because there's something intrinsically wrong with them.

The Left seems to forget that tolerance is a virtue if you're talking about listening to other points of view. But it's a vice if you're talking about letting evil behavior overrun your society. The truth is, if we don't fight evil—behaviors that destroy lives—our society will not survive. We can't tolerate behavior that destroys innocent people, our families, and our communities.

Ironically, for all their moral piousness, the Left comes up short in their demand that we tolerate other people. Tolerance is too weak; it doesn't go far enough. Love should be our goal. Tolerance says, "Hold your nose and put up with them." Love says, "Reach out and help them." We should *love people* but *hate the evil* that they do. For example, we should hate homosexual acts but love the people who engage in them.

How do we "love" people from a public policy perspective? Love isn't necessarily giving people what they *want*. It is giving them what they *need* for long-term health and prosperity. Certain drivers may *want* to drive too fast all the time, but a responsible government will nevertheless set speed limit laws. In other words, love means defining the boundaries in which one must live to prosper and maintain good health. That's why even some homosexuals do not want public encouragement of homosexuality. As George Gilder points out in *Men and Marriage*, "Some gays ... are not helped by the aggressive gay liberation movement that wants to flush them out of the closet and into the street where they can be exploited by the gay rights brigade. They want to live quietly and productively and are thoughtful enough not to want to inflict their problem on others."[19]

In the final analysis, the most loving thing we can do for ourselves and our fellow citizens—homosexuals included—is to discourage and, if necessary, outlaw behavior that will devastate them, their families, and the community at large. Look at it this way: If a foreign government imposed a disease on us that cut our life-span to the age of forty, we'd go to war. We surely wouldn't "tolerate" it. Likewise, when it comes to dealing with evil behavior in our society today—behavior that destroys—tolerance is the one thing we can't tolerate. Love requires better.

WHY HOMOSEXUAL ACTS VIOLATE THE MORAL LAW

In the debate over homosexual marriage, conservatives argue that no lasting society in the history of humankind has formally recognized homosexuality as a legitimate lifestyle choice. With that assertion certainly true, the real question is "Why have virtually all civilizations throughout history condemned homosexuality?" Has it been pure prejudice, as those on the Left claim, or has it been grounded in some consistent, self-evident standard of right and wrong, what we have been calling "the Moral Law"?

Certainly, the dramatically shorter life-span of homosexuals calls the naturalness of homosexuality into question (the first principle we set forth at the end of chapter 8). In fact, we believe that there are at least three reasons why homosexual acts violate the Moral Law: (1) The natural anatomy of the body including organ function and reproduction rejects the naturalness of homosexual acts; (2) The medical consequences of homosexual acts indicate that the behavior itself is selfish rather than loving; (3) The evidence of personal guilt experienced by those who engage in homosexual acts. We believe that these reasons from the Moral Law, and those from written moral creeds, account for the universal condemnation of homosexuality throughout history. We'll look at each of these three reasons in turn.

Anatomy, Organ Function, and Biology

In terms of anatomy, organ function, and biology, homosexuality is, of course, contrary to the facts of life. The natural design of the body affirms the union of a man and a women. Only men and women can procreate, and their parts fit perfectly together for the act of heterosexual intercourse.

Conversely, the natural design of the body rejects the very act of male homosexual intercourse. The rectum clearly was not designed for male sexual intrusion. It's thin internal wall is too easily ruptured during anal sex, which is why homosexual contact provides an extremely efficient means of transmitting disease. It is in this way that bacteria and viruses from semen or fecal matter can make direct contact with blood.

Now think about what happens during the act of male homosexuality. So as not to risk offense we will describe it no further. But our question is this: "Do you *honestly* believe that such an act is a natural act—that the body was designed with this in mind?" How could it be? The act destroys the function of the rectum. Instead of getting rid of waste and disease to keep the body healthy, the homosexual's rectum actually becomes a conduit for the spread of bacteria and disease. How can an act that produces this result honestly be considered a "natural" act? Results speak for themselves.

Those arguing for the morality of homosexual activity often attempt to refute this kind of Moral Law argument by claiming that sex is simply an alternative use of the rectum. Just because the primary function isn't sex, they say, doesn't mean that anal sex is "unnatural." Using an analogy, they'll argue that the natural functions of your nose are smelling and breathing, yet we don't claim you're violating nature if you also use your nose to hold up eyeglasses. In other words, even though the rectum may be designed to expel waste, we can also use it for sexual activity.

Unfortunately for them, their analogy doesn't hold up. There's a crucial difference between using the nose for eyeglasses and the rectum for sex—one is benign and the other is harmful. The nose is unaffected by eyeglasses, but the rectum is damaged by homosexual contact—so much so that the rectum often can't accomplish its primary function effectively. If wearing eyeglasses damaged our ability to smell and breathe, we would universally condemn such behavior as unhealthy and unnatural. Since the penis destroys the ability of the rectum to function properly, why don't we come to the same conclusion about anal sex?

In truth, anal sex isn't at all like using your nose to wear eyeglasses—anal sex is more like using your nose to sand unfinished wood. You may scrape your nose a little the first time, but the more you sand the more damage you'll do. Common sense tells us that a person won't survive very long if he continues to use his body against its natural design.

Such anatomical problems undeniably plague male homosexual activity. But what about lesbian contact? While lesbian relations do not present the same anatomical problems as male homosexual relations, lesbians tend to engage in unnatural practices that are nearly as damaging to the body. A 1993 CDC study on 498 lesbian women in the San Francisco Bay area had some startling findings:[20]

- Fifteen percent of these women reported "participating in

piercing, cutting, or whipping to the point of bleeding" with their female partners.

- Eleven percent admitted to IV drug use at some time since 1978 (the rate for the general population is less than 1 percent).

Moreover, as we mentioned earlier, the median age of death for lesbians discovered by the *Omega* study was forty-four. So while the nature of lesbian relations may appear benign anatomically, the acts performed and the lifestyle led are unnatural and empirically harmful.

Love or Selfishness?

Those who engage in homosexual acts claim they have a right to engage in the sexual activity of their choice, and they have a right to have their unions recognized by the state. They argue that their movement is simply about recognizing loving relationships. They say society shouldn't prevent two people "in love" from marrying each other. They insist that the current marriage law is bigotry.

But is it? In order to have a rational discussion about this we need to define what is meant by "love." While there are many types of love (the ancient Greeks identified three), most would agree that the most supreme form of love seeks the ultimate good of its object. That is, if you really love someone, you'll want what's ultimately best for him or her even if that means you will be inconvenienced in the process.

We know this is true of love because the Moral Law tells us it is so—it's exactly the kind of love we want others to show us. We all want to be treated as "ends," not "means to an end." We don't want people to use us merely for their own sexual or psychological gratification. (To be sure, people use one another all the time, but most would agree that a relationship based on mutual respect and sacrificial giving is far superior.) The love we expect from others is that which seeks the best for us.

The question is, "What kind of love typifies a homosexual relationship?" Are there men who really feel drawn romantically to other men? No doubt. Are there men who really have a deep sense of commitment to other men, who wish to care for them, and desire to be intimate with them? No doubt. But the same might be said of a man and his daughter, a man and a child, or three men and a woman. Should those people act on their sexual desires? If they did, would their actions truly be seeking the ultimate good of the person or persons they were trying to "love?" While you may want to have sex with someone other than your heterosexual spouse, the most loving thing you can do is *not* to have sex with that person.

Some may argue, "When two adults consent to engage in homosexual acts they are each seeking the good of the other. Each person wants it and chooses it." But if you truly love someone, will you do something that will seriously hurt or kill that person? Having homosexual sex with someone does just that. It's been documented to cause disease and death at an extremely early age. With the consequences so severe, if a man really "loved" another man, he wouldn't engage in homosexual acts with him. Sex isn't the only way you can demonstrate your love for someone. Men may demonstrate their love for one another without having sex.

Now some might say, "If consenting adults want to risk their health and lives engaging in homosexual acts, that's their choice—they should be free to do it." The problem with that argument is this: It ignores the fact that no person is an island— that two people committing homosexual acts in their bedroom *can and will* adversely affect innocent people.

Ryan White was one of homosexuality's many innocent victims. As you recall, Ryan was not a homosexual himself; he was an innocent child who received HIV-tainted blood from a homosexual donor. Ironically, the homosexual community used the occasion of young Ryan's illness to lobby for more AIDS research money while their own behavior caused his death. In fact, virtually every case of AIDS can be traced back to homosexual acts. While the disease has made its way into the heterosexual community, it has done so through homosexual blood donations and infected bisexual men. Today, homosexuals still comprise more than 85 percent of new AIDS cases in the U.S. (By the way, the PR efforts of the homosexual community have been successful: AIDS now gets twenty times as much federal research and education dollars per death as cancer!)

But what if two monogamous homosexuals keep to themselves and stay free of disease—shouldn't that be accepted? After all, aren't the libertarians and liberals right when they say that "you should be able to do whatever you want as long as you don't hurt someone else"? Let's assume this moral absolute *is* true. The question remains, "What does 'hurt' mean?" Does it only pertain to physical harm? Is it right to bring psychological, emotional, or even moral harm against someone? Certainly not, and many people in our nation sue for such non-physical damages and win huge monetary paybacks in court.

It is not only the physical consequences of homosexual acts that affect innocent people. There is also the psychological, emotional, and moral harm that those who choose to engage in homosexual acts inflict on others. For example, parents are hurt emotionally when their children choose the homosexual lifestyle. They hurt and grieve not merely because they wish that their children would marry the opposite sex, but because they fear for their children's safety. Exhibiting the highest form of love, they simply want what will bring the best long-term consequences to their children.

Contrary to the negative aspersions cast by the "homophobia" police, the fear that parents and loved ones feel regarding homosexuality has little to do with bigotry, ignorance, or a lack of understanding. *Rather, it has everything to do with a complete understanding of the facts.* In light of the overwhelming evidence of the dangers of homosexuality, family and friends have every reason to be upset over their loved ones becoming involved in this lifestyle. The health dangers, social dysfunctions, and inability to procreate are conditions no sane parent wants any child to choose.

In addition to families and friends, the community at large also has a legitimate claim that it is being harmed by homosexual acts. These acts generate huge economic costs, including medical care for AIDS victims and ballooning insurance premiums that have been passed on to us all. They inflict painful social costs by taking our fellow citizens—homosexuals and non-homosexuals (like Ryan White)—from this world prematurely.

Finally, they impose long-lasting moral costs on us by establishing an immoral climate for our children. After all, we all have to breathe the same moral air. And just as we shouldn't tolerate people polluting the physical air we must breathe, why should we tolerate pollution of the moral air that helps form the character of our children? An immoral environment for our children—one that tolerates or encourages destructive behavior— will eventually lead to the behavior that ultimately burdens our society with the economic and social costs mentioned above.

What we promote in our society today will tangibly affect our society tomorrow (i.e., just as the sexual revolution of the '60s helped to destroy the morality and health of the '90s; we're feeling the effects of yesterday's actions today).

In short, homosexual acts are inherently selfish acts. They are not consistent with the Moral Law or with true love, which is to seek the ultimate good of the loved one. Homosexuality is wrong because it negatively affects those involved in such a relationship as well as other loved ones and the community at large.

One might say, "If homosexual relationships are wrong for this reason, then so are some heterosexual relationships." It is true that any behavior that is inherently selfish and harmful to others is wrong. The difference here is that—in light of the known dangers of homosexuality—homosexual acts are *always* wrong, *always* selfish; whereas heterosexual acts are often loving and right.

Guilt

In their effort to legitimize their behavior, homosexuals often claim that they were born homosexuals; that if given a choice, they would never choose to be homosexuals. They say they have literally experienced many years of guilt struggling with their sexual identity, only to feel liberation after accepting their homosexual orientation and embracing it as "natural."

But if homosexuality is "natural," why the intense struggle with guilt? Some may say that the guilt is a result of "homophobia," a product of our unenlightened, prejudiced environment. But virtually all societies throughout history have condemned homosexuality. Why is this true?

How plausible is it to assume that virtually every society in the history of mankind has come to the same conclusion about homosexuality by chance? Statistically, the chances of this conclusion are infinitesimal. It's much more plausible to believe that they have come to the same conclusion because they've all been endowed with the same self-evident moral values, which are derived from the standard we've been calling "the Moral Law." In other words, societies throughout history have condemned homosexuality precisely because this moral intuition has evoked a sense of guilt in those who practice it.

Some may ask, "If it's self-evidently wrong, then why do so many homosexuals no longer feel guilty about it? In fact, why are so many of them actively promoting homosexuality and recruiting others to do it?" The answer lies with the propensity of human beings to suppress what condemns their behavior while aggressively concocting rationalizations to support it. No one wants to admit their behavior is wrong, especially if they don't *want* to stop doing it. The heart, like the hands, can become callused.

In fact, those who finally succumb to homosexual desires are no different than anyone else who decides to engage in an immoral activity—they ultimately *choose* to suppress their conscience and guilt. When they finally do so, they feel liberated—free from the restraints of their conscience. In order to validate their decision and free themselves completely from any flickering remnant of guilt, they seek others who have made the same choice. Organizing their numbers, they launch a full-scale effort to demand not merely tolerance but approval from society. Why? Because being tolerated doesn't make anyone feel right or accepted. Only through society's full acceptance and approval will the homosexual's choice be validated and his conscience be suppressed completely. After all, once you've finally made a choice to keep doing something that deep down in your heart you know is wrong, you basically have two options: (1) Keep your shameful behavior in the closet, away from the disapproving scrutiny of mainstream society; or (2) Muster your numbers to launch an all-out "in your face" effort to redefine right and wrong in the minds of mainstream society. With suppressed guilt and slick rationalizations, many of those who engage in homosexual acts are now engaged in the latter.

SUMMARY

Before concluding, we will review what we've covered so far:

- The median homosexual life-span is about forty years—a little over half that of the general population.
- Monogamous homosexuals tend to engage in more risky sexual behavior than those who are not monogamous. More body fluids are exchanged in such relationships. As a result, homosexuals in this category further shorten their life-span.
- Since monogamy further shortens the life-span of homosexuals, homosexual marriage would not improve their health. It would only encourage more risky behavior among them, and

it would legitimize destructive behavior for children.

- Homosexual acts are anatomically unnatural and unhealthy. They hurt and kill homosexuals and often lead to the injury or death of innocent people. Hence, they are inherently selfish, not loving, acts. As such, they are contrary to the Moral Law.

We have seen that arguments in support of homosexuality are flawed or miss the point:

- *"We are consenting adults!"* Consent doesn't necessarily make an act right. Homosexuality is wrong—a violation of the Moral Law. It is not simply a matter of preference, as evidenced by (1) the natural anatomy of the body, including organ function and reproduction, which rejects the naturalness of homosexual acts; (2) the harmful consequences of homosexual acts, which demonstrate that the behavior itself is selfish rather than loving; and (3) the consistent sense of guilt that has been experienced by those who engage in homosexual acts throughout all of human history.
- *"You can't legislate morality!"* All laws legislate morality; the only question is, "Whose morality should we legislate?" Should we legislate the morality that kills people by about the age of forty, or the one that preserves them to seventy-five or eighty?
- *"We were born this way!"* Welcome to the human race—we were all born with weaknesses and imperfections! And while the research into a genetic cause for homosexual tendencies is inconclusive, its outcome is irrelevant anyway. Law standards cannot be relaxed for those in the population who may be genetically bent toward harmful behavior. Genetics do not excuse harmful behavior because a free choice is still made to engage in that behavior. "Orientation" does not turn immoral acts into moral acts.
- *"What about tolerance?"* Tolerance may be a virtue, but love is a greater one. Tolerance is weak ("put up with them"); love must be our standard ("reach out to them"). We must love people by seeking to minimize the behavior that is destroying them. Tolerating harmful behavior is unloving.

CONCLUSION

When we take an honest look at the empirical data regarding homosexuality, the correct public policy stance we should demand from our government is unequivocal: discourage homosexuality. As with many political issues, reasonable people may disagree on how to discourage it (the means), but the fact that we must discourage it for the health and well-being of all concerned (the end) is beyond question. Certainly the repeal of sodomy laws, the funding of sex education programs that advance homosexuality, and the acceptance of homosexual marriage are the wrong direction for our country.

The truth is clear: Homosexual acts hurt and kill people. The worst thing we can do from a public policy perspective is to encourage behavior that destroys our citizens. Unfortunately, that's exactly what homosexual activists are demanding.

Common sense tells us that a nation will not survive very long if it encourages its people to engage in harmful behavior. We can't afford to suppress the truth any longer. Instead of fooling ourselves into thinking that we are helping people by encouraging what's killing them, we must plainly admit that the best solution is to resurrect traditional Moral Law standards and encourage their achievement through hard work and personal responsibility. We must strive for moral excellence rather than hide behind fallacious excuses. The future of our nation and our children depends on the public policy path we choose right now.

One final note: Homosexual activists have been known to classify people such as us—those who identify the dangers of homosexuality—as enemies of homosexuals. These activists often resort to name-calling (which is a good indication that they've run out of valid arguments) by tagging principled opponents as "bigots" and "homophobes" who are on the same par as racists. Nothing could be further from the truth. Disagreement with the radical gay political agenda does not make someone an enemy of homosexuals. To the contrary—those of us who are reasonably pointing out the known dangers of homosexual activity should be considered friends, not foes. After all, we're the ones trying to spare homosexuals from further disease and death by telling the truth about the issue. The activists who are suppressing that truth are their real enemies.

10. ABORTION: CHOOSING OURSELVES TO DEATH

"Convenience is becoming the theme of our culture."
—Judge Robert Bork

There are few issues more emotional in our nation today than abortion. Contemporary thinker and speaker Ravi Zacharias has experienced the agitation some people express simply when they think the subject *may* come up. A recent exchange Zacharias had on a call-in radio program illustrates the point:

> At Ohio State University, I did an open forum on a radio talk show. The host was an atheist. From the start, the callers were antagonistic. I could feel the tension as soon as the lines lit up. One angry woman caller said, "All you people have is an agenda you're trying to promote." Referring to abortion, she said, "You want to take away our rights and invade our private lives." Abortion had not even been brought up. "Just a minute," I replied. "We didn't even raise the subject." I said, "Can I ask you a question? On every university campus I visit, somebody stands up and says that God is an evil God to allow all this evil into our world. This person typically says, 'A plane crashes: Thirty people die,

and twenty people live. What kind of a God would arbitrarily choose some to live and some to die?' " I continued, "But when we play God and determine whether a child within a mother's womb should live [or die], we argue for that as a moral right. So when human beings are given the privilege of playing God, it's called a moral right. When God plays God, we call it an immoral act. Can you justify this for me?" That was the end of the conversation.[1]

What could the caller say? Zacharias had hit on the central problem that relativism presents to a community—everyone gets to play God. Everyone decides what is right and wrong for themselves because there is no standard beyond themselves. We have already seen why this is logically self-defeating and practically impossible for any civilized society. There is a real right and wrong that we *discover* rather than *determine*, so that no one needs to play God.

The question is: "What's the real right and wrong regarding abortion? Should abortion be protected as a right or outlawed as wrong?" We will now take a pointed and factual look at the subject and hope that you will be open to the facts. Whether you're pro-life or pro-choice, your position should be based on the truth. There is no way this issue will ever be resolved if people aren't honest enough to investigate and accept the facts.

THE FACTS ABOUT THE UNBORN

As we mentioned in chapter 6, *Roe v. Wade* was the 1973 Supreme Court case that overturned the laws against abortion in all fifty states. In doing so, the *Roe* Court failed to address the central issue in the abortion debate, which is, of course, the question of whether or not an unborn baby is a human being. Justice Harry Blackmun casually brushed off that question when he wrote, "We need not resolve the difficult question of when life begins."[2] In other words, *in ruling on the legality of abortion, the Supreme Court incredibly denied that it was necessary to discover when life begins!* Of course, by allowing abortion at virtually any time during pregnancy, the Court had by implication declared that life does not begin until birth. But were they right? Does life begin at birth or before? Let's take a look at the facts.

There are a number of medical facts that prove life begins at conception. First, at the moment a male sperm unites with a female ovum, each having 23 chromosomes, a new and unique 46 chromosome human "zygote" is created. Though tiny, this new creature has all of the genetic information that a fully developed person has. No new genetic information will be added throughout the baby's lifetime. (In fact, according to Nobel laureate and biophysicist Francis Crick, the genetic content of a newly fertilized ovum is equivalent to *fifty complete sets* of *Encyclopedia Britannica!*[3] This is no tissue blob. It is an incredibly complex new individual creation.) "Her genetic makeup is established at conception, determining to a great extent her own individual characteristics—gender, eye color, bone structure, hair color, skin color, susceptibility to certain diseases."[4] In other words, there is nothing genetically different between a human zygote and the person reading this sentence. Both you and the baby have a distinctive genetic code. As a result, you are each unique, you are each 100 percent human being, and you are each unlike any other creature ever conceived.

Second, because of this unique genetic code, we know that the baby in the womb is not merely a part of its mother's body. This is evident for a number of other reasons as well: (1) About half the babies are male (and the mother is always a female); (2) Many babies have a different blood type than their mother; and (3) Fertilized ova maintain their own genetic characteristics when transplanted into a different mother (for instance, if a black woman is implanted with a fertilized egg from a white couple, she will give birth to a white baby).

Third, the developmental requirements of the baby in the womb are exactly those of babies outside the womb. There are four basic things that an unborn child needs to reach adulthood: time, air, water, and food. These are the same four things that a two-year-old child needs to reach adulthood.

These facts have led world renowned scientists and geneticists to testify before Congress that life begins at conception. Their testimony could not be more clear.

> In biology and in medicine, it is an accepted fact that the life of any individual organism produced by sexual reproduction begins at conception, or fertilization (Dr. Micheline M. Mathew-Roth, Harvard University).
>
> To accept the fact that after fertilization has taken place a new human has come into being is no longer a matter of taste or opinion. The human nature of the human being

from conception to old age is not a metaphysical contention, it is plain experimental evidence (world famous French geneticist Jerome LeJeune).

But now we can say, unequivocally, that the question of when life begins is no longer a question for theological or philosophical dispute. It is an established scientific fact. Theologians and philosophers may go on to debate the meaning of life or the purpose of life, but it is an established fact that all life, including human life, begins at the moment of conception (Dr. Hymie Gordon, professor of medical genetics and physician at Mayo Clinic).[5]

It is important to note that "no witness [who testified before the Senate subcommittee] raised any evidence to refute the biological fact that from the moment of conception there exists a distinct individual being who is alive and is of the human species."[6] In other words, no witness challenged the scientific consensus that life begins at conception. Medical experts know that an unborn child is not a "potential life" as the *Roe* Court would have us believe. Rather, it is a life with great potential.

In addition to this expert medical testimony, there is the added testimony of plain old common sense. Dogs conceive dogs, cats conceive cats, and humans conceive humans. Sonograms, and now even actual video footage of a baby in the womb,[7] show us a tiny but amazing human being. We witness thousands of babies—not "tissue blobs"—born prematurely each year. And expectant mothers who miscarry are distressed not because they have lost a "choice," but because they have lost a child. Despite the inconvenience these facts might bear, we must be honest enough with ourselves not to suppress them. Unfortunately, many on the pro-abortion side have suppressed them. Let's take a look at how they avoid the facts to justify abortion.

WORD GAMES

Given the evidence that human life begins at conception— and since everyone agrees that innocent human life should not be taken (this is obvious from the Moral Law)—it seems there would be a consensus in this country to outlaw abortion except where the mother's life is in danger. That, in fact, was the consensus before the *Roe* Court legalized and legitimized abortion on demand. As we indicated in chapter 2, legalization helped to change the minds of many from believing abortion is wrong to believing it is acceptable. As a result, our country is virtually split down the middle over this issue.

But legalization has not been the only cause for the split. There has been a very skillful public relations campaign from the powerful abortion lobby in this country to justify abortion. That lobby has two major elements: intense ideological support from the Left who value radical individualism over all else, and significant financial backing from the beneficiaries of what is now a multibillion-dollar industry. In fact, *abortion is the most common elective surgical procedure currently performed in the U.S. And 93 percent of all abortions in the United States are birth control (convenience) abortions.*[8] They have nothing to do with rape, incest, health of the baby, or health of the mother.

One primary tactic of the abortion lobby is to hide the truth about abortion in attractive euphemisms—pleasant words that conceal a harsh reality. You are not killing your baby; you are "terminating your pregnancy." You are not pregnant with a child; you have a "product of conception." You don't have a responsibility; you have a "choice." But fanciful language does not change reality. As much as we might like to avoid the reality, abortion is the intentional taking of an innocent human life.

Please don't emotionally short-circuit here. We are not saying that all women who have abortions are murderers. Most women who get abortions are not murderers but victims themselves, deceived by the euphemisms of the abortion propaganda machine. The point is this: Medically and scientifically, abortion ends the life of an innocent human being. Because this conclusion is inescapable, pro-abortionist activists use every tactic imaginable to avoid any discussion of the status of the fetus. As *Roe* author Justice Harry Blackmun showed us, they avoid the question of when life begins and emphasize friendly terms such as "choice," "reproductive health," and "privacy."

Another euphemism used by pro-abortion activists is the very name of their cause. They call themselves "pro-choice" but nothing could be further from the truth. They are not truly interested in choice. They are interested in advancing abortion. If the "pro-choicers" were truly "pro-choice" they would invite pro-life advocates to their meetings and into their clinics. After all, life is the only other choice a woman can make. Instead, pro-abortion advocates greet pro-lifers with court orders to keep them as far away as possible. The pro-abortionists have only one choice in mind. The other choice isn't good for business.

Now let's take a look at the major justifications abortion rights advocates use to keep business going. As we'll see, they all collapse under the weight of truth.

LOGIC OF THE LEFT: ARGUMENTS FOR ABORTION

There are many arguments advanced by the Left to justify abortion. We have identified seventeen of the more common pro-abortion arguments and placed them into four major categories: Rights, Solutions, Ignorance, and Relativism. Below is the complete list. We'll cover these arguments by category.

Rights: Abortion is a right.
1. "Women must have the freedom to choose!"
2. "It's my body! Abortion is a matter of privacy!"
3. "Abortion is a right that helps women advance their careers."
4. "Abortion is a constitutional right!"

Solutions: Abortion solves a problem.
5. "Abortion is appropriate for unwanted babies, those with birth defects, or those being born into poverty."
6. "Abortion is justified to help relieve over-population."
7. "Abortion helps avoid child abuse."
8. "Abortion should remain legal or women will die from back-alley abortions!"
9. "Abortion should not be outlawed because some women get pregnant by rape or incest."
10. "Abortion should not be outlawed because pro-lifers won't adopt all the babies."

Ignorance: Ambiguity makes abortion acceptable.
11. "Abortion is acceptable because the fetus is tiny, undeveloped, and unconscious."
12. "Abortion is acceptable before viability."
13. "We really don't know if the unborn are human."
14. "Okay, the unborn are human but they're not 'persons'!"

Relativism: Abortion is only wrong if you think it's wrong.
15. "Don't like abortion? Don't have one!"
16. "I'm personally opposed to abortion, but we shouldn't legislate our values on others."
17. "Don't cram your morals down my throat! Keep abortion legal!"

Rights: Abortion Is a Right

1. "Women must have the freedom to choose!"

When Al Gore debated Dan Quayle back in the 1992 vice-presidential debate, he repeatedly challenged Quayle to say, "I support a woman's right to choose." Quayle, of course, refused, and the debate resumed as a war of slogans rather than a rigorous intellectual pursuit of the truth. Quayle would have been better served by answering Gore's challenge with a question: "A right to choose *what*, Al?"

In fact, Quayle should have exposed the blatant hypocrisy of Gore and the Democrats right there. In 1992 Quayle and the Republicans were advancing school choice—the idea that parents should have the right to choose which school their children attend. But since Clinton and Gore were captive to the National Education Association—an organization committed to keeping competition (and thus excellence) out of our government schools—they were opposed to school choice. With this in mind, Quayle's complete rebuttal to Gore could have gone this way:

"Al, when you claim that a woman should have the freedom to choose, I must ask you: freedom to choose *what?* After all, it is a scientific fact that an unborn child is a human being. You know it, I know it, and the medical community knows it. So why do you insist that a mother has a right to choose the death of her innocent baby? The blunt term we use for such an act is murder. If that term is offensive to you, Al, it should be. The act is offensive, especially to the baby. No one has a right to choose murder. In fact, no one has the moral right to choose *anything* that directly ends the life of another innocent human being. The right to life is the right to all other rights. Without life we'd all have no rights whatsoever.

"Furthermore, Al, if you are for a woman's right to choose, then why aren't you for a woman's right to choose a school for her child? Why should a woman have the right to choose the death of her child but not the right to choose a school for her child? And what about the father? Why doesn't he have a 'right to choose'?

"Al, you know as well as I do that the phrase 'freedom to choose' is nothing more than a smoke screen, a euphemism to hide the real truth about abortion. If the freedom to choose was really highest on your hierarchy of values, then you wouldn't condemn racists for choosing to discriminate, rapists for choosing to rape, or companies for choosing to pollute (those polluters were terrible villains in your book, Al, weren't they?). The bottom line is that you *know* that the unborn are human beings worthy of protection, but you just don't *want* to admit it. Come clean, Al! Your position is indefensible."

2. "It's my body! Abortion is a matter of privacy!"

As we mentioned before, the baby is not a part of its mother's body. Although the baby resides there, he or she is genetically unique. Even if it is granted that a mother has the right to control her body, she does not have the right to destroy someone else's body in the process. That's exactly what happens in abortion. The question that never gets asked is, "What about the baby's body?"

Appealing to privacy does not solve the problem either. Wrongs do not become rights because they are committed in private. It doesn't matter how many or how few people are involved in the decision to steal a car, abuse a spouse, or abort a child. The acts and the results are still wrong. Moreover, why is the privacy of the child never defended? The pain and death caused by the abortion device certainly violate the child's privacy. University of Rhode Island ethicist Stephen Schwarz points out: "The child's right to live, not to be killed, especially by the painful methods of abortion . . . surely outweighs anyone's claim to a right to privacy. And the state must protect that right, just as it protects other civil rights."[9]

3. "Abortion is a right that helps women advance their careers."

First, while few would admit this crass way of putting it, this latent argument seems to be at the bottom of much of the feminist support for abortion. Certainly the option of abortion can help free women from the burden of unwanted pregnancies, thereby allowing them to advance their careers. But this is like arguing that the option of murdering workplace competitors would help women advance their careers. The ends do not justify the means.

Second, what is often forgotten is that more than two thousand women's careers are ended every day by abortion—at least half of the babies who die in abortion clinics are females who are never given an opportunity to have a career. Moreover, the proportion of female to male deaths will increase as abortion becomes more commonly used for sex selection. As we saw in chapter 4, this is already the case in China.

Finally, instead of advancing respect for women, abortion has led to more disrespect for women. Because of the legality of abortion, family and friends often feel free to pressure women into killing their babies when they wouldn't otherwise do so. The same is true of some men with whom women are sexually active. Such men favor abortion because it frees them of what would normally be a long-range responsibility. In effect, abortion makes women more susceptible to predatory males who want to use women for sex but aren't really interested in making long-term commitments to them. With abortion on demand the law of the land, is it any wonder why respect for life, commitment, and responsibility have waned?

4. "Abortion is a constitutional right!"

Those who argue that there should be a constitutional right to abortion because seven Supreme Court justices said so might not want to press that argument too far. As we have seen, the Court has been wrong on many issues. In fact, in a case with striking similarities to *Roe v. Wade*, the Court was wrong on March 6, 1857, when it voted seven to two in *Dred Scott v. Sandford* that blacks were not "persons" under the Constitution and thus had no rights as citizens. According to the Court, blacks were the "chattel" (property) of their owners, not "persons" with rights of their own under the Constitution.

In the same way, *Roe v. Wade* ruled that the unborn are the "property" of their mothers with no rights of their own under the Constitution. For this reason, the unborn can be disposed of in any way their mothers see fit. The similarities of the two cases are unavoidable:

DRED SCOTT V. SANDFORD (1857)	ROE V. WADE (1973)
Slavery is legal	Abortion is legal
7 to 2 decision	7 to 2 decision
Blacks are nonpersons	Unborn are nonpersons
Blacks are property of owner (master)	Unborn are property of owner (mother)
Abolitionists should not impose morality on the slave owner	Pro-lifers should not impose morality on the mother

The Supreme Court was wrong about blacks in 1857, and it was wrong about unborn babies in 1973. Unborn children *are* persons with a protected right to life. The Fourteenth Amendment explicitly says that the state shall not "deprive any person of life, liberty, or property, without due process of law; nor deny any person within its jurisdiction the equal protection of the laws." The *Roe* Court suggested that this amendment does not recognize an unborn child as a "person." But the Court was wrong for a number of reasons.

First, there were legal references to the unborn as a "child" during the time when the Fourteenth Amendment was written.[10] Second, the dictionaries of the day defined a fetus as a "child in the womb." Third, the killing of the unborn was called "manslaughter." Fourth, at that time all abortions were prohibited, except for saving the life of the mother. Fifth, at that time the same range of punishments existed for killing the baby as for killing the mother. Sixth, the Supreme Court as late as 1970 (in *Steinberg v. Ohio*), only three years before *Roe v. Wade*, called the unborn a "person" protected under the Fourteenth Amendment. Seventh, some of the congressmen who voted for and helped draft the Fourteenth Amendment also approved of strong anti-abortion laws in some United States territories, which were all under the jurisdiction of the Constitution. And finally, "the most direct piece of federal legislation relating to abortion in this period was enacted by Congress in 1873, five years after the Fourteenth Amendment was proposed." This legislation "prohibited the selling, lending, or giving away of 'any article . . . for causing unlawful abortion' as defined by the criminal law of the state in which the federal enclave was located."[11]

The bottom line is this: If the Fourteenth Amendment was meant to include the right to abortion and exclude the unborn from legal protection, it was completely unknown to those who were responsible for the amendment's existence. In other words, the *Roe* Court usurped the will of the people by ignoring the original intent of the Fourteenth Amendment and by overturning the abortion laws of all fifty states. The Court legislated their own meaning into the law instead of upholding the meaning the people had approved.[12]

Commenting on *Roe*'s majority opinion, Justice William Rehnquist wrote in dissent that the Court's illegitimate reasoning "partakes more of judicial legislation than it does of a determination of the intent of the drafters of the Fourteenth Amendment.... To reach its result, the Court necessarily has had to find within the scope of the Fourteenth Amendment a right that was apparently completely unknown to the drafters of the Amendment."[13]

As we indicated in chapter 6, when the Court ignores the intent of a particular law it is ignoring the will of the people. Instead of the people governing themselves, they are governed by the imposed will of unelected judges. That's not representative democracy, that's closer to tyranny.

Solutions: Abortion Solves a Problem.

5. "Abortion is appropriate for unwanted babies, those with birth defects, or those being born into poverty."

Once again, this justification ignores the fact that the baby is a human being. How does being unwanted nullify a person's humanness? There are unwanted two-year-olds and even some unwanted teenagers! If abortion is appropriate because an unborn child is unwanted, handicapped, or poor, then why is it not permissible to kill unwanted, handicapped, or poor children who are already born? If it is more merciful to kill the unborn for these reasons, then we should round up all children in these conditions and exterminate them immediately. After all, unlike those still in the womb, we know for sure who is actually unwanted, poor, and handicapped.

We don't do this precisely because it is a repulsive violation of the Moral Law. Murder is not a solution to social ills. Perhaps the reason abortion doesn't repulse us like this suggestion does is due to the fact that we don't see the bodies from the four thousand-plus abortions performed in this country every day. It's a hidden practice. Out of sight, out of mind. If we did see them, perhaps the conscience of the nation would be awakened.

6. "Abortion is justified to help relieve overpopulation."

This is more illicit logic from the pro-abortion side. First, murdering a portion of the population is not the solution to overpopulation. The end doesn't justify the means. Second, while many metropolitan areas are overcrowded, the world is not over-populated. The entire population of the world could live eight per house on small lots within the state of Texas.[14] The entire world could stand side-by-side within the city limits of Jacksonville, Florida. Moreover, the well-known famines in Ethiopia, for example, have been the result of political infighting, not inadequate food production. World food production has grown twice as fast as population growth since 1961.[15] Third, in the United States, there are more couples wanting to adopt than there are abortions. Fourth, our birth rate is 1.8 for every couple. We are literally a dying nation that would be declining in population if it were not for immigration.

It's very interesting to note that the pro-abortionists who propose this justification never volunteer to kill themselves in order to alleviate the "population problem"! They only claim that we should kill the helpless to solve this perceived problem.

7. "Abortion helps avoid child abuse."

Question: If a parent beats a child so badly that the child dies, would you consider that child abuse? Of course! Murder is the worst kind of child abuse. It is strange logic to suggest that killing a child is better than letting her live because she might be abused in the future. Moreover, since abortion on demand became the law of the land, child abuse has risen by some reports as much as 500 percent.[16] Disrespect for life is permeating our culture. One woman who stabbed two children in a South Carolina mall summed up the attitude partially brought on by abortion. When asked why she stabbed the children, she responded, "So what? . . . People can always make more babies."[17]

8. "Abortion should remain legal or women will die from back-alley abortions!"

On April 20, 1998, President Clinton declared, "We are fighting for the lives of our children!" Was he referring to abortion?

No. Cigarettes! Implying that outlawing abortion would be dangerous, President Clinton has said repeatedly that he would like to keep abortion "safe, legal, and rare." Questions for the President: "Why do you want to keep abortion *rare?* There must be something morally wrong with it if you want to keep it *rare.* But if there's something morally wrong with it, then why do you want to keep it legal?" Nothing morally wrong is ever politically right, especially when lives are at stake.

The problem with the "back-alley" justification—in fact, the problem with all abortion justifications except saving the life of the mother—is that the unborn child is a 100 percent human being. Why should we keep crime safe and legal? Should we allow "murdering facilities" in every town so the murdering process will be safer? How about bomb-making facilities so terrorists don't accidentally blow themselves up making their bombs? What's safe about a *legal* procedure that kills more than half its patients? After all, some women and all babies die today from legal abortions.

Moreover, the "back-alley" scare has been grossly exaggerated if not completely fabricated. First, women getting abortions were not rescued from death by *Roe,* but by the availability of antibiotics, which began in the '40s. Second, according to one of Planned Parenthood's own medical conferences, more than 90 percent of illegal abortions before 1973 were done with medical equipment by doctors in their offices, not back alleys.[18] In fact, Bernard Nathanson, one of the original pro-abortion leaders and co-founder of the N.A.R.A.L. (the National Association for the Repeal of Abortion Laws, now known as the National Abortion Rights Action League), admits that he made up exaggerated statistics of women dying from illegal abortions in order to get abortion legalized:

> I confess that I knew the figures [five thousand to ten thousand per year] were totally false, and I suppose the others did too if they stopped to think of it. But in the "morality" of the revolution, it was a *useful* figure, widely accepted, so why go out of our way to correct it with honest statistics? The overriding concern was to get the laws eliminated, and anything within reason that had to be done was permissible.[19]

According to the United States Bureau of Vital Statistics, the actual number of women dying from illegal abortions in 1972 (the year before *Roe*) was thirty-nine.[20] That's *thirty-nine*. Even if ten times that number were not reported, it's a long way from five thousand to ten thousand! According to the Center for Disease Control, a similar number of women are dying today from *legal* abortions (the average was fourteen deaths per year between 1973 and 1991).[21] And due to the sheer volume of abortions (1.2–1.6 million per year), more women incur abortion-related injuries today than at any time before *Roe*.[22]

The truth is that pro-abortion zealots have proven time and time again that they depend on lies to deceive the public. In fact, in 1995 Norma McCorvey, the "Roe" of *Roe v. Wade*, revealed that the case itself was built on a lie. McCorvey admitted that she lied about being gang raped in order to improve her chances of getting an abortion (she never did get the abortion but gave birth to a baby girl). Her own experience working in an abortion clinic haunted her and played a part in her conversion to Christianity and the pro-life position. In an interview with *Newsweek* she said, "Have you ever seen a second-trimester abortion? It's a baby. It's got a face and a body, and they put him in a freezer and a little container."[23]

The deceitful streak of the pro-abortionists was reaffirmed in 1997 when Ron Fitzsimmons, executive director of the National Association of Abortion Providers, which represents more than two hundred clinics, admitted that abortion-rights advocates misled the public by talking primarily about the few hundred partial-birth abortions performed in the last trimester rather than the thousands done in the second trimester."[24] Fitzsimmons confessed that he had "lied through his teeth" when he told *Nightline*'s Ted Koppel in 1995 that there were only five hundred "partial-birth abortions" in America each year. In March 1997 he admitted that there are really more like five thousand done each year. Of course, even if there were only one done each year it still wouldn't be justified.

During the recent partial-birth abortion debate, pro-abortionists were caught in still another lie: They maintained that victims of that gruesome procedure are horribly deformed or are aborted to save the life of the mother. The truth was later revealed by the very doctor who invented the procedure. He asserted that about 80 percent of partial birth abortions are purely elective.[25] At least one other abortion provider confirmed this.[26]

In other words, most of the babies who are nearly fully delivered—only to have a hole drilled in their skulls and their brains sucked out—are perfectly healthy babies whose mothers are not in danger.

In fact, there is no legitimate medical need for partial-birth abortion. Former Surgeon General C. Everett Koop maintains that there is no circumstance by which partial-birth abortion would ever be needed to save the life of a mother.[27] Think about it. How does killing the baby help the mother? If the baby needs to come out, a routine Cesarean section can be performed. The truth is this: Partial-birth abortion isn't needed to save the life or health of the mother; partial-birth abortion is needed because it's the only way to legally kill a baby that large and remove its body from the mother. But the abortion rights industry doesn't want this truth to be known. Like the facts about illegal abortions, the facts about partial-birth abortions hurt their cause and their business.

9. "Abortion should not be outlawed because some women get pregnant by rape or incest."

Before we discuss whether abortion is justified in these hard cases, let us investigate why the pro-abortionists bring this up. Do they bring it up because they are truly concerned about keeping abortion legal for rape and incest victims, or do they bring it up because they want to use these hard cases to assert that all abortions should remain legal? There's a simple way to find out. Simply ask pro-abortionists if they would support a law that would ban all abortions except in case of rape, incest, or to save the life of the mother. Chances are you'll get a *"no,"* which means they really want *all* abortions to remain legal, not just those pertaining to rape and incest. In effect, they are using rape and incest as an emotional smoke screen to compensate for their inability to justify their real position by the facts. So after you have uncovered their real position, ask them why all non-rape and non-incest abortions should be legal. They will have a difficult time justifying it.

Back to our question: Is abortion justified for rape and incest? Let's start by saying that rape and incest are morally vile acts, and those who commit them should be punished to the maximum extent of the law. Conversely, women who are victims of these crimes need our love and compassion. While most victims of rape or incest do not conceive, a very small percentage do. So we are talking about a very small number of possible abortion cases, *far less than 1 percent of the total.*

Now we must be brutally honest here: If our wives were raped and conceived, emotionally we might want—at least initially—to have the baby aborted. But emotions don't always lead us to the right conclusion. There's a difference between the act and the product of the act. While the act was horrible, the product is not. The product is an innocent human being. It makes sense to punish the guilty rapist, but it doesn't make sense to give capital punishment to the innocent baby. Why should the child be punished for the crime of the father?

One reason, presented by the pro-abortionists, is to spare the mother the emotional and physical burden of carrying the baby to term. Prohibiting abortion in such cases appears to add insult to injury. The poor woman has already been degraded by a rape and now we're saying that she must give birth as well. How can this be justified?

First, if the victim gets immediate medical treatment, conception can be avoided in all cases (since conception does not occur immediately after intercourse). This seems like the best solution to the problem. But if a woman does conceive, while this is certainly a difficult situation, we cannot forget that we are dealing with a human life here. The murder of an innocent human being to relieve the suffering of another is never justified. As Stephen Schwarz points out, sometimes the moral thing to do is not the most pleasant:

> A person in a concentration camp may have the opportunity to become an informer, which means a better life for him. But it also means betraying his friends and causing them additional suffering. Morally, he is forced to remain in his present, pitiable state, rather than do a moral evil, namely, betraying his friends, perhaps causing their deaths. If a woman is forced to continue a pregnancy, the case is similar in this respect, that she too is forced to remain in a pitiable state because the alternative is a moral evil, the killing of an innocent child.[28]

Second, if the removal of emotional distress from the mother is justification for aborting babies of rape, then so is the killing of children already born who are products of rape. While these children may remind the mother of the rape, this certainly doesn't justify killing them.

Third, while abortion is intended to remove emotional distress, there is good evidence that abortion actually *adds* emotional, psychological, and even physical distress. One study of 252 women who had abortions concluded that in these hard cases, which "are generally very difficult psychological circumstances, abortion almost invariably tends to aggravate and complicate the women's problems."[29] A doctor from Planned Parenthood's own association of physicians concludes, "There are no known psychiatric diseases which can be cured by abortion.... Paradoxically, the very women for whom legal abortion may seem most justifiable are also the ones for whom the risk is highest of post-abortion psychic insufficiency...."[30] Moreover, a 30 percent increased incidence of breast cancer has been discovered in women who have had abortions.[31] In short, the indignity of a rape is not helped by adding the guilt and harmful medical consequences of an abortion.

If all of this still doesn't convince you that rape and incest babies should be protected, please don't lose sight of the fact that such cases are the extreme exception (again, far less than 1 percent of all abortions). These cases should not be the basis of our nation's abortion laws. As we indicated in chapter 8, one of the principles of good law-making is to realize that laws cannot be written with the extreme exception in mind. We shouldn't do away with all speed limits because on a rare occasion we might need to rush someone to the emergency room. Likewise, we shouldn't do away with all laws limiting abortion because we can't bring ourselves—despite the evidence—to prevent the deaths of babies conceived by rape or incest. Indeed, any restriction would be better than the abortion-on-demand policy now in place. More than four thousand convenience deaths per day do not have to take place to keep abortion available for a handful.

10. **"Abortion should not be outlawed because pro-lifers won't adopt all the babies."**

This is not really a direct argument against abortion, but one that is advanced, nevertheless. Attacking the person holding a position does not necessarily destroy the validity of the position itself. Indeed, there are good, well-meaning people (and also a few extremist nuts) on both sides of this debate. In truth, it doesn't matter what pro-lifers (or pro-abortionists) do. Their actions, good or bad, have no bearing on the morality of abortion. Nevertheless, let's respond directly to the charge.

First, if no one were ready to adopt these babies, killing them still would not be justified. If it were, we would be justified in executing all orphans. Second, as we have mentioned, there *are* people waiting to adopt—more babies are wanted for adoption than are aborted. And finally, what pro-lifers fail to do does not give pro-abortionists justification for murder. This was communicated beautifully during a debate on abortion. A question directed at the pro-life side came from an angry woman in the audience that went this way: "Are you going to adopt the children I'm forced to give birth to after you make abortion illegal!?" The scholar arguing the pro-life position approached the microphone and calmly said, "I have three children asleep at home right now. After this debate, I will go home, and at midnight tonight I will kill all three of those children *unless* you agree to adopt them. If you don't agree to adopt them, am I justified in killing them?"[32] That was the end of the conversation.

Ignorance: Ambiguity Makes Abortion Acceptable

11. "Abortion is acceptable because the fetus is tiny, undeveloped, and unconscious."

Underlying this justification is the "quality of life" view that only "normal" life is worth protecting. If it doesn't look like a normal person or function like a normal person, it may not be worth protecting like a normal person. As we'll see in the next chapter, this is the same logic behind some of the euthanasia arguments. Proponents claim that a comatose man who is only a shell of his former self no longer has a valuable life, so his life can be ended. But suppose the doctor told us that in eight months the comatose man would wake up, recover, and then live a normal life as a unique individual. Would we even consider euthanasia? Of course not. Then why do we accept abortion?[33]

The truth is, size, development, or consciousness do not determine humanness. Are small people less human than large ones? Are underdeveloped children less human than mature adults? Does murder cease being murder if the victim is unconscious? If so, then every murderer should simply knock out his victims before he kills them. Ethicist Francis Beckwith writes, "It may be true that it is psychologically easier to kill something that does not resemble the human beings we see in everyday life, but it does not follow from this that the being in question is any less human or that the executioner is any more humane."[34]

12. "Abortion is acceptable before viability."

You've heard this before. Once a child can survive on its own, then we shouldn't abort it; but before that time, abortion is okay. This justification is invalid for a number of reasons. First, viability has absolutely nothing to do with essential humanness. The unborn are genetically 100 percent human from their conception regardless of their stage of development or state of viability. Viability is an arbitrary measure of what someone can do, not what someone is. We are in great danger as a society if we value people merely for what they can *do* rather than who they *are*. Second, children already born are not viable. If you leave a two-month-old baby alone, it will die. (Come to think of it, many teenagers aren't viable, either!) Third, even if viability were the standard, technology keeps moving the standard back. Will the pro-abortionists give up their stand on abortion when modern medicine can grow a child in an artificial womb? Not a chance.

13. "We really don't know if the unborn are human."

As we have seen, we really *do* know. But for the sake of argument let's assume some ambiguity there. Let's assume we really don't know if the unborn are human. Doesn't prudence demand that we err on the side of life? Put it this way: If you were unsure whether it was a prowler or your teenage daughter trying to open your front door late at night, would you shoot first and ask questions later? Of course you wouldn't. You would verify the identity of the person on the other side before pulling the trigger because a mistake would be devastating. Likewise, if you are out hunting deer and hear a rustling in the bush, you don't shoot first and ask questions later. You may have killed your hunting partner! So when it comes to life in the womb, if you're not sure, *don't shoot!*

14. "Okay, the unborn are human but they're not 'persons'!"

Some pro-abortionists admit that the unborn are 100 percent human beings from conception, but they try to wiggle out of the implications of that admission by claiming that the unborn are not "persons," so they're not protected by the Fourteenth Amendment. This justification merely plays the semantics game.

First, any distinction between a human being and a person is an arbitrary one. They are trying to make a distinction when there's no distinction to be made. It's a distinction without a real difference.

Second, any distinction between humans and persons on the grounds they lack certain functions would justify killing children and adults who have lost these same functions. For example, if the unborn are not considered persons because they are unconscious, then adults should not be considered persons when they are unconscious. But this is absurd. Can we kill adults simply because they lack consciousness?

Third, even if one were to agree that the unborn are not "persons," they are still innocent human beings and innocent human beings should not be killed. An unborn child doesn't lose its humanness simply because the Supreme Court refuses to call it a "person."

Fourth, the distinction is probably legally irrelevant anyway. Unborn eagles receive legal protection and they're not considered persons. Why shouldn't unborn humans get the same protection? Moreover, innocent human life was protected in this country before the Fourteenth Amendment ever existed. So even if unborn babies aren't considered "persons" protected by the Fourteenth Amendment, they should still be protected as innocent human beings by criminal law.

Finally, if the Supreme Court can recognize a corporation as a person (*Santa Clara v. Sanford*, 1886), then surely they should recognize an unborn child as a person. The bottom line is that this justification is nothing but more fanciful language intended to cover an evil deed. It really gets the pro-abortionists nowhere.

Relativism: Abortion Is Only Wrong If You Think It Is.

15. "Don't like abortion? Don't have one!"

This is nothing more than an emotive outburst found on the car bumpers of pro-abortion activists. To see its absurdity, let's make up some of our own: "Don't like slavery? Don't own a slave!" "Don't like murder? Don't commit one!" "Don't like theft? Don't steal!" According to this kind of pro-abortionist logic, nothing would be worth outlawing. As long as you don't commit acts that you find offensive, you should let everyone else do whatever they want. This is relativism—and a recipe for anarchy.

16. "I'm personally opposed to abortion, but we shouldn't legislate our values on others."

You hear this argument especially from evasive politicians who want to have it both ways. "I may be personally opposed, but I do not want to impose my values on others." This is more anti-intellectual nonsense.

First, to see the absurdity of the argument, apply the logic to any immoral activity: "I'm personally opposed to killing two-year-olds, but I don't want to impose my values on others. If you want to kill two-year-olds, that's okay with me" or "I'm personally opposed to rape, but if you want to rape someone, go right ahead. Far be it from me to object."

Second, the objection to imposing values assumes that all values are personal—that they are merely a matter of taste or opinion, that there is no objective right or wrong. This entire book has shown why this is absurd. Murder is wrong not simply because you object to it, but because it violates the Moral Law. Abortion is wrong whether you are personally opposed to it or not. Hence, pro-lifers are not imposing *their* morality, but *our* morality—the one given to us all.

Third, as we have seen, all moral positions impose values. Even the moral position that you should not impose values on others does just that: it imposes values on others. For if we are not to restrain people legally from doing wrong, then we impose on others the effects of the wrongdoing. In the case of abortion, the effects are felt by the baby, in some cases by the father, and by the mother who is often misled and must suffer the emotional and physical scars for the rest of her life. The effects are also felt by innocent people who are victims of crime spawned by our nation's blatant disrespect for life.

17. "Don't cram your morals down my throat! Keep abortion legal!"

This makes no sense. Pro-abortionists are doing the same thing. As we discussed in chapter 3, both sides want to impose "their" values. Laws favoring abortion impose values on the *life* of the unborn; pro-life laws impose values on the *liberty* of the mother. In other words, the pro-life side wants to impose *continued pregnancy* on the mother, while the pro-abortion side wants to impose *death* on the baby.

While some of you may not *like* the conclusion, it is obvious from medical facts that the morality that should be imposed is the pro-life one. This is the morality inherited by all of us but only accepted by some of us. It is our common morality. Facts are sometimes hard.

WARPED OUTCOMES

Liberalized abortion laws have resulted in the following warped outcomes:

- Unborn eagles are protected by law. Unborn humans are not.
- A teenage girl at a public school must get permission from her parents to take an aspirin, but she needs no permission if she wants to get an abortion.
- A corporation is a "person" protected by the Fourteenth Amendment, but an unborn child is not.
- A mother who takes drugs can be prosecuted for harming her baby during pregnancy, but that same mother has a "right" to have her baby dismembered, scalded, or suffocated in her womb by abortion.
- Doctors in one room can operate to "save the life" of a five-month-old baby in the womb. In the next room, they can deliver a full-term baby feet first, drill a hole in the back of her skull and remove her brains!
- Outside of a few state laws against partial-birth abortion, humans can be killed in any gruesome manner while animals are legally protected. George Will points this out clearly: "Americans are proud of their humane feelings and are moved by empathy. Thus, we regulate the ways animals can be killed. Certain kinds of traps are banned. Cattle cannot be slaughtered in ways deemed careless about pain. Stray dogs and cats must be killed in certain ways. . . . But no laws regulate the suffering of the aborted."[35]
- Children know the unborn are people but adults do not. In May 1984 Milwaukee police descended on four children, ages four to eleven, after receiving reports that the suspects were throwing stones from a bridge. According to one of the officers on the scene, the police discovered that the children were "throwing fetuses around." The youngsters had retrieved twenty-two aborted infants from a nearby dumpster. When asked what they were doing, the children replied that they

were playing with "little people."[36] Question: If it is so easy for children to see that the unborn are people, why is it so hard for many adults to admit the same? Is it possible that the little people know something that the big people don't know?

- Staying in the womb can be more dangerous than coming out. On October 15, 1994 Simone Keys gave birth to her premature son Timothy who weighed one pound, fourteen ounces. Doctors skillfully prevented the birth of Timothy's twin sister, Celeste, who stayed in the womb for another ninety-five days, and was born at full term on January 18, 1995.[37] Had Ms. Keys so desired, she could have exercised her "right" to an abortion and killed Celeste at any time during the remainder of her pregnancy, even though Celeste was obviously just as much an innocent human being as her twin brother. Thankfully, Ms. Keys recognized the higher right to life. (Incidentally, Ms. Keys said that Celeste became active— squirming and wiggling in the womb—whenever she visited Timothy in the hospital.[38])

- Doctors have performed gruesome experiments on live aborted babies. Heads have been cut off babies and experiments performed on them; live hearts have been taken out and kept alive; kidneys and sex organs of aborted babies have been transplanted; stomachs have been cut open and studied—all without any anesthesia for the baby, in spite of the known fact that between eight and thirteen weeks after conception babies have a nervous system that can feel organic pain.[39]

WHAT'S THE SOLUTION?
HOW FAR CAN THE LAW GO?

So what should we do with these facts? Some believe that legal remedies would not be effective even if they were passed. "People will do it anyway," they say. We debunked that fallacy in chapter 2 but we'll say another word about it here. The truth is, legal remedies against abortion *have* been effective and probably would be again if enacted: One survey showed that the law had played a "major role" in shaping the moral perception of abortion for 70 percent of the women who had had abortions; moreover, *75 percent of those who had an abortion said they definitely would not have sought an illegal abortion.*[40] Abortion statistics bear this out. Upon legalization, the number of abortions exploded and soon reached approximately sixteen times the pre-legalization level.[41] The law obviously had an effect on behavior.

But how far can the law go? Since the unborn are innocent human beings, a complete ban on abortions (except those to save the life of the mother) should be our goal. Such a ban worked in this country for years. Unfortunately, it appears that such legislation cannot be achieved politically at this time. That's why we should embrace any law that would reduce the number of abortions. For example, a ban that would allow for exceptions in cases of rape, incest, or life of the mother would be far better than the current situation. Some pro-lifers view this as an intolerable compromise, an abandonment of the goal. But it is not. It is simply an admission that the complete goal cannot be attained immediately. Given the political reality that attitudes about abortion will not change overnight, we must remember that half a loaf is better than no loaf. Saving some lives is better than saving none.

CONCLUSION

The morality of our country is best judged by how we treat our own children. Sadly, with nearly one out of every three pregnancies ending in abortion, the most dangerous place to be in America is in the womb. But the freedom to choose an abortion only makes sense if unborn children are not alive—if they are not human beings. We have reviewed the irrefutable medical (and common sense) evidence that the unborn are living human beings. As a result, virtually every argument for abortion rights collapses under the weight of this truth. Justice Blackmun himself wrote, "If this suggestion of personhood is established, the appellant's case [for abortion rights], of course, collapses. . . ."[42]

We have news for Justice Blackmun and his supporters: The personhood of the unborn *has* been established. The simple logic is this: (1) Our common moral law teaches us that it is morally wrong to intentionally take the life of an innocent human being; (2) The fact is, unborn babies are innocent human beings from the moment of conception; and (3) Therefore, abortion, which takes the life of an innocent human being, is morally wrong.

As we work to change laws and change hearts, we must speak

the truth respectfully. Violence against pro-abortionists is *never* the answer. Two wrongs do not make a right. Norma McCorvey was "won by love" (the title of her 1998 book),[43] not by finger-wagging self-righteousness. We must work peacefully through love and logic to persuade others to accept the truth. This admittedly will be a difficult task because the truth is being suppressed in our country. Most pro-abortionists aren't willing to discuss the status of the baby, nor are they willing to admit that virtually every argument for abortion is an argument for infanticide. Instead of admitting the obvious, the pro-abortionists are sacrificing children on the altar of convenience and selfish personal autonomy. May God help the country that suppresses the Moral Law in order to kill inconvenient children.

We shall let Mother Teresa have the last word:

> By abortion, the mother does not learn to love, but kills even her own child to solve her problems. And by abortion, the father is told that he does not have to take any responsibility at all for the child he has brought into the world. That father is likely to put other women into the same trouble. So abortion just leads to more abortion. Any country that accepts abortion is not teaching its people to love, but to use any violence to get what they want.[44]

11. EUTHANASIA: EXTERMINATING OURSELVES TO DEATH

"Today, no unwanted baby. Tomorrow, no unwanted grand-parent."

Former governor of Colorado Richard Lamm once said that elderly people who are terminally ill "have a duty to die. . . . Like leaves which fall off a tree forming the humus in which other plants can grow, we've got a duty to die and get out of the way with all of our machines and artificial hearts, so that our kids can build a reasonable life."[1]

Once it hit the news, the governor tried desperately to get his two feet out of his mouth, insisting that he was not for killing the elderly. Yet this would leave the elderly with a moral "duty" to kill themselves!

Unfortunately, Lamm's sentiments are gaining momentum in our nation, and they reflect the logical outworking of the abortion movement. In fact, in order to understand the emergence of Kevorkian on the cultural landscape, we need to take a look back at an event that helped crystallize the transition from abortion to euthanasia in this country. That event took place in an Indiana hospital in 1982.

FROM ROE TO DOE

At 8:19 P.M., on April 9, 1982, Dr. Walter Owens, an obstetrician, delivered a baby boy in Bloomington, Indiana—a boy that ignited a nationwide controversy. The baby, who became known as "Baby Doe," suffered from Down's syndrome and an obstruction in his esophagus. Dr. James Schaeffer and Dr. Paul Windsler, the parents' family practitioners, recommended that the baby be referred to Riley Hospital for Children for lifesaving surgery to clear the blocked esophagus. The problem was serious but correctable.

Dr. Owens, whose job should have been over after delivery, told the parents that the child was a "blob" and would be severely retarded. He said that the boy only had a 50 percent chance of surviving the surgery (despite the fact that the success rate on *premature* babies was 88 percent at the time). Dr. Owens advised the parents to refuse consent for the surgery and predicted that the boy would die from pneumonia in a few days. This prediction was a sure thing. Without the surgery, Baby Doe would eventually drown in his own secretions after experiencing severe chemical irritation from stomach acids spilling into his lungs.

By 10:00 P.M., after only a half hour of discussion, the parents of Baby Doe decided, "We don't want the baby treated." The pediatrician, Dr. Schaeffer, asked, "Do you realize what you're doing?" The parents acknowledged that they did. Dr. Owens told them, "You have made a wise and courageous decision."

Unable to stand by and do nothing, Dr. Schaeffer persuaded Dr. Owens to speak with a pediatric surgeon at Riley Hospital for Children. Despite the fact that the pediatric surgeon called Owens' intentions "infanticide," the conversation did not change Dr. Owens' resolve. Abandoning his normal role as an obstetrician once again, Owens ordered the nurses to feed Baby Doe orally even though feeding him might cause him to choke and die. Owens also expressly prohibited intravenous feeding— which would have kept Baby Doe alive—and ordered the nurses to keep the boy sedated. At the time, Baby Doe did not need sedation because he was not yet uncomfortable. The sedation would only diminish his choke reflex and thereby speed his demise.

Wary of the legal implications, the hospital attorney requested and received a bedside hearing to determine the fate of Baby Doe. In a shocking ruling, Superior Court Judge John Baker ruled that the parents had the right to choose to follow the opinion of either Owens or Schaeffer. In other words, the parents could choose the boy's death!

On Sunday, two days after the birth, the nurses revolted against the instructions of Dr. Owens because those instructions clearly violated medical ethics. As a result, Baby Doe was transferred to a private room where private nurses gave him further injections of morphine and phenobarbital.

By Monday Baby Doe was weak, parched, and spitting blood. Further legal action, including an appeal to the Indiana Supreme Court, failed to stop the madness. Meanwhile, several couples lined up to adopt the boy. It was becoming clear that Baby Doe was very much a wanted child despite what his parents thought.

On Thursday, April 15, with Baby Doe severely dehydrated and barely clinging to life, Attorney Lawrence Brodeur flew to Washington where Supreme Court Justice John Paul Stevens was to hear a request to overrule the decision of the Indiana Court. Back in Bloomington, with the hospital staff in an uproar, the chief of staff ordered Dr. Schaeffer to start an IV to give Baby Doe the fluids he needed. This resulted in an altercation between Schaeffer and Owens. But it was all to no avail. Baby Doe died that night at 10:01 P.M.[2]

INESCAPABLE LOGIC: FROM ABORTION TO INFANTICIDE TO EUTHANASIA

While there is a lot that remains unclear about the life and death of Baby Doe, there is one thing we know for sure: The justifications used to kill Baby Doe are the same justifications used to kill babies in the womb. The logic is inescapable. Abortion leads to infanticide, and infanticide leads to euthanasia. Killing babies we do not want before they are born leads to killing babies we do not want after they are born. And infanticide of the young leads to euthanasia of the old. Abortion, infanticide, and euthanasia have no substantial difference. Indeed, the father of modern situational ethics, Joseph Fletcher, said it best: "Abortion is prenatal euthanasia, and euthanasia is post-natal infanticide."[3]

The parallel is striking. They have the same *subject* (a human being), the same *reason* (unwanted), and the same *result* (death).

The logic demands that if tiny human beings can be killed because they are unwanted, deformed, unaffordable (or whatever) before they are born, they can be killed for the same reasons when they are older. As former Surgeon General C. Everett Koop put it, every argument for abortion is an equally good argument for euthanasia. In fact, Koop claims he foresaw what was coming when *Roe v. Wade* was decided. He wrote:

> Physicians know [that] the actual moment of birth changes but little in the condition of the baby. If abortion is allowed a few days before birth, how is that different from killing a few days after [birth]? Abortion, I saw, was leading to infanticide. And infanticide was euthanasia. What would keep it from extending to older people?[4]

Koop's predictions were indeed prophetic. Respect for life has diminished as infanticide today seems almost commonplace. Unfortunately, the treatment of babies since *Roe* has been even worse than that given to Baby Doe.

Gruesome Realities

Since *Roe* ended legal protection of the unborn, some doctors have combined infanticide with experimentation. They've experimented on aborted babies. (We apologize for the gruesome nature of the following examples, but the truth must be known.)

- Six months after the *Roe v. Wade* decision, Dr. Peter A. J. Adam, a professor of pediatrics at Case Western Reserve University, conducted an experiment in which he cut off the heads of twelve live aborted babies, pumped blood to their brains and kept them alive by machine to observe them.[5] Responding to criticism, Dr. Adam defended his experiment by commenting, "Once society's declared the fetus dead, and abrogated its rights, I don't see any ethical problem.... Whose rights are we going to protect once we've decided the fetus won't live?"[6]
- In a series of experiments conducted at Stanford University, Dr. Robert C. Goodlin cut open the chests of live aborted babies and observed their hearts directly. "The thorax [chest] was opened and the heart was observed directly," he explained. All of the babies died within eleven hours.[7]
- In three studies at the University of Manitoba beginning in

1973, Dr. Francisco Reyes cut open the stomachs and skulls of 249 live aborted babies. The first study involved the delivery of live, normal babies whose abdomens were cut open and their sex and adrenal glands examined. The second study involved seventy-nine babies aborted alive and later killed by a heart puncture. The third study involved 116 babies also aborted alive. Their skulls were opened and their pituitary glands removed. They also were later killed by heart puncture.[8]

- According to a June 1972 Reuters News Agency report, testicles were successfully transplanted from a six-month-old aborted baby into a twenty-eight-year-old Lebanese man. The donor baby was then killed.[9]
- In 1974 Dr. Bela A. Resch cut the hearts out of aborted babies and observed them beating outside their bodies for hours.[10]
- In 1980 Dr. Martti Kekomaki cut open the stomachs and severed the heads of several live aborted babies.[11] He later remarked, "An aborted baby is just garbage and that's where it ends up. Why not make use of it for society?"[12]
- In a bizarre process called cryonics, even adults have been the victims of experimentation. Cryonics is the process of freezing the body in the hopes of bringing it back to life one day. One woman, Dora Kent, had her head surgically removed from her body and frozen in the hopes she could one day be brought back to life with a new body. According to the *American College of Surgeons Bulletin,* "She was apparently still alive when the procedure was started. Her son is a believer in cryonics, and he supervised the removal of his mother's head. The coroner has classified the death as a homicide."[13] (While this practice is not yet widespread, it does occur and illustrates the bizarre extremes to which disrespect for life may take us.)

The Unthinkable Is Happening—Parents Are Doing It!

Unfortunately, it's not just the doctors that have lost respect for life. Mothers are committing infanticide as well. The following are just a few of numerous cases:

- One year before Baby Doe, on April 4, 1981, a baby was born alive and well a month and a half before its scheduled birth. Sadly, the mother threw the baby from the seventh floor of her room in the downtown Sheridan-Dallas Hotel. The autopsy showed that the baby died on impact. The case was taken to court, but the charges were dismissed. After all, she could have walked into any abortion clinic in Texas and killed her baby in the womb within the next two months! Ironically, sometime later in the same city, a young girl left her newborn baby at a local hospital. The papers reported that the police had a warrant out for her arrest because of "child abuse." If she had only killed the baby in her womb a day earlier it would have been called a woman's right to privacy!

- More recently, in 1994, Susan Smith drowned her two little boys in a lake in South Carolina, just a couple of years after she could have had them killed legally.

- In 1996 two college students allegedly murdered their baby boy in a Delaware Hotel, just minutes after they could have killed him legally.

- And in 1997 a teenage girl allegedly killed her baby after giving birth at her class prom. Reports say the young mother left the strangled newborn in the rest room trash can and then rejoined her friends on the dance floor.

We've slid a long way since we devalued life. Unless we make some drastic changes in our country soon, things will only get worse. With cases of infanticide growing today, cases of adult euthanasia certainly will be growing tomorrow.

Kevorkian: the "Orkin Man" for Pesky Humans

Thankfully, the American public was outraged enough by the Baby Doe story that they demanded and got legislative action. On October 9, 1984, the Baby Doe amendment became part of Public Law 98–475 when it was signed by President Reagan. The law expanded the definition of child abuse to include the withholding of fluids, nutrition, and medically indicated treatment for disabled infants.

Despite this bright spot in the Baby Doe story, clouds are looming large on the horizon for our elderly and infirmed. As Dr. Koop predicted, infanticide is now extending into adult euthanasia. This is obvious by the very public antics of Dr. Jack Kevorkian—the "Orkin Man" for pesky humans. By March 1998 Kevorkian had admitted to helping some one hundred people die.[14] And, incredibly, he seems happy about killing people. When a reporter asked him if there was any distinction between hooking up Mrs. Adkins to his suicide machine and leaving a loaded .45 on her bed table, Kevorkian "cheerfully" conceded, "None."[15]

Kevorkian is trying to move the U.S. in the direction of the Netherlands, where euthanasia is legal. (It is estimated that there are now around 11,800 cases of euthanasia in the Netherlands each year.[16]) And Kevorkian seems to be making some progress. While more than forty states ban doctor-assisted suicide, Oregon voters have upheld a doctor-assisted suicide law. And the existence of the Hemlock Society and other pro-euthanasia groups, boasting as they do of assisted suicide and writing "how-to" manuals on death, provide ample proof that there is a growing market for this deadly service.

According to a report in the *New England Journal of Medicine*, euthanasia is happening in our hospitals right now. The report claims that 20 percent of 850 intensive care nurses admitted having deliberately hastened the death of a patient.[17] One proponent of euthanasia notes that 23 percent of 600 California doctors polled said they had helped at least one person die, and 62 percent approved of a physician doing so. In fact, 68 percent of them favored a law legalizing it.[18]

These recent developments indicate that there is certainly a growing acceptance of euthanasia in our country. As "Dr. Death" swoops over the elderly, looking for a weak member on whom to prey, the time has come to reexamine the deadly logic that got us here. But first a few terms need to be defined.

WHAT IS EUTHANASIA?

We will use the term "euthanasia" to mean an act that intentionally and directly causes a patient's death. This definition of euthanasia includes active euthanasia, voluntary euthanasia, aid-in-dying, and physician-assisted suicide. By this latter term we mean an act in which a patient is given the means and specific instructions to take his or her own life.

A Fatal Difference

It is important to note a crucial difference between taking a life intentionally and allowing a death naturally. The first is homicide, and the second is a natural death. *Withholding artificial life-sustaining means from terminally ill patients or hastening death through treatments aimed at controlling symptoms does not necessarily constitute either euthanasia or assisted suicide.*[19] If these acts are with the informed consent of the patient, and if the purpose of these acts is to comfort the patient or allow the natural dying process to continue, then they are not morally wrong. In such cases their purpose is not to deliberately end his or her life. Where there is no intention to kill there is no moral culpability. For example, if someone intends to kill a person but the bullet misses, we believe he was morally wrong. But if a hunter's stray bullet accidentally hits someone we do not hold him morally responsible. In other words, administering morphine *to relieve pain*, while it may hasten death, does not constitute euthanasia. There is an important difference between mercy dying and mercy killing.

A 1997 Clinton Administration brief to the Supreme Court recognized the difference between responsible medical treatment and euthanasia:

> There is a very significant distinction between removing artificial supports—and thereby allowing the underlying disease to progress to its inevitable end—and providing chemicals to kill someone. In one case, the cause of death can reasonably be viewed as the underlying disease; in the other, the cause of death can only be viewed as the lethal medication. That important, common-sense distinction is reflected in the laws of at least forty states that permit the withdrawal of life-sustaining treatment but prohibit the prescription of lethal drugs.[20]

Since administering pain-relieving drugs or withdrawing artificial treatment does not intentionally and directly cause a patient's death, we will focus the remainder of our attention on active euthanasia.

LOGIC OF THE LEFT: ARGUMENTS FOR ACTIVE EUTHANASIA

Like the pro-abortionists, proponents of euthanasia have a number of common arguments that they present for their position. They are as follows:

- Euthanasia shows mercy in avoiding needless suffering.
- Euthanasia ensures patient autonomy and respects the wishes of the dying.

- Euthanasia enables people to "die with dignity."
- Euthanasia is in the best interest of the patient.
- Euthanasia provides just treatment.
- Euthanasia relieves the financial burden of the family.
- Euthanasia is justified by the Golden Rule.

We'll address each of these arguments in order. But before we do, we must deal with the old "Don't judge a man unless you've walked in his shoes" objection. Or, in this case, "Don't condemn euthanasia if you're not terminally ill!"

Don't Judge Unless You've Been There!

This argument takes the moral position that you should not assess a moral issue unless you've experienced it yourself. But this claim is obviously nonsense. For if one can only discover the right thing to do if presented with the situation personally, then few of us could say that slavery is wrong because we haven't experienced the daunting task of harvesting a large crop by ourselves!

Right and wrong is *not determined* by our experience with the moral issue in question. It is *discovered* by right reasoning from the Moral Law. In other words, the morality *of* the act exists independently of our experience *with* the act. In fact, the best time to assess moral issues is when you're thinking clearly and not hampered by emotional or physical distress. In other words, this objection actually backfires—those most capable of discovering the morality of euthanasia are probably those who are *not* terminally ill!

Now let's move on to the more serious arguments in favor of euthanasia. We'll answer these arguments after we present them.

Does Euthanasia Show Mercy by Avoiding Needless Suffering?

The argument stated: One of the first defenses proponents of euthanasia offer is the argument from the standpoint of mercy. They insist that sometimes euthanasia is the only way to avoid needless suffering, so to refuse the plea of a terminally ill patient to be put to rest is merciless. Situation ethicist Dr. Joseph Fletcher argued that we would shoot a horse trapped in a burning barn to relieve its suffering. So why wouldn't we put a human being out of his/her misery who is in a hopeless situation of suffering?[21]

In fact, since some terminal patients suffer excruciating and prolonged pain, it is argued that euthanasia would prevent such a cruel and inhumane situation. Dr. David C. Thomasma asks, "If, from time to time, pain control proves fruitless, does not the quality of mercy and compassion compel us to accede to a patient's request for active euthanasia?"[22]

The argument refuted: In response to this argument, we must note several things. First of all, and we don't mean to be glib, but this argument assumes without justification that there is no value in suffering. Since we quite naturally avoid pain at all costs, we forget that it sometimes has value. Important lessons can be taught and learned by enduring suffering, even if it is the last lesson learned. In fact, some virtues—such as courage and perseverance—can only be developed and expressed through difficulty. So even if the sufferer passes on, he can set a moral example for others to live by and can provide inspiration to his family and community by not giving up on life. In other words, suffering can have value, both for the dying patient and for those around him.

The second answer to the "needless" suffering argument is that current medical science can alleviate most kinds of physical pain. Exceptions to this are rare. Former Surgeon General C. Everett Koop observed that "we can alleviate the unbearable in life better than ever before."[23] Indeed, it is ironic that euthanasia is becoming more popular as pain is becoming more manageable. Yet even if there remains a few cases where pain is difficult to control, recall from chapter 8 that the law cannot be built on a few isolated cases. Virtually no laws would stand if extreme exceptions could nullify them.

Third, research from the Netherlands shows that 95 percent of all requests for euthanasia are due to mental illness, not physical suffering. And the majority of those that get psychiatric help later feel grateful to be alive (more on this later in the chapter).[24]

Fourth, as we saw in the last chapter, a common justification for abortion is to avoid suffering. But if killing newborn or dying people to avoid suffering is justified, then why isn't killing everyone to avoid suffering justified? After all, literally *every* human being is terminal and every human being has suffering in his or her future. If avoiding suffering is really a valid justification for ending someone's life, then we should commend every act of murder as an act of mercy!

Finally, to respond to Fletcher's illustration, it is precisely because humans are not animals that we do not kill them in difficult situations. That is, since we believe human life has a higher value than that of animals, we do not treat humans like laboratory rats. Moreover, human beings don't lose their value when they lose their health. People are valuable because of their humanity, not because they lack an infirmity.

Does Euthanasia Ensure Patient Autonomy and Respect the Wishes of the Dying?

The argument stated: The argument for euthanasia from patient autonomy is similar to the "freedom to choose" rhetoric that dominates the abortion movement. Freedom, they insist, implies human autonomy, which includes the right to avoid interminable suffering. As Dr. Robert Wood argued, it "is a serious attempt by patients to increase their own options when faced with terminal illness. . . ."[25] One proponent, Dr. Anne David, argued that denying euthanasia to a dying patient is like telling a patient that they were in charge of their life all along and then in the most crucial moment saying, "No, we are in charge, and we won't do what you ask because it is not in our best interest."[26] In short, if dying is a part of life, how can we say a person has control over his life and then deny him his wish to terminate it?

The argument refuted: In response to this argument, several things come to mind. First, this justification—which is based on the radical autonomy demanded by the Left—assumes that the highest good is what the person wishes. But is this true? Should the wishes of the dying be granted even if those wishes are morally wrong? For example, should we grant a dying man his wish that his mortal enemy be murdered? Of course not. So why then should we grant a dying man the wish that he himself be murdered? That's the question.

Here's where the clash of worldviews between the Left and Right is most evident. The Left's absolute is personal autonomy. Since the Left believes that there is no authority higher than the individual, a dying man has the right to kill himself. People owe their existence to themselves so they should legally have control over their own life and death. On the other hand, the Right's absolute is life. Since the Right believes that life is given from above, a dying man doesn't have the moral authority to take his own life. Life is the domain of God.

So the question over the morality of voluntary euthanasia seems based on the origin of life. Do we owe our lives to ourselves or to some power beyond us? Which view is correct? The Left believes the former, but our country was founded on the view that life comes from God, as the *Declaration of Independence* asserts. Moreover, our laws have reflected that belief throughout our nation's history—suicide has consistently been legally prohibited (despite recent developments in Oregon).[27]

Believe it or not, even the Supreme Court has recognized this fact (thankfully). In a unanimous 1997 opinion (*Washington v. Glucksberg*), the court rejected the claim that assisted suicide is a constitutionally protected right. The Court rightly appealed to the nation's legal history regarding suicide to come to its decision:

> The history of the law's treatment of assisted suicide in this country has been and continues to be one of the rejection of nearly all efforts to permit it. That being the case, our decisions lead us to conclude that the asserted "right" to assistance in committing suicide is not a fundamental liberty interest protected by the Due Process Clause.[28]

In effect, the Court agreed that life is a higher value than liberty. Those who believe in euthanasia invert the natural hierarchy of values by holding more awe for liberty than for life. But our inclinations tell us that such an inversion is false. We know we have a higher obligation to protect innocent life, including our own life. In other words, the Moral Law tells us to do good and shun evil. And this applies not only to how we treat other people but how we treat ourselves, as well. Even if we consent to being treated with euthanasia, that doesn't justify it. As we covered in chapter 9, consent does not necessarily make a particular action right or wrong. Adults can consent to evil, but that doesn't make evil right. And willfully destroying ourselves is evil. In short, patient autonomy does not include the right to do evil to others or to ourselves.

Second, how can intentionally induced death be called an act of freedom when it destroys all freedom? The very notion of autonomy presumes a will to live. But suicide is the end of autonomy, not its goal. Control over one's life is one thing—and even that is limited; control over one's death is quite another thing.

Dead people don't have autonomy.

Third, the perverse result of the euthanasia movement is not advancement of individual autonomy, but rather contempt for the sick and dying. The society that legalizes euthanasia says to the dying, "You may continue to live if you like, but *we* see no reason why you must." In such an environment the dying come to feel that it is not only their *right* but their *duty* to no longer linger; to hurry up and get out of the way. Should euthanasia be legalized, this sentiment surely will be exacerbated because of the growing managed health care environment that rewards physicians for doing less for their patients.

This is important because patients generally listen to their doctors. Dr. Rosemary Anton notes, "Doctors greatly influence patient's treatment decisions by the information they give and the way they give it." Consequently, "how many debilitated and depressed patients will be misled to request aid in dying when assured that it is really for the best?"[29] And those that don't listen to their doctors may be killed against their will. This is already happening in the Netherlands. "By 1990, about 11,800 deaths (9 percent of all deaths) were inflicted by doctors, *about half of them without the patients consent*" (emphasis added).[30]

Fourth, it is a fatal mistake to assume that patient autonomy encompasses the right to euthanasia. As Dr. Michael Levy correctly observes, "Patient autonomy does not ... guarantee that a patient can demand therapies that are futile or, in the case of euthanasia, fatal."[31] If it did, it would both destroy the basis for the medical profession as well as many of its patients.

Finally, if you've ever worked on anything complicated, you know that you should never take something apart unless you *know* you can put it back together. This wisdom certainly applies to human life. Doctors can do amazing things to help the body heal itself: They can prescribe medication; they can repair organs; they can even replace organs that have gone bad. But despite all of these amazing feats, no doctor can create life or bring life back once it's gone. Neither can doctors explain the source of life by some kind of scientific equation. Life is a mystery that is frankly out of our control and should therefore be respected. Suicide and euthanasia are serious moral wrongs because they take away the gift of life that can never be replaced. Once carried out they are irreversible. Life cannot be put back together again.

Does Euthanasia Enable People to "Die With Dignity?"

The argument stated: Some proponents of euthanasia insist that the dignity of life takes precedence over life itself. Let us "die with dignity" has become a motto of the euthanasia movement. Dean of law at Florida State, Sheldon F. Kurtz, argues that the pro-euthanasia view "incorporates an ethic that values personal integrity and human dignity more than mere biological existence."[32]

The argument refuted: It is strange logic to claim that one is affirming life by eliminating it. How can one dignify life by terminating it? We are reminded of the answer to suicide by the late French existentialist, Jean-Paul Sartre, who declared that an act against one's self can never be an act for one's self. No act that extinguishes a life dignifies that life. Rather, it destroys it.

Commenting on the euthanasia movement, Dr. Robert Bernhoft observed, "This whole thing is 'social Darwinism' in liberal clothing. . . . My idea of death with dignity is facing it with courage and humor. *Putting one to sleep like a rat is not dignified*" (emphasis added).[33] Indeed, what's dignified about cowardice?

Is Euthanasia in the Best Interest of the Patient?

The argument stated: Proponents claim that euthanasia is in the best "interest" of the patient because it relieves the suffering of the patient and the family without violating anyone's rights.

The argument refuted: In replying to this argument, it is important to note three things. First, ending a person's life ends all of his "interest." How can the death of a person improve his "interest" in life?

Second, even if we assume that a painless state is a good state, it is still morally wrong to accomplish a good end by an evil means. Certainly a person would not be justified if he murdered his parents in order to receive a good inheritance. Evil means are not justified by good ends. The means must be just themselves.

Third, not everything a person believes to be in his own best interest actually is. A person in the midst of extreme pain is usually not the best judge of whether or not he should be given death-producing drugs. To assume otherwise is like claiming that the best time to ask a woman if she wants to have more children is at the height of her labor pains. Pain clouds reasoning.

Finally, even if a person opts for euthanasia during a lucid period, the act is still morally wrong. As we indicated earlier, consent doesn't turn a moral wrong into a moral right.

Does Euthanasia Provide Just Treatment?

The argument stated: Some who favor legalizing euthanasia go so far as to claim that it is the only way to guarantee fair treatment for all. Since not everyone can afford expensive care for prolonging life, euthanasia would offer an alternative that all could afford.

The argument refuted: This justification is nonsensical. First of all, euthanasia is an alternative we can *ill* afford because it is an attack on the very nature of human life itself. How can we say that we are helping life when we are really eliminating it?

Second, calling euthanasia "a just treatment" because all can afford it is like insisting that anyone who can't afford the comfort of a Cadillac should be allowed to self-destruct in his Yugo. That everyone can't afford the best treatment does not mean that no one should get it. By this logic no one should enjoy a good Thanksgiving meal because there are people starving in Ethiopia.

Third, rather than providing just treatment, if anything, legalized euthanasia would provide more *unjust* treatment. Think about it. Who is more likely to get recommended for euthanasia—someone who can pay his medical bills or someone who can't? If euthanasia is ever legalized, there will be a great temptation to recommend those patients whose disease, family system, financial status, or community resources denies them access to good medical care. In other words, *euthanasia would likely become a penalty for being too sick, too isolated, or too poor.*

Does Relieving the Financial Burden of the Family Justify Euthanasia?

The argument stated: It is insisted that prolonging the life of those needing intensive care can and often does drain the financial resources of the family. For many this can be an overwhelming burden. Surely the decision to stop this financial bleeding and burden in the case of those who are inevitably going to die anyway cannot be considered an evil.

The argument refuted: Once again, this argument for euthanasia inverts the hierarchy of values. It values money more than life. When carried to its logical end, you can see why the argument is absurd. Consider this: Every dependent person is a financial burden; the young are financial burdens to their parents; aging parents can be financial burdens to the young. Therefore, since everyone is going to die, and since everyone costs money, then why aren't we justified in killing anyone who is costing us money?

Second, this argument is based on the fallacious premise that a price tag can be placed on human life. It wrongly assumes that we should protect and preserve life only if we can afford it. But this materialistic view overlooks the intrinsic value of an individual human life and wrongly assumes that the end (saving money) justifies the means (killing the patient). While there is no moral obligation to make heroic financial efforts to artificially sustain a life, it is certainly morally wrong to end a life in order to save money. Is life worth nothing more than dollars and cents?

Is Euthanasia Justified by the Golden Rule?

The argument stated: Some proponents of euthanasia use the Golden Rule—"Do unto others as you would have them do unto you"—to argue their position. They believe everything they personally desire should be universalized. If they personally desire euthanasia, then they should have access to it and so should other people. Hence, they argue that euthanasia should be legalized.

The argument refuted: The problem with this justification is that it misconstrues the point of the Golden Rule, which does not demand that we universalize or legalize our *desires* but only our *rights* and *duties*. A person may have a desire to die, but he has an obligation to live. And if it is right to protect life, then it is wrong to promote death.

In other words, what we *want* to do is not always what we *ought* to do. Just because we desire something does not mean we ought to do it. For example, when someone cuts us off in traffic, we may *desire* to do the same to him, but we *ought* not to do so. Likewise, that someone gets so desperate she *feels* like dying does not mean that she *should* precipitate her death or ask a physician to assist her. What we *ought* to do is to preserve life, not destroy it, whether it is our life or someone else's life.

WHY EUTHANASIA VIOLATES THE MORAL LAW

There is a strange and tragic irony in our postmodern world. Many contend earnestly for animal rights and overlook human wrongs. They work to save baby seals but overlook the mass slaughter of baby humans (by abortion). They literally give their lives to save dying trees but are not willing to save living humans. Beneath all the inconsistency is the premise that *it is morally wrong* to waste plant and animal life. It is this same Moral Law to which we appeal in showing it is morally wrong to waste human life.

In answering the arguments for euthanasia above, we have already given numerous reasons why euthanasia violates the Moral Law command to do good and shun evil. The following summarizes what we've said so far:

- Euthanasia does not show mercy for the sufferer—it destroys the sufferer.
- Euthanasia does not uphold patient autonomy—it ends patient autonomy.
- Euthanasia does not enable people to "die with dignity"—it enables them to be killed like laboratory rats.
- Euthanasia is not in the best "interest" of the patient—it ends all "interests" of the patient.
- Euthanasia does not provide just treatment—it encourages unjust murder.
- Euthanasia does not relieve financial strain—it encourages materialism, devalues life, and adds guilt.
- Euthanasia is not justified by the Golden Rule—it is condemned by the Golden Rule.

In addition to these refutations of pro-euthanasia arguments, here are six more reasons why euthanasia should remain illegal:

- Euthanasia makes false and fatal assumptions.
- Euthanasia violates the Hippocratic Oath—the "moral law" of medicine.
- The "choice" of euthanasia will not be fully informed, and it may be coerced.
- Voluntary euthanasia will lead to involuntary euthanasia.
- Legalized euthanasia devalues life.
- Euthanasia assumes death ends suffering.

Now let's take a look at each one of these.

Euthanasia Makes False and Fatal Assumptions.

There is a fatal assumption behind most arguments for euthanasia. The assumption presupposes that a person does not, or will not, have a meaningful existence. This can take several forms. If the patients are fatally ill, it is assumed that they will not be cured. If they are not cured, it assumes that they cannot have a meaningful life while suffering with the illness. If they are being kept alive on machines, it assumes that they will never be able to live without the machines. And if they are in a coma, it assumes they will never come out of it. All of these assumptions have been proven wrong in a number of cases. Consider the following examples:

"Dental Tranquilizer Revives 'Vegetative Man' "

The above headline catches one's attention. It was reported that "after eight years in a 'vegetative state,' a Wisconsin accident victim has become lucid and active following the administration of a tranquilizer for routine dental work. . . ." According to the attending physician, neurologist Andres M. Kranner, Valium was given to the patient and "he woke up and started talking." The *Sentinel* reported that "he was able to answer questions, say his name, feed himself, and walk."[34] Is this not a meaningful life?

" 'Medical Vegetable' Regains a Full Life"

This 1975 headline in the *Chicago Tribune* is right next to a picture of a happy mother with her bouncing baby boy on her lap. Under the photo are these words: "Mrs. Carol Rogman, whose life would have ended had her mother decided to 'pull the plug,' holds her son, Larry Jr., 19 months."

Carol was a former beauty queen who was plunged into a coma after an auto accident. The doctor informed her mother that even if Carol survived she would "only be a vegetable." However, four months later she was gradually coaxed out of the coma and, as the headline put it, she regained "a full life."[35]

"North Carolina Man Wakes After Eight Years Unconscious"

This headline describes the day Conley Holbrook, apparently beaten almost to death by a man with a log, awakened from his coma after eight years and cried, "Momma!" According to the report, "At about 10:30, I was gonna go and get some juice for us.... I started out the door and he said, 'Momma.' So I went back to the bed and I said, 'Conley, you're talking!' And he said, 'Yes, Momma, I want to tell you he hurt me.' "[36]

Mrs. Holbook's message to others with loved ones in comas: "Don't give up," and "Always hope in the Lord. Just hang in there."[37]

Life Is Worth Living

One woman who has turned her suffering into a source of inspiration for millions is well-known quadriplegic Joni Eareckson Tada. Read what she has said regarding euthanasia and the quality of life:

> Having lived in a wheelchair for twenty-four years, unable to feed myself, brush my teeth, or go to the bathroom, I am following the reports about Kevorkian with intense interest. Unfortunately, the public is no longer outraged by Kevorkian's dealings with terminally ill or disabled people. Society's sensibilities are becoming dulled. *We are now accepting a dangerous premise: that life lived in pain or in a wheelchair is not worth living, that you are better dead than disabled.... Instead of making it easier for people to die, let's make it easier for them to live* (emphasis added).[38]

Indeed, as these few examples show, many of the assumptions behind the euthanasia movement are dangerous and false.

Euthanasia Violates the Hippocratic Oath—the "Moral Law" of Medicine.

While doctors are not required to take the Hippocratic Oath, for nearly 2,500 years the Oath has functioned as a kind of "moral law" of medicine. It has helped build trust in the medical profession. One section of it says, "I will neither give a deadly drug to anybody if asked for it, nor will I make a suggestion to this effect."[39] As the Oath proclaims, physicians have a responsibility to their patients to prevent death, not precipitate it. Medicine practiced in any other way is contrary to the Moral Law.

Respect and trust is one very positive effect the Hippocratic Oath has had on the medical profession. Unfortunately, this trust will be severely eroded if euthanasia is legalized, especially in the area of terminal care. As Dr. Michael Levy observes, "The very presence of active euthanasia as a fail-safe option can erode trust that the health care system will do everything possible to relieve suffering prior to terminating life."[40]

This is already happening in the Netherlands, where euthanasia is legal. Studies of the Netherlands show that "intolerable physical symptoms are *not* the reason most patients request physician-assisted suicide or euthanasia."[41] Instead, more than 95 percent of those who commit suicide have a major psychiatric illness at the time of death.[42] "Research indicates, however, that many people who request physician-assisted suicide withdraw that request if their depression and pain are treated. Suicidal, terminally ill patients 'usually respond well to treatment for depressive illness and pain medication and are then grateful to be alive.' "[43]

The problem is this: With euthanasia available, doctors in the Netherlands are not taking the time to evaluate their patients for mental illness. "Psychiatric consultation for medical patients who request physician-assisted death is relatively rare [about 3 percent]."[44] In other words, "because depression is difficult to diagnose, physicians and medical professionals often fail to respond adequately to seriously ill patients' needs. Thus, legal physician-assisted suicide [in the United States] could make it more difficult for the state to protect depressed or mentally ill persons, or those who are suffering from untreated pain, from suicidal impulses."[45]

Did you grasp that? *Most patients who request suicide in the Netherlands are mentally ill, but doctors are not being thorough enough to detect it. So instead of getting the psychiatric help they need, patients are going to their deaths!* The option of legal euthanasia naturally allows the doctors to make hasty, incorrect diagnoses. After all, if you're a doctor with no moral objection to euthanasia, why seek to help someone who is really sick when death is a much easier and cheaper option?

Think about this in personal terms. Can you imagine having to wonder if the doctor caring for your mother has done everything reasonably possible to correctly evaluate her condition? Or can you imagine having to fear that he's actually trying to kill her rather than make her well? This is the real possibility that legalized euthanasia will give us. With the option available, and managed health care squeezing budgets, doctors face a great temptation to "play God."

But doctors who "play God" clearly cross the ethical line.

Not only does euthanasia take an innocent life, but it also does not allow for mistakes in diagnosis and prognosis to be corrected. After all, many "terminal" patients don't die when doctors say they will. In a recent large study of severely ill patients, 28 percent of those who were told they'd be dead within six months actually lived longer than a year.[46]

Moreover, euthanasia prevents patients from experiencing the benefits of skilled symptom and pain control. Aggressive care can improve the quality and quantity of remaining life. So even assuming a quality of life premise, one can justify caring over killing. Judge Bork writes, "When my first wife was diagnosed with cancer, the doctor told me she would live only six months to two years. She lived *nine and a half years*, and those were good years, for her, for me, for our children, and for her friends" (emphasis added).[47]

Finally, as you might imagine, legalized euthanasia will force many doctors into situations that compromise their personal ethical standards. Abortion has provided a dilemma for some medical students, and it's quite likely that legalized euthanasia would present the same problem. Of course, no doctor in theory would be forced to commit euthanasia, but its very availability might serve to corrupt the integrity of individual doctors and the health care profession as a whole. This already appears to be happening. As euthanasia gains wider support, some doctors are privately helping patients die. Preliminary data from the largest survey to date on physician's attitudes toward assisted suicide suggest that "doctors with the most experience prescribing lethal doses of drugs to patients tend to be more comfortable with their decisions."[48] Diane Meier of Sinai Medical Center finds that result disturbing. Ideally, she says, physicians committing such acts should never "get over their fear and trembling."[49] Unfortunately, now it's only the patients who should have the fear and trembling.

Legalization will only worsen this problem. As we showed in chapter 2, the mere existence of a law helps restrain evil behavior by preventing most people from even considering it. Conversely, that which becomes legal also becomes moral in the eyes of many. If death is made an option to a profession once committed to preserving life, we will be sliding down the slippery slope to abuse.

The "Choice" of Euthanasia Will Not Be Fully Informed, and It May Be Coerced.

A pregnant women who visits an abortion clinic is rarely given accurate information regarding the life in her womb. As we have seen, the pro-abortion industry masks the truth in deceiving euphemisms: The baby is not a unique human being with the genetic information of fifty sets of *Encyclopedia Britannica*; it is a "blob of tissue" or "product of conception." You're not killing your baby, you're "terminating a pregnancy," etc. There's no reason to think such abuses won't infest the euthanasia market.

Euthanasia proponents claim that administrative rules can prevent such abuse. But this has proven to be untrue in other areas. First, administrative rules haven't stopped abuse in the abortion industry. In fact, the personal rights mentality is so pervasive that few rules have been imposed on the abortion industry. (The average tattoo parlor is more closely regulated and better run than the average abortion clinic.) Why will the euthanasia industry be any different?

Second, many rules already in place to protect the terminally ill aren't working. As some hospice professionals have noted, "The failure of policies, procedures, rules, and regulations to guarantee the safety and efficacy of the care currently being rendered to terminally ill patients in this country offers little security that proposed administrative 'safeguards' will protect the public from such potential dangers."[50] It's certainly not difficult to find older patients today being suckered.

Think about a situation where euthanasia has become as accepted as abortion in our country. Grandpa is terminally ill and his family has already made subtle hints, if not overt suggestions, about saving medical expenditures for Junior's education or some other pressing need. Can you imagine the distress that terminally ill man might feel if he refuses to accept legal euthanasia? (Don't think this situation is far-fetched. As we have seen, financial considerations are already a common justification for abortion. And what's the difference between inconvenient babies and inconvenient adults to people willing to make such choices?)

Just like pregnant women and the option of abortion, if euthanasia becomes a legally accepted option, terminally ill patients will be pressured by family members and health care providers to consent to it. But such pressure during their weakened condition hardly makes the decision truly voluntary. As Dr. Eric Chevlen pointedly notes, "For a society to approve euthanasia is no different from a crowd chanting to a man hesitating on a ledge: 'Jump!' "[51] This is especially frightening because it is a decision that affords no possibility of correcting a mistake. There is no return from the choice of euthanasia.

It is one thing to allow inevitable death to occur naturally; it is quite another to choose euthanasia as a convenient way out of a difficult situation. At a time when the family and community should be minimizing suffering by giving care and compassion, the patient's suffering and mental anguish will be compounded by guilt and thoughts of "getting out of the way" for the good of his loved ones. What could be more selfish behavior on the part of the family and more inhumane treatment to the dying loved one?

As Dr. Michael Levy bluntly observes, "Active euthanasia is more a cowardly response to incompetence than a brave final act of compassion."[52] Further, it "is a desperate act of ultimate failure on the part of the patient's family to provide or to obtain adequate supportive care for their dying loved one."[53] We owe the dying members of our family treatment, not termination.

Voluntary Euthanasia Will Lead to Involuntary Euthanasia.

In 1991 Professor Rosemary Anton predicted that once euthanasia is legalized for the competent, the principle of "substituted judgment will be used to kill the incompetent."[54] In other words, "loved ones" will be able to decide to kill their "incompetent" relatives.

In late 1997, with only one state (Oregon) allowing doctor-assisted suicide, Anton's prediction began its fulfillment. In a December 3, 1997 press release, the Hemlock Society advocated the idea that euthanasia should be performed on those terminal patients (including children) who are considered incompetent or disabled. The criteria for death? If the patient's "agent" believes that life is "too burdensome to continue."[55]

This led Burke Balch, Director of Medical Ethics for the National Right to Life Committee, to observe, "Groups such as the Hemlock Society, which in the past publicly claimed to advocate only assisted suicide—clearly have an agenda that includes non-voluntary euthanasia for those who cannot speak for themselves. The very euthanasia advocates who scoffed at warnings about the 'slippery slope' are now providing direct evidence of it."[56]

What a can of worms this opens up—from the definition of "incompetent" to the assessment of what kind of life is "too burdensome." Should individuals really be making those life and death judgments, especially about someone else? As we mentioned earlier, they already are doing this in the Netherlands. "By 1990, about 11,800 deaths (9 percent of all deaths) were inflicted by doctors, *about half of them without the patients consent*" (emphasis added).[57]

Moreover, in 1994, the slope steepened when the Dutch Supreme Court ruled that physician-assisted suicide might be justifiable for patients with "unbearable" mental suffering but *no physical illness*.[58] The speed at which the Dutch Parliament moved from approving voluntary euthanasia to considering involuntary euthanasia was alarming. "*Exactly one week* after the lower house of the Dutch Parliament 'codified' existing medical guidelines to allow 'mercy killing' of patients who 'voluntarily' ask to be euthanized, the government said it would consider non-voluntary euthanasia of patients, including newborns with serious medical problems and the mentally ill (emphasis added)."[59]

We're playing with fire here, friends. But that doesn't seem to bother the hard-core proponents of euthanasia. Apparently they don't think it's enough for adults to "play God" with their own lives. Adults should also get to "play God" with the lives of others.

Legalized Euthanasia Devalues Life.

As we saw in chapter 2, laws help advance and protect what a society values. As a result, legalization of euthanasia would further devalue life and add to the growing decay of moral values in America. In fact, we have arrived at this point of legalization precisely because we have devalued life in other areas, namely abortion. Judge Bork rightly observes, "The movement to make assisting suicides legal was made virtually inevitable by the Supreme Court's creation of a right to abortion."[60] Indeed the two are linked.

Professor Anton argues that euthanasia will viciously undermine our sense of responsibility and love for others. For "as it becomes first allowed, and then expected, that the unfit will get out of the way so as not to burden the rest of us, we will be unwilling to support those who stubbornly refuse to cooperate." In this way, "our willingness to sacrifice for the good of others will be diminished. . . ."[61] What we owe the dying is not "a seductively efficient death, but support for the remainder of their lives."[62] Indeed, the entire culture is harmed when we devalue life.

As an alternative to euthanasia, what is needed is an ethically sound model of compassionate, cost-effective, quality-assured, patient/family oriented, terminal care. Such care, as is provided by hospice facilities, should be expanded to reach more eligible patients.

Euthanasia Assumes That Death Ends Suffering.

This final observation may seem a little strange, but did you ever stop to think: "How does Dr. Kevorkian know that death ends suffering?" Obviously it ends suffering as we know it in this life, but isn't it possible that Kevorkian is ushering some of his victims into a more permanent realm of suffering? Could this not be the fatal error?

Kevorkian's assumption that there is nothing beyond the grave isn't noticed by many because it is part of the secular humanist worldview that has been dominating our culture for decades.[63] The humanists, of course, roll their eyes when anyone suggests that their dogmatic worldview—that there is no God or afterlife—could be wrong. Unfortunately for them, their worldview isn't supported by the evidence.[64]

This is an extremely important point, because if our country gets the wrong answer to the worldview question, then it will get the wrong answer to moral questions, as well. And that's exactly why our culture is where it is today. We've allowed the atheistic worldview to take over without challenging its validity. Homosexuality, abortion, and euthanasia are symptoms of a wrong worldview. The correct worldview recognizes that life isn't all about me! me! me!—it recognizes that we have a duty to others, as well. We're not here to simply please ourselves—to take the easy way out of difficult and inconvenient situations—but to bravely serve God and others as the Moral Law instructs. The Moral Law mandates that we protect life, not destroy it. Until we accept this truth and act on it, our nation will teeter on the brink of self-destruction.

WHAT SAITH THE SUPREME COURT?

On June 15, 1990 the U.S. Supreme Court (in a 5–4 decision) denied the guardians of Nancy Cruzan the authority to withhold from her food and fluids provided through a tube in Cruzan's stomach.[65]

In the Court's words,

> While recognizing a right to refuse treatment embodied in the common law doctrine of informed consent, the court questioned its applicability in this case.... It also declined to read into the State Constitution a broad right to privacy that would support an unrestricted right to refuse treatment and expressed doubt that the Federal Constitution embodied such a right.[66]

This decision is a mixed blessing for those opposed to euthanasia.

On the One Hand ...

On the one hand, (1) The high Court refused to recognize a constitutional right to die (as we saw earlier, this was unanimously reaffirmed in the 1997 *Washington v. Glucksberg* case); (2) They ruled the states have the right to protect the life of the terminally ill; (3) The Court also refused to recognize the right to privacy as a basis for the decision of the patient to refuse life-sustaining treatment (they based it rather on the liberty interest in the Fourteenth Amendment); (4) They insisted that there must be "clear and convincing" evidence (somewhere "between a preponderance of evidence" and "beyond a reasonable doubt") that the incompetent patient desired to refuse life-sustaining treatment; and (5) They refused to give an inherent right of "surrogate" or "substituted" judgment contrary to the "clear and convincing" evidence of what the patient wished.

On the Other Hand ...

On the other hand, (1) The Court did not find a constitutional right to live, that is, a constitutional mandate that the law must protect every citizen's life from termination by the withholding of life-sustaining treatment; (2) The Court left open the "state's right" to pass laws that permit people to refuse to receive life-sustaining means. This could open the door to voluntary euthanasia efforts (Indeed, as mentioned above, Oregon has already done this); (3) They allowed refusal of life-sustaining means when there was "clear and convincing" evidence that the incompetent patient desired to die; (4) The Court "assumed" that "the

United States Constitution would grant a competent person a constitutionally protected right to refuse lifesaving hydration and nutrition;"[67] and (5) They allowed for states to pass laws giving "surrogate" or "substituted" judgment that may be contrary to the patient's wishes.

In short, the Supreme Court transferred the whole battle to the states. If human life is to be protected against further encroachment by the forces of death, it must be done on a state-by-state level. In brief, the "unalienable Right to Life" guaranteed by the *Declaration of Independence* and the Constitution (Fifth and Fourteenth Amendments) has now been alienated from every citizen. It remains to be seen how far this will go. Unfortunately, both the logic (of abortion leading to euthanasia) and historical trends seems to favor the euthanasia forces.

CONCLUSION

Where does this trend to legalize euthanasia leave us? Many in our country are suppressing the truth. Instead of admitting that we should love and care for those who are dying, proponents spin euthanasia in a positive light to cover up their unwillingness to do the hard, and often inconvenient, work of love. That attitude has naturally followed from legalized abortion. Instead of asking pregnant women to love their babies by bringing them to term (when parenthood or adoption could take place), proponents of abortion cover up their deed and sacrifice children on the altar of convenience. As Judge Bork observes, "Convenience is becoming the theme of our culture. Humans tend to be inconvenient at both ends of their lives."[68]

But the arguments in favor of euthanasia, like those for abortion, overlook one all-important fact: We're dealing with a human life that we did not create and that we have no right to take. Or, to put it in the words of the *Declaration of Independence*, "The Right to Life" (young or old) is an "unalienable Right of the Creator."

We now arrive at the same conclusion about euthanasia that we did concerning abortion: (1) Our common Moral Law teaches us that it is morally wrong to take the life of an innocent human being (whether they request it or not); (2) The dying are innocent human beings (who deserve love, not lethal injections); and (3) Therefore, euthanasia, which takes the life of an innocent human being, is morally wrong and should remain illegal.

We know we don't owe our lives to ourselves. Life is a special gift that is beyond our control, and everyone knows it. However, once again, our main problem is not that we don't *know* what's right; our main problem is that we don't have the will to *do* what's right. We've suppressed the Moral Law and lost our respect for life because we desire autonomy and convenience above all else. Consequently, we've lost our concern for others so that the ultimate "virtue" in our culture is now selfishness rather than love. Instead of meeting the challenge to love, we respond to these opportunities with acts of evil and selfishness. The result is a cold and dangerous society that rationalizes evil and continues to slide further into moral oblivion. The end of that slide starts with a vocal commitment to Truth by every concerned American, including you. If we don't speak up, we could be next: "Do not ask for whom the bell tolls—it tolls for thee."

EPILOGUE

WHERE DO WE GO FROM HERE?

*"Those who cannot remember the past
are condemned to repeat it."*

Throughout this book, we have extolled the writings and actions of our Founding Fathers. But even they were not without fault. While they clearly recognized and legislated the Moral Law into their new government, they suppressed that same Moral Law on the issue of slavery. Their failure to obey the Moral Law on this issue had devastating consequences on our country—millions of lives were ruined and lost.

Tragically, the same dreadful consequences are resulting today because our country is again suppressing the truth. Practices such as abortion, euthanasia, and homosexuality are directly responsible for shortened, ruined, and lost lives. Yet many Americans seem concerned only about the economy. In fact, the most popular slogan for recent presidential elections has been "It's the economy, stupid!" But if money made people happy, the United States would be the happiest place on earth. Instead, we lead the world in indicators of unhappiness such as suicide, drug use, and divorce.

Our priorities are all messed up. Why are we so eager to work on our national economy but afraid to work on our national morality? *We are like misguided parents who have one child on drugs, another with an unwanted pregnancy, and a third already dead from suicide, yet who still believe that the solution to all of their problems is their next pay raise!*

What ails us is morality, not money. People are not committing crimes or engaging in rampant immorality because the capital gains tax is too high or interest rates aren't quite where they should be. Don't get us wrong: Money and the economy are important. But money alone will not save us from ourselves. Money without morality leads to the kind of materialistic madness we've been experiencing: We have everything to live *with* and nothing to live *by!*

What can we do about all of this? It's not our intention here to suggest specific legislation that should be passed. You know the moral issues plaguing this country, and you know the cultural and legislative battles that need to be fought. What we want to do is equip you to win those battles. At the end of chapter 8 we laid out nine principles for applying the Moral Law to legislation. Here we would like to suggest nine more principles that will equip you to engage effectively in the public debate:

First, stop being paranoid about legislating morality. Show that all laws legislate morality, and that everyone in the public debate is trying to do so. We've seen that all political perspectives—including libertarian, liberal, moderate, and conservative—are based on moral beliefs. Despite claims to the contrary, everyone has a basic morality that undergirds their position on political issues. For many it's the freedom to do whatever you want "as long as you don't hurt someone else." Even those who say "morality should not be legislated" are sure *that* is the right moral position. The fact is, everyone advocating a political position is attempting to legislate morality. Which morality is the right one to legislate? We have shown it to be the common Moral Law.

Second, don't be defensive about charges of being "judgmental." Those who claim that "you should not judge" are inconsistent because that very statement is a moral judgment about you. So when someone says, "Who are you to judge?" the proper response is, "Since we are both rational people, who are aware of certain fundamental principles of logical and moral reasoning, we are both qualified to judge. In fact, I'm simply using the same standard you are using to judge me. All of us *must* make moral judgments. Laws couldn't be made if we didn't make judgments. And if we never judged between behaviors that are good and those that are evil, then we all would have destroyed ourselves years ago."

Third, love people, but don't accept their false ideas as true or their evil behavior as moral. Contrary to popular wisdom, not all ideas and lifestyles are equally true, moral, or beneficial. Yet the kind of "tolerance" demanded in today's society tells us that we must tolerate everything, even evil. But, of course, we must *never* tolerate evil. Tolerating evil is unloving because evil hurts innocent people and destroys lives. Through reasoned debate, *using verifiable evidence,* we must defeat bad ideas and bad legislation while we show love and respect to the people promoting them.

Fourth, remember that character does *matter.* There's been a great debate recently about whether character and morality really matter for a political leader. The truth is, character and morality not only matter, they are absolutely essential. Why? Two reasons:

(1) The moral content of leadership is provided by the leader himself. Leadership, by itself, is amoral because the skills of goal-setting and persuasion can be mastered by both the good and the evil. For example, Adolf Hitler was a great leader but he had poor character. People followed him *because* of his leadership skills. But the *direction* in which they followed him was determined by his character.

(2) Public character cannot be separated from private character. The leader's entire life is an example to the nation and its children. Being a good moral example *is part of the leader's job.* Moreover, the notion that what a leader does in his private life is of no consequence to his public life flies in the face of common sense:

- Do people get new minds and wills when they go out in public? By what miraculous process do private liars suddenly become public saints? The *same* psychological and moral person exists in both places.
- Why won't those who use immoral means to get what they want in their private lives use immoral means to get what they want in their public lives? Those who refuse to restrain

their appetites in private are unlikely to resist the enormous temptation to abuse their political power to get what they want (and to use that power to cover up their "private" indiscretions). They also open themselves up to blackmail.

- Why should a leader who cannot be trusted by his own family be trusted by a nation of families?
- Finally, how can those responsible for legislating morality do so when they have trouble discerning right from wrong? Are such people really qualified to make decisions of the highest moral consequence, such as sending our military men and women into battle?

Fifth, vote morals over money, principle over party, character over cash. A leader's moral views are more important than his economic views. You can't have the latter without a firm foundation in the former. For how can you trust a leader to implement his *promised* economic program when he sees nothing morally wrong with breaking *promises*? And even if you can trust him on economics, are not morals more important? If you lived in Germany during the 1930s, and a candidate had a great program for the economy (in fact, his program might help make you rich) but he also wanted to kill Jews, would you vote for him? Of course not! Then why criticize pro-lifers for automatically ruling out candidates who are pro-abortion? After all, they are rightly concluding that if a candidate cannot support the highest value of every rational human being, then why consider where he or she stands on the other values that pale in comparison?

Sixth, emphasize unity more than diversity. Instead of magnifying our superficial differences, we must unify socially around our essential agreements. The Moral Law provides that unity. This is important because a civilized community cannot be maintained unless there is some moral unity in the community. While it's nice to remember that some of us are "Native," "African," "Irish," "Italian," or "German" Americans, etc., we must never forget that we are all of one race—the human race—united by one Moral Law. Unfortunately, the Left has been trying to drive our citizens into narrow little ethnic and cultural corners, leaving us fractured and wrongly doubting that the Moral Law exists to unite us all.

Seventh, support religious freedom and religious expression. We have argued that we should base our laws on the Moral Law, not religion or some "Holy Book" (be it the Bible, Quran, or any other such book). However, we must not forget that inspiration to obey those laws is best provided by religion. As George Washington correctly proclaimed in his farewell address: "Reason and experience both forbid us to expect that a national morality can prevail in exclusion of religious principle" (see chapter 5).

Indeed, a devout belief in God motivates most people *from within* to live by principles consistent with the Moral Law. Conversely, as we saw in chapter 4, when we kill a belief in God, we create an environment conducive to untold human evil. Religion should be encouraged. What could be better for our country than its citizens being religiously committed to doing the right thing?

If we continue to exorcise all religious expression from public life, especially our public schools, we will be removing the very force that can help turn our country around. In fact, as we showed in chapter 6, removing all references to traditional religion: (1) violates the free exercise clause of the First Amendment; and (2) doesn't demonstrate neutrality but favors and establishes atheism/Secular Humanism as the "religion" of the land. Our nation can't survive too much more of the immorality that "religion" has spawned.

Eighth, remember not to over*legislate morality.* The unvarying standard of the Moral Law should always be the goal of civil legislation. For acts that are intrinsically evil, such as murder and rape, the law must demand zero tolerance even when it's difficult to enforce. However, zero tolerance is not always attainable for acts that may be harmful but are not obvious intrinsic evils, especially if most people would not obey such a strict law. For example, given the overwhelming evidence concerning the dangers of smoking, it would certainly be better if no one smoked. However, since large numbers of people continue to smoke, we permit smoking as long as non-smokers are protected from the dangers of passive smoke.

The principle is this: When the ideal is not realizable, then we should legislate the optimum achievable within the existing conditions. That is, when the *maximum* is not possible, we should not settle for the *minimum* but should legislate the *optimum*. Even though ideally a whole loaf is the best, realistically a part of a loaf is better than no loaf at all. America will not stand for extreme Puritanism, nor will it survive radical Libertarianism.

Nonetheless, we must maintain an optimum Moralism.

While there will be disagreement as to precisely what the optimum is, two things should be kept in mind. First, we shouldn't give up all legislative efforts to achieve good *ends* because there is disagreement over where to draw the legal line (the *means*). For example, if preventing death from smoking is a good *end*, we shouldn't give up all legislative *means* just because there is disagreement over how far anti-smoking laws should go. We should continue to press for the optimum. Second, factual disagreements should not dissuade us from legislating laws which, in our best judgment, help enforce the Moral Law in our society. For example, murder is wrong because it intentionally takes the life of an innocent human being. And if it can be shown to be a *fact* that the unborn are innocent human lives, then there should be laws against abortion (see chapter 10). On the other hand, if the unborn are not innocent human beings, then anti-abortion laws should not exist. The same reasoning should be applied to addictive drugs, including alcohol and nicotine. If they do kill people, we should seek optimum legislation against them.

Finally, even if liberals charge that every law they don't like is "overlegislating morality," we should not stop legislating what is morally right. *No* legislation against evil is not the answer to *over*legislating. *Better* legislation is the answer. And better legislation does not settle for the minimum nor always demand the maximum, but helps achieve the optimum good as measured by the common Moral Law.

Ninth, the bottom line: Turn your opponent's argument on itself. As we have seen, those who argue against absolute morality set up absolute moral standards of their own. You've probably noticed by now that the best tactic is to challenge the assumption behind their claim, and, if possible, turn their own argument against them. Ask questions like:

- "Who said 'consent' makes something right? Is that just your opinion or did you get that from a higher source?"
- "Why should we tolerate everything? And if we should, why are you intolerant of my position?"
- "If we are not to judge, why are you judging me? And if we can't judge, why are we even here tonight to debate this issue?"

The first thing to do is to see what the argument is claiming and then to turn that claim on itself. Bad arguments kill themselves if you know how to reverse their direction.

CONCLUSION

As we conclude, the challenge from the preface still stands. We welcome a well-reasoned rebuttal from those of you who believe our arguments are all wrong—just be sure to tell us the standard by which you judge them wrong. After all, if you're "morally outraged" by what we've said, you must have some moral standard that you believe we've violated. The minute you say that your ideas are better than anyone else's, you are comparing them to a standard independent of them both. Any assessment you make of our arguments—or counterarguments you make against them—implies that standard. Is your standard merely your opinion, or is it based on something beyond yourself such as the unchanging Moral Law?

In the meantime, we are well aware that legislation will not solve all of our problems. A country will only be as good as the individuals in it. In fact, if everyone lived their personal lives according to the Moral Law standard, we wouldn't need legislation. And if that were the case, this book would have no need to exist.

But as we all know, people continue to do many wrong things. And as we have seen, the law acts as a great teacher. Good laws invite good behavior and bad laws invite bad behavior. If we are going to leave our children a safe and productive society, we must not be afraid to legislate the morality that will help shape that society. If we fail at this task, others will continue to legislate the immorality that is bringing our country such pain and suffering.

"The only thing necessary for the triumph of evil is for good men to do nothing."

—Edmund Burke

APPENDICES

I. THE DECLARATION OF INDEPENDENCE

II. THE CONSTITUTION

III. TRANSCULTURAL EXAMPLES OF THE COMMON MORAL LAW

APPENDIX I

THE DECLARATION OF INDEPENDENCE

ACTION OF SECOND CONTINENTAL CONGRESS, JULY 4, 1776.
THE UNANIMOUS DECLARATION OF THE THIRTEEN UNITED STATES OF AMERICA.[1]

WHEN in the Course of human events, it becomes necessary for one People to dissolve the Political Bands, which have connected them with another, and to assume, among the Powers of the Earth, the separate and equal Station to which the Laws of Nature and of Nature's GOD entitle them, a decent Respect to the Opinions of Mankind requires that they should declare the Causes which impel them to the Separation.

WE hold these Truths to be self-evident, that all Men are created equal, that they are endowed, by their CREATOR, with certain unalienable Rights, that among these are Life, Liberty and the Pursuit of Happiness—That to secure these Rights, Governments are instituted among Men, deriving their just Powers from the Consent of the Governed, that whenever any Form of Government becomes destructive of these Ends, it is the Right of the People to alter or to abolish it, and to institute new Government, laying its Foundation on such Principles, and organizing its Powers in such Form, as to them shall seem most likely to effect their Safety and Happiness. Prudence, indeed, will dictate, that Governments long established, should not be changed for light and transient Causes; and accordingly all Experience hath shewn, that Mankind are more disposed to suffer, while Evils are sufferable, than to right themselves by abolishing the Forms to which they are accustomed. But when a long Train of Abuses and Usurpations, pursuing invariably the same Object, evinces a Design to reduce them under absolute Despotism, it is their Right, it is their Duty, to throw off such Government, and to provide new Guards for their future Security. Such has been the patient Sufferance of these Colonies; and such is now the Necessity which constrains them to alter their former Systems of Government. The History of the present King of Great-Britain is a History of repeated Injuries and Usurpations, all having in direct Object the Establishment of an absolute Tyranny over these States. To prove this, let Facts be submitted to a candid World.

HE has refused his Assent to Laws, the most wholesome and necessary for the public Good.

HE has forbidden his Governors to pass Laws of immediate and pressing Importance, unless suspended in their Operation till his Assent should be obtained; and when so suspended, he has utterly neglected to attend to them.

HE has refused to pass other Laws for the Accommodation of large Districts of People, unless those People would relinquish the Right of Representation in the Legislature, a Right inestimable to them, and formidable to Tyranny only.

HE has called together Legislative Bodies at Places unusual, uncomfortable, and distant from the Depository of their public Records, for the sole Purpose of fatiguing them into Compliance with his Measures.

HE has dissolved Representative Houses repeatedly, for opposing with manly Firmness his Invasions on the Rights of the People.

HE has refused for a long Time, after such Dissolutions, to cause others to be elected; whereby the Legislative Powers, incapable of Annihilation, have returned to the People at large for their exercise; the State remaining, in the mean Time, exposed to all the Dangers of Invasion from without, and Convulsions within.

HE has endeavoured to prevent the Population of these States; for that Purpose obstructing the Laws for Naturalization of Foreigners; refusing to pass others to encourage their Migrations hither, and raising the Conditions of new Appropriations of Lands.

HE has obstructed the Administration of Justice, by refusing his Assent to Laws for establishing Judiciary Powers.

HE has made Judges dependent on his Will alone, for the Tenure of their Offices, and the Amount and Payment of their Salaries.

HE has erected a Multitude of new Offices, and sent hither Swarms of Officers to harrass our People, and eat out their Substance.

HE has kept among us, in Times of Peace, Standing Armies, without the Consent of our Legislatures.

HE has affected to render the Military independent of and superior to the Civil Power.

HE has combined with others to subject us to a Jurisdiction foreign to our Constitution, and unacknowledged by our Laws; giving his Assent to their Acts of pretended Legislation:

FOR quartering large Bodies of Armed Troops among us:

FOR protecting them, by a mock Trial, from Punishment for any Murders which they should commit on the Inhabitants of these States:

FOR cutting off our Trade with all Parts of the World:

FOR imposing Taxes on us without our Consent:

FOR depriving us, in many Cases, of the Benefits of Trial by Jury:

FOR transporting us beyond Seas to be tried for pretended Offences:

FOR abolishing the free System of English Laws in a neighbouring Province, establishing therein an arbitrary Government, and enlarging its Boundaries, so as to render it at once an Example and fit Instrument for introducing the same absolute Rules into these Colonies:

FOR taking away our Charters, abolishing our most valuable Laws, and altering fundamentally the Forms of our Governments:

FOR suspending our own Legislatures, and declaring themselves invested with Power to legislate for us in all Cases whatsoever.

HE has abdicated Government here, by declaring us out of his Protection, and waging War against us.

HE has plundered our Seas, ravaged our Coasts, burnt our Towns, and destroyed the Lives of our People.

HE is, at this Time, transporting large Armies of foreign Mercenaries to complete the Works of Death, Desolation, and Tyranny, already begun with Circumstances of Cruelty and Perfidy, scarcely paralleled in the most barbarous Ages, and totally unworthy the Head of a civilized Nation.

HE has constrained our Fellow Citizens, taken Captive on the high Seas, to bear Arms against their Country, to become the Executioners of their Friends and Brethren, or to fall themselves by their Hands.

HE has excited domestic Insurrection amongst us, and has endeavoured to bring on the Inhabitants of our Frontiers, the merciless Indian Savages, whose known Rule of Warfare, is an undistinguished Destruction, of all Ages, Sexes and Conditions.

IN every stage of these Oppressions we have Petitioned for Redress in the most humble Terms: Our repeated Petitions have been answered only by repeated Injury. A Prince, whose Character is thus marked by every Act which may define a Tyrant, is unfit to be the Ruler of a free People.

NOR have we been wanting in Attentions to our British Brethren. We have warned them, from Time to Time, of Attempts by their Legislature to extend an unwarrantable Jurisdiction over us. We have reminded them of the Circumstances of our Emigration and Settlement here. We have appealed to their native Justice and Magnanimity, and we have conjured them by the Ties of our common Kindred to disavow these Usurpations, which would inevitably interrupt our Connexions and Correspondence. They too have been deaf to the Voice of Justice and of Consanguinity. We must, therefore, acquiesce in the Necessity, which denounces our Separation, and hold them, as we hold the rest of Mankind, Enemies in War, in Peace Friends.

WE, therefore, the Representatives of the UNITED STATES OF AMERICA, in GENERAL CONGRESS Assembled, appealing to the Supreme Judge of the World for the Rectitude of our Intentions, do, in the Name, and by Authority of the good People of these Colonies, solemnly Publish and Declare, That these United Colonies are, and of Right ought to be, FREE AND INDEPENDENT STATES; that they are absolved from all Allegiance to the British Crown, and that all political Connexion between them and the State of Great-Britain, is, and ought to be totally dissolved; and that as FREE AND INDEPENDENT STATES, they have full Power to levy War, conclude Peace, contract Alliances, establish Commerce, and to do all other Acts and Things which INDEPENDENT STATES may of Right do. And for the support of this Declaration, with a firm Reliance on the Protection of DIVINE PROVIDENCE, we mutually pledge to each other our LIVES, our FORTUNES, and our SACRED HONOR.

John Hancock.

GEORGIA, *Button Gwinnett, Lyman Hall, Geo. Walton.*

NORTH-CAROLINA, *Wm. Hooper, Joseph Hewes, John Penn.*

SOUTH-CAROLINA, *Edward Rutledge, Thos Heyward, junr., Thomas Lynch, junr., Arthur Middleton.*

MARYLAND, *Samuel Chase, Wm. Paca, Thos. Stone, Charles Carroll, of Carrollton.*

VIRGINIA, *George Wythe, Richard Henry Lee, Ths. Jefferson, Benja. Harrison, Thos. Nelson, jr., Francis Lightfoot Lee, Carter Braxton.*

PENNSYLVANIA, *Robt. Morris, Benjamin Rush, Benja. Franklin, John Morton, Geo. Clymer, Jas. Smith, Geo. Taylor, James Wilson, Geo. Ross.*

DELAWARE, *Caesar Rodney, Geo. Read.*

NEW-YORK, *Wm. Floyd, Phil. Livingston, Frank Lewis, Lewis Morris.*

NEW-JERSEY, *Richd. Stockton, Jno. Witherspoon, Fras. Hopkinson, John Hart, Abra. Clark.*

NEW-HAMPSHIRE, *Josiah Bartlett, Wm. Whipple, Matthew Thornton.*

MASSACHUSETTS-BAY, *Saml. Adams, John Adams, Robt. Treat Paine, Elbridge Gerry.*

RHODE-ISLAND AND PROVIDENCE, *C. Step. Hopkins, William Ellery.*

CONNECTICUT, *Roger Sherman, Saml. Huntington, Wm. Williams, Oliver Wolcott.*

IN CONGRESS, JANUARY 18, 1777.

THE CONSTITUTION

(includes Bill of Rights and Amendments 11–27)[1]

WE the PEOPLE of the UNITED STATES, in order to form a more perfect union, establish justice, ensure domestic tranquility, provide for the common defence, promote the general welfare, and secure the blessings of liberty to ourselves and our posterity, do ordain and establish this Constitution for the United States of America.

ARTICLE I

Section 1. ALL legislative powers, herein granted, shall be vested in a Congress of the United States, which shall consist of a Senate and House of Representatives.

Section 2. The House of Representatives shall be composed of Members chosen every second year by the people of the several States, and the Electors in each State shall have the qualifications requisite for Electors of the most numerous branch of the state Legislature.

No person shall be a Representative who shall not have attained to the age of twenty five years, and been seven years a citizen of the United States, and who shall not, when elected, be an inhabitant of that state in which he shall be chosen.

Representatives and direct taxes shall be appointed among the several States which may be included within this Union, according to their respective numbers, which shall be determined by adding to the whole number of free persons, including those bound to service for a term of years, and excluding Indians not taxed, three fifths of all other persons. The actual enumeration shall be made within three years after the first meeting of the Congress of the United States, and within every subsequent term of ten years, in such manner as they shall by law direct. The number of Representatives shall not exceed one for every thirty thousand, but each State shall have at least one Representative; and until such enumeration shall be made, the State of New-Hampshire shall be entitled to choose three, Massachusetts eight, Rhode-Island and Providence Plantation one, Connecticut five, New-York six, New-Jersey four, Pennsylvania eight, Delaware one, Maryland six, Virginia ten, North-Carolina five, South-Carolina five, and Georgia three.

When vacancies happen in the Representation from any State, the Executive authority thereof shall issue writs of election to fill such vacancies.

The House of Representatives shall choose their Speaker and other officers, and shall have the sole power of impeachment.

Section 3. The Senate of the United States shall be composed of two Senators from each State, chosen by the Legislature thereof, for six years; and each Senator shall have one vote.

Immediately after they shall be assembled in consequence of the first election, they shall be divided as equally as may be into three classes. The seats of the Senators of the first class shall be vacated at the expiration of the second year, of the second class at the expiration of the fourth year, and the third class at the expiration of the sixth year, so that one third may be chosen every second year, and if vacancies happen, by resignation or otherwise, during the recess of the Legislature of any State, the Executive thereof may make temporary appointments until the next meeting of the Legislature, which shall then fill such vacancies.

No person shall be a Senator who shall not have attained to the age of thirty years, and been nine years a citizen of the United States, and who shall not, when elected, be an inhabitant of that State for which he shall be chosen.

The Vice-President of the United States shall be President of the Senate, but shall have no vote, unless they be equally divided.

The Senate shall choose their other officers, and also a President pro tempore, in the absence of the Vice-President, or when he shall exercise the office of President of the United States.

The Senate shall have the sole power to try all impeachments. When sitting for that purpose, they shall be on oath or affirmation. When the President of the United States is tried, the Chief Justice shall preside; and no person shall be convicted without the concurrence of two thirds of the members present.

Judgement, in cases of impeachment, shall not extend further than to removal from office, and disqualification to hold and enjoy any office of honour, trust or profit, under the United States; but the party convicted shall nevertheless be liable and subject to indictment, trial, judgement and punishment, according to law.

Section 4. The times, places, and manner, of holding elections for Senators and Representatives, shall be prescribed in each State by the Legislature thereof; but the Congress may at any time, by law, make or alter such regulations, except as to the place of choosing Senators.

The Congress shall assemble at least once in every year, and such meeting shall be on the first Monday in December, unless they shall by law appoint a different day.

Section 5. Each House shall be the judge of the elections, returns and qualification of its own members, and a majority of each shall constitute a quorum to do business; but a smaller number may adjourn from day to day, and may be authorized to compel the attendance of absent members, in such manner, and under such penalties, as each House may provide.

Each House may determine the rules of its proceedings, punish its members for disorderly behavior, and, with the concurrence of two thirds, expel a member.

Each House shall keep a journal of its proceedings, and from time to time publish the same, excepting such parts as may in their judgment require secrecy; and the yeas and nays of the members of either House on any question shall, at the desire of one fifth of those present, be entered on the journal.

Neither House, during the session of Congress, shall, without the consent of the other, adjourn for more than three days, nor to any other place than that in which the two Houses shall be sitting.

Section 6. The Senators and Representatives shall receive a compensation for their services, to be ascertained by law, and paid out of the treasury of the United States. They shall in all cases, except treason, felony and breach of peace, be privileged from arrest during their attendance at the session of their respective Houses, and in going to and returning from the same; and for any speech or debate in either House, they shall not be questioned in any other place.

No Senator or Representative shall, during the time for which he was elected, be appointed to any civil office under the authority of the United States, which shall have been created, or the emoluments whereof shall have been increased, during such time; and no person holding any office under the United States shall be a member of either House during his continuance in office.

Section 7. All bills for raising revenue shall originate in the House of Representatives; but the Senate may propose or concur with amendments, as on other Bills.

Every bill which shall have passed the House of Representatives and the Senate shall, before it become a law, be presented to the President of the United States; if he approve; he shall sign it; but if not, he shall return it, with his objections, to that House in which it shall have originated, who shall enter the objections at large on their journal, and proceed to reconsider it. If after such reconsideration two thirds of that House shall agree to pass the bill, it shall be sent, together with the objections, to the other House, by which it shall likewise be reconsidered, and if approved by two thirds of that House, it shall become a law. But in all such cases the votes of both Houses shall be determined by yeas and nays, and the names of the persons voting for and against the bill shall be entered on the journal of each House respectively. If any bill shall not be returned by the President within ten days (Sundays excepted) after it shall have been presented to him, the same shall be a law in like manner as if he had signed it, unless the Congress by their adjournment prevent its return, in which case it shall not be a law.

Every order, resolution or vote, to which the concurrence of the Senate and House of Representatives may be necessary (except on a question of adjournment) shall be presented to the President of the United States; and before the same shall take effect, shall be approved by him, or being disapproved by him, shall be re-passed by two thirds of the Senate and House of Representatives, according to the rules and limitations prescribed in the case of a bill.

Section 8. The Congress shall have power to lay and collect taxes, duties, imposts and excises, to pay the debts and provide for the common defence and general welfare of the United States; but all duties, imposts and excises, shall be uniform throughout the United States;

To borrow money on the credit of the United States;

To regulate commerce with foreign nations, and among the several States, and with the Indian tribes;

To establish a uniform rule of naturalization, and uniform laws on the subject of bankruptcies throughout the United States;

To coin money, regulate the value thereof, and of foreign coin, and fix the standard of weights and measures;

To provide for the punishment of counterfeiting the securities and current coin of the United States;

To establish post-offices and post-roads;

To promote the progress of science and useful arts, by securing for limited times to authors and inventors the exclusive right to their respective writings and discoveries;

To constitute tribunals inferior to the Supreme Court;

To define and punish piracies and felonies committed on the high seas and offences against the law of nations;

To declare war, grant letters of marque and reprisal, and make rules concerning captures on land and water;

To raise and support armies, but no appropriation of money to that use shall be for a longer term than two years;

To provide and maintain a navy;

To make rules for the government and regulation of the land and naval forces;

To provide for calling forth the militia to execute the laws of the Union, suppress insurrections, and repel invasions;

To provide for organizing arming, and disciplining the militia, and for governing such part of them as may be employed in the service of the United States, reserving to the States respectively the appointment of the officers, and the authority of training the militia according to the discipline prescribed by Congress;

To exercise exclusive legislation, in all cases whatsoever, over such district (not exceeding ten miles square) as may, by cession of particular States, and the acceptance of Congress, become the seat of the government of the United States, and to exercise like authority over all places purchased by the consent of the Legislature of the State in which the same shall be, for the erection of forts, magazines, arsenals, dock-yards, and other needful buildings;—and,

To make all laws which shall be necessary and proper for carrying into execution the foregoing powers, and all other powers vested by this Constitution in the government of the United States, or in any department or officer thereof.

Section 9. The migration or importation of such persons as any of the States now existing shall think proper to admit, shall not be prohibited by the Congress prior to the year one thousand eight hundred and eight, but a tax or duty may be imposed on such importation, not exceeding ten dollars for each person.

The privilege of the writ of habeas corpus shall not be suspended, unless when in cases of rebellion or invasion the public safety may require it.

No bill of attainder, or ex post facto law, shall be passed.

No capitation or other direct tax shall be laid, unless in proportion to the census or enumeration herein before directed to be taken.

No tax or duty shall be laid on articles exported from any State.

No preference shall be given by any regulation of commerce or revenue to the ports of one state over those of another: Nor shall vessels bound to or from one State, be obliged to enter, clear, or pay duties, in another.

No money shall be drawn from the treasury, but in consequence of appropriations made by law; and a regular statement and account of the receipts and expenditures of all public money shall be published from time to time.

No title of nobility shall be granted by the United States: And no person holding any office of profit or trust under them shall, without the consent of the Congress, accept of any present, emolument, office or title, of any kind whatever, from any King, Prince, or foreign State.

Section 10. No State shall enter into any treaty, alliance or confederation; grant letters of marque and reprisal; coin money; emit bills of credit; make anything but gold and silver coin a tender in payment of debts; pass any bill of attainder, ex post facto law, or law impairing the obligation of contracts, or grant any title of nobility.

No State shall, without the consent of the Congress, lay any imposts or duties on imports or exports, except what may be absolutely necessary for executing its inspection laws; and the new produce of all duties and imposts, laid by any State, on imports or exports, shall be for the use of the treasury of the United States; and all such laws shall be subject to the revision and control of the Congress. No state shall, without the consent of Congress, lay any duty of tonnage, keep troops or ships of war in time of peace, enter into any agreement or compact with another State, or with a foreign power, or engage in war, unless actually invaded, or in such imminent danger as will not admit of delay.

ARTICLE II

Section 1. The executive power shall be vested in a President of the United States of America. He shall hold his office during the term of four years, and, together with the Vice President, chosen for the same term, be elected as follows:

Each state shall appoint, in such manner as the Legislature thereof may direct, a number of Electors, equal to the whole number of Senators and Representatives to which the State may be entitled in the Congress; but no Senator or Representative, or person holding an office of trust or profit under the United States, shall be appointed an Elector.

The Electors shall meet in their respective States, and vote by ballot for two persons, of whom one at least shall not be an inhabitant of the same state with themselves. And they shall make a list of all the persons voted for, and of the number of votes for each; which list they shall sign and certify, and transmit sealed to the seat of the government of the United States, directed to the President of the Senate. The President of the Senate shall, in the presence of the Senate and House of Representatives, open all the certificates, and the votes shall then be counted. The person having the greatest number of votes shall be the President, if such number be a majority of the whole number of Electors appointed; and if there be more than one who have such majority, and have an equal number of votes, then the House of Representatives shall immediately choose by ballot one of them for President; and if no person have a majority, then from the five highest on the list the said House shall in like manner choose a President. But in choosing the President the votes shall be taken by States, the representation from each State having one vote; a quorum for this purpose shall consist of a member or members from two thirds of the States, and a majority of all the States shall be necessary to a choice. In every case, after the choice of the President, the person having the greatest number of votes of the Electors shall be the Vice-President. But if there should remain two or more who have equal votes, the Senate shall choose from them by ballot the Vice President.

The Congress may determine the time of choosing the Electors, and the day on which they shall give their votes; which day shall be the same throughout the United States.

No person, except a natural born citizen, or a citizen of the United States at the time of the adoption of this Constitution, shall be eligible to the office of President; neither shall any person be eligible to that office, who shall not have attained to the age of thirty five years, and been fourteen years a resident within the United States.

In case of the removal of the President from office, or of his death, resignation, or inability to discharge the powers and duties of the said office, the same shall devolve on the Vice-President; and the Congress may by law provide for the case of removal, death, resignation or inability, both of the President and Vice-President, declaring what officer shall then act as President, and such officer shall act accordingly, until the disability be removed, or a President shall be elected.

The President shall, at stated times, receive for his services a compensation, which shall neither be increased nor diminished during the period for which he shall have been elected, and he shall not receive within that period any other emolument from the United States, or any of them.

Before he enter on the execution of his office, he shall take the following oath or affirmation:

"I do solemnly swear (or affirm) that I will faithfully execute the office of President of the United States, and will, to the best of my ability, preserve, protect and defend, the Constitution of the United States."

Section 2. The President shall be Commander in Chief of the army and navy of the United States, and of the militia of the several states, when called into the actual service of the United States; he may require the opinion, in writing, of the principal officer in each of the executive departments, upon any subject relating to the duties of their respective offices, and he shall have power to grant reprieves and pardons for offences against the United States, except in cases of impeachment.

He shall have power, by and with the advice and consent of the Senate, to make treaties, provided two thirds of the Senators present concur; and he shall nominate, and by and with the advice and consent of the Senate shall appoint Ambassadors, other public Ministers, and Consuls, judges of the Supreme Court, and all other officers of the United States, whose appointments are not herein otherwise provided for, and which shall be established by law. But the Congress may by law vest the appointment of such inferior officers as they think proper in the President alone, in the courts of law, or in the heads of departments.

The President shall have power to fill up all vacancies that may happen during the recess of the Senate, by granting commissions, which shall expire at the end of their next session.

Section 3. He shall from time to time give to the Congress information of the state of the Union, and recommend to their consideration such measures as he shall judge necessary and expedient; he may, on extraordinary occasions, convene both Houses, or either of them, and in case of disagreement between them, with respect to the time of adjournment, he may adjourn them to such time as he shall think proper; he shall receive Ambassadors and other public Ministers; he shall take care that the laws be faithfully executed, and shall commission all the officers of the United States.

Section 4. The President, Vice-President and all civil officers of the United States, shall be removed from office, on impeachment for, and conviction of, treason, bribery, or other high crimes and misdemeanors.

ARTICLE III

Section 1. The judicial power of the United States, shall be vested in one Supreme Court, and in such Inferior Courts as the Congress may from time to time ordain and establish. The Judges, both of the supreme and Inferior Courts, shall hold their offices during good behaviour and shall, at stated times, receive for their services a compensation, which shall not be diminished during their continuance in office.

Section 2. The judicial power shall extend to all cases in law and equity, arising under this Constitution, the laws of the United States, and treaties made, or which shall be made, under their authority; to all cases affecting Ambassadors, other public Ministers and consuls; to all cases of admiralty and maritime jurisdiction; to controversies to which the United States shall be a party; to controversies between two or more States; between a State and citizen of another State; between citizens of different States; between citizens of the same State claiming lands under grants of different States, and between a State, or the citizens thereof, and Foreign states, citizens or subjects.

In all cases affecting Ambassadors, other public Ministers and consuls, and those in which a State shall be party, the Supreme Court shall have original jurisdiction. In all the other cases before mentioned, the Supreme Court shall have appellate jurisdiction, both as to law and fact, with such exceptions and under such regulations as the Congress shall make.

The trial of all crimes, except in cases of impeachment, shall be by jury; and such trial shall be held in the State where the said crimes shall have been committed; but when not committed within any State, the trial shall be at such place or places as the Congress may by law have directed.

Section 3. Treason against the United States, shall consist only in levying war against them, or in adhering to their enemies, giving them aid and comfort. No person shall be convicted of treason, unless on the testimony of two witnesses to the same overt act, or on consession in open court.

The Congress shall have power to declare the punishment of treason, but no attainder of treason shall work corruption of blood, or forfeiture, except during the life of the person attainted.

ARTICLE IV

Section 1. Full faith and credit shall be given in each State to the public acts, records, and judicial proceedings, of every other State. And the Congress may by general laws prescribe the manner in which such acts, records and proceedings, shall be proved, and the effect thereof.

Section 2. The citizens of each State shall be entitled to all privileges and immunities of citizens in the several states.

A person, charged in any State with treason, felony, or other crime, who shall flee from justice, and be found in another State, shall, on demand of the executive authority of the State from which he fled, be delivered up, to be removed to the State having jurisdiction of the crime.

No person, held to service or labour in one State, under the laws thereof, escaping into another, shall, in consequence of any law or regulation therein, be discharged from such service or labor; but shall be delivered up, on claim of the party to whom such service or labour may be due.

Section 3. New States may be admitted by the Congress into this Union; but no new State shall be formed or erected within the jurisdiction of any other State; nor any State be formed by the junction of two or more States, or parts of States, without the consent of the Legislatures of the States concerned, as well as of the Congress.

The Congress shall have power to dispose of and make all needful rules and regulations, respecting the territory or other property belonging to the United States; and nothing in this Constitution shall be so construed, as to prejudice any claims of the United States, or of any particular State.

Section 4. The United States shall guarantee, to every State in this Union, a republican form of government, and shall protect each of them against invasion; and, on application of the Legislature, or of the executive (when the Legislature cannot be convened) against domestic violence.

ARTICLE V

The Congress, whenever two thirds of both Houses shall deem it necessary, shall propose amendments to this Constitution; or, on the application of the Legislatures of two thirds of the several States, shall call a Convention, for proposing amendments; which, in either case, shall be valid to all intents and purposes, as part of this Constitution, when ratified by the Legislature of three fourths of the several States, or by conventions in three fourths thereof, as the one or the other mode of ratification may be proposed by the Congress: Provided that no amendment which may be made prior to the year one thousand eight hundred and eight shall in any manner affect the first and fourth clauses, in the ninth section of the first article; and that no State, without its consent, shall be deprived of its equal suffrage in the Senate.

ARTICLE VI

All debts contracted, and engagements entered into, before the adoption of this Constitution, shall be as valid against the United States under this Constitution, as under the Confederation.

This Constitution, and the laws of the United States which shall be made in pursuance thereof, and all treaties made, or which shall be made, under the authority of the United States, shall be the supreme law of the land; and the Judges in every State, shall be bound thereby; anything in the Constitution or laws of any State to the contrary notwithstanding.

The Senators and Representatives before mentioned, and the members of the several State Legislatures, and all executive and judicial officers, both of the United States and of the several States, shall be bound by oath or affirmation to support this Constitution; but no religious test shall ever be required as a qualification to any office, or public trust, under the United States.

ARTICLE VII

The ratification of the Conventions of Nine States shall be sufficient for the establishment of this Constitution, between the States so ratifying the same.

Done in Convention by the unanimous consent of the States present, the seventeenth day of September, in the year of our Lord one thousand seven hundred and eighty seven and of the independence of the United States of America the twelfth.

In witness whereof, We have hereunto subscribed our Names. George Washington-Presidt., and deputy from Virginia; *New Hampshire:* John Langdon, Nicholas Gilman; *Massachusetts:* Nathaniel Gorham, Rufus King; *Connecticut:* Wm. Saml. Johnson, Roger Sherman; *New-York:* Alexander Hamilton; *New-Jersey:* Wil. Livingston, David Brearly, Wm. Paterson, Jona Dayton; *Pennsylvania:* B. Franklin, Thomas Mifflin, Robt. Morris, Geo.

Clymer, Thos. FitzSimons, Jared Ingersoll, James Wilson, Gouv. Morris; *Delaware:* Geo. Read, Gunning Bedford jun, John Dickinson, Richard Bassett, Jacob Broom; *Maryland:* James McHenry, Dan of St Thos. Jenifer, Danl. Carroll; *Virginia:* John Blair, James Madison jun.; *North-Carolina:* Wm. Blount, Richd. Dobbs Spaight, Hugh Williamson; *South-Carolina:* J. Rutledge, Charles Cotesworth Pinckney, Charles Pinckney, Pierce Butler; *Georgia:* William Few, Abr. Baldwin.

THE BILL OF RIGHTS

Amendments 1–10 of the Constitution

The Conventions of a Number of the States having, at the Time of adopting the Constitution, expressed a Desire, in Order to prevent misconstruction or Abuse of its Powers, that further declaratory and restrictive Clauses should be added: And as extending the Ground of public Confidence in the Government will best insure the beneficent Ends of its Institution; Resolved, by the Senate and House of Representatives of the United States of America, in Congress assembled, Two Thirds of both Houses concurring, That the following Articles be proposed to the Legislatures of the several States as Amendments to the Constitution of the United States: All, or any of, which Articles, when ratified by Three Fourths of the said Legislatures, to be valid to all Intents and Purposes as Part of the said Constitution, namely:

AMENDMENT I

Congress shall make no Law respecting an Establishment of Religion, or prohibiting the free Exercise thereof; or abridging the Freedom of Speech, or of the Press, or the Right of the People peaceably to assemble, and to petition the Government for a Redress of Grievances.

AMENDMENT II

A well regulated Militia being necessary to the Security of a free State, the Right of the People to keep and bear Arms shall not be infringed.

AMENDMENT III

No Soldier shall, in Time of Peace, be quartered in any House without the Consent of the Owner, nor, in Time of War, but in a Manner to be prescribed by Law.

AMENDMENT IV

The Right of the People to be secure in their Persons, Houses, Papers, and Effects, against unreasonable Searches and seizures shall not be violated, and no Warrants shall issue but upon probable Cause supported by Oath, or affirmation, and particularly describing the Place to be searched, and the Persons or Things to be seized.

AMENDMENT V

No Person shall be held to answer for a Capital, or otherwise Infamous Crime, unless on a Presentment or Indictment of a Grand Jury, except in Cases arising in the Land or Naval Forces; or in the Militia, when in actual Service in Time of War or public Danger: nor shall any Person be subject for the same Offence to be Twice put in Jeopardy of Life or Limb; nor shall be compelled, in any criminal case to be a witness against himself, nor be deprived of Life, Liberty, or Property, without due Process of Law: nor shall private Property be taken for public Use, without just Compensation.

AMENDMENT VI

In all Criminal Prosecutions, the accused shall enjoy the Right to a speedy and public Trial, by an impartial Jury of the State and District wherein the Crime shall have been committed, which District shall have been previously ascertained by Law; and to be informed of the Nature and Cause of the Accusation; to be confronted with the Witnesses against him; to have compulsory Process for obtaining Witnesses in his favour, and to have the Assistance of counsel for his Defence.

AMENDMENT VII

In Suits at Common Law, where the Value in Controversy shall exceed Twenty Dollars, the Right of Trial by Jury shall be preserved, and no Fact tried by a Jury shall be otherwise re-examined in any Court of the United States, than according to the Rules of the Common Law.

AMENDMENT VIII

Excessive bail shall not be required; nor excessive Fines imposed; nor cruel and unusual Punishments inflicted.

AMENDMENT IX

The Enumeration in the Constitution of certain Rights shall not be construed to deny or disparage others retained by the People.

AMENDMENT X

The Powers not delegated to the United States by the Constitution, nor prohibited by it to the States, are reserved to the States respectively or to the People.

AMENDMENTS TO THE CONSTITUTION

(Amendments 11–27)

AMENDMENT XI

(1798) The judicial power of the United States shall not be construed to extend to any suit in law or equity, commenced or prosecuted against one of the United States by citizens of another state, or by citizens or subjects of any foreign state.

AMENDMENT XII

(1804) The electors shall meet in their respective states and vote by ballot for President and Vice-President, one of whom, at least, shall not be an inhabitant of the same state with themselves; they shall name in their ballots the person voted for as President, and in distinct ballots the person voted for as Vice-President, and they shall make distinct lists of all persons voted for as President, and of all persons voted for as Vice-President, and of the number of votes for each, which lists they shall sign and certify, and transmit sealed to the seat of the government of the United States, directed to the President of the Senate;—The President of the Senate shall, in the presence of the Senate and House of Representatives, open all the certificates and the votes shall then be counted;—the person having the greatest number of votes for President, shall be the President, if such number be a majority of the whole number of electors appointed; and if no person have such majority, then from the persons having the highest numbers not exceeding three on the list of those voted for as President, the House of Representatives shall choose immediately, by ballot, the President.

But in choosing the President, the votes shall be taken by states, the representation from each state having one vote; a quorum for this purpose shall consist of a member or members from two-thirds of the states, and a majority of all the states shall be necessary to a choice. And if the House of Representatives shall not choose a President whenever the right of choice shall devolve upon them, before the fourth day of March next following, then the Vice-President shall act as President, as in the case of the death or other constitutional disability of the President. The person having the greatest number of votes as Vice-President, shall be the Vice-President, if such number be a majority of the whole number of electors appointed, and if no person have a majority, then from the two highest numbers on the list, the Senate shall choose the Vice-President; a quorum for the purpose shall consist of two-thirds of the whole number of Senators, and a majority of the whole number shall be necessary to a choice. But no person constitutionally ineligible to the office of President shall be eligible to that of Vice-President of the United States.

AMENDMENT XIII

(1865) *Section 1.* Neither slavery nor involuntary servitude, except as a punishment for crime whereof the party shall have been duly convicted, shall exist within the United States, or any place subject to their jurisdiction.

Section 2. Congress shall have power to enforce this article by appropriate legislation.

AMENDMENT XIV

(1868) *Section 1.* All persons born or naturalized in the United States, and subject to the jurisdiction thereof, are citizens of the United States and of the state wherein they reside. No state shall make or enforce any law which shall abridge the privileges or immunities of citizens of the United States; nor shall any state deprive any person of life, liberty, or property, without due process of law; nor deny to any person within its jurisdiction the equal protection of the laws.

Section 2. Representatives shall be apportioned among the several states according to their respective numbers, counting the whole number of persons in each state, excluding Indians not taxed. But when the right to vote at any election for the choice of electors for President and Vice President of the United States, Representatives in Congress, the executive and judicial officers of a state, or the members of the legislature thereof, is denied to any of the male inhabitants of such state, being twenty-one years of age, and citizens of the United States, or in any way abridged, except for participation in rebellion, or other crime, the basis of representation therein shall be reduced in the proportion which the number of such male citizens shall bear to the whole number of male citizens twenty-one years of age in such state.

Section 3. No person shall be a Senator or Representative in Congress, or elector of President and Vice President, or hold any office, civil or military, under the United States, or under any state, who, having previously taken an oath, as a member of Congress, or as an officer of the United States, or as a member of any state legislature, or as an executive or judicial officer of any state, to support the Constitution of the United States, shall have engaged in insurrection or rebellion against the same, or given aid or comfort to the enemies thereof. But Congress may by a vote of two-thirds of each House, remove such disability.

Section 4. The validity of the public debt of the United States, authorized by law, including debts incurred for payment of pensions and bounties for services in suppressing insurrection or rebellion, shall not be questioned. But neither the United States nor any state shall assume or pay any debt or obligation incurred in aid of insurrection or rebellion against the United States, or any claim for the loss or emancipation of any slave; but all such debts, obligations and claims shall be held illegal and void.

Section 5. The Congress shall have power to enforce, by appropriate legislation, the provisions of this article.

AMENDMENT XV

(1870) *Section 1.* The right of citizens of the United States to vote shall not be denied or abridged by the United States or by any state on account of race, color, or previous condition of servitude.

Section 2. The Congress shall have power to enforce this article by appropriate legislation.

AMENDMENT XVI

(1913) The Congress shall have power to lay and collect taxes on incomes, from whatever source derived, without apportionment among the several states, and without regard to any census of enumeration.

AMENDMENT XVII

(1913) The Senate of the United States shall be composed of two Senators from each state, elected by the people thereof, for six years; and each Senator shall have one vote. The electors in each state shall have the qualifications requisite for electors of the most numerous branch of the state legislatures.

When vacancies happen in the representation of any state in the Senate, the executive authority of such state shall issue writs of election to fill such vacancies: Provided, that the legislature of any state may empower the executive thereof to make temporary appointments until the people fill the vacancies by election as the legislature may direct.

This amendment shall not be so construed as to affect the election or term of any Senator chosen before it becomes valid as part of the Constitution.

AMENDMENT XVIII

(1919) *Section 1.* After one year from the ratification of this article the manufacture, sale, or transportation of intoxicating liquors within, the importation thereof into, or the exportation thereof from the United States and all territory subject to the jurisdiction thereof for beverage purposes is hereby prohibited.

Section 2. The Congress and the several states shall have concurrent power to enforce this article by appropriate legislation.

Section 3. This article shall be inoperative unless it shall have been ratified as an amendment to the Constitution by the legislatures of the several states, as provided in the Constitution, within seven years from the date of the submission hereof to the states by the Congress.

AMENDMENT XIX

(1920) The right of citizens of the United States to vote shall not be denied or abridged by the United States or by any state on account of sex.

Congress shall have power to enforce this article by appropriate legislation.

AMENDMENT XX

(1933) *Section 1.* The terms of the President and Vice President shall end at noon on the 20th day of January, and the terms of Senators and Representatives at noon on the 3rd day of January, of the years in which such terms would have ended if this article had not been ratified; and the terms of their successors shall then begin.

Section 2. The Congress shall assemble at least once in every year, and such meeting shall begin at noon on the 3rd day of January, unless they shall by law appoint a different day.

Section 3. If, at the time fixed for the beginning of the term of the President, the President elect shall have died, the Vice President elect shall become President. If a President shall not have been chosen before the time fixed for the beginning of his term, or if the President elect shall have failed to qualify, then the Vice President elect shall act as President until a President shall have qualified; and the Congress may by law provide for the case wherein neither a President elect nor a Vice President elect shall have qualified, declaring who shall then act as President, or the manner in which one who is to act shall be selected, and such person shall act accordingly until a President or Vice President shall have qualified.

Section 4. The Congress may by law provide for the case of the death of any of the persons from whom the House of Representatives may choose a President whenever the right of choice shall have devolved upon them, and for the case of the death of any of the persons from whom the Senate may choose a Vice President whenever the right of choice shall have devolved upon them.

Section 5. Sections 1 and 2 shall take effect on the 15th day of October following the ratification of this article.

Section 6. This article shall be inoperative unless it shall have been ratified as an amendment to the Constitution by the legislatures of three-fourths of the several states within seven years from the date of its submission.

AMENDMENT XXI

(1933) *Section 1.* The eighteenth article of amendment to the Constitution of the United States is hereby repealed.

Section 2. The transportation or importation into any state, territory, or possession of the United States for delivery or use therein of intoxicating liquors, in violation of the laws thereof, is hereby prohibited.

Section 3. This article shall be inoperative unless it shall have been ratified as an amendment to the Constitution by conventions in the several states, as provided in the Constitution, within seven years from the date of the submission hereof to the states by the Congress.

AMENDMENT XXII

(1951) *Section 1.* No person shall be elected to the office of the President more than twice, and no person who has held the office of President, or acted as President, for more than two years of a term to which some other person was elected President shall be elected to the office of the President more than once. But this article shall not apply to any person holding the office of President when this article was proposed by the Congress, and shall not prevent any person who may be holding the office of President, or acting as President, during the term within which this article becomes operative from holding the office of President or acting as President during the remainder of such term.

Section 2. This article shall be inoperative unless it shall have been ratified as an amendment to the Constitution by the legislatures of three-fourths of the several states within seven years from the date of its submission to the states by the Congress.

AMENDMENT XXIII

(1961) *Section 1.* The District constituting the seat of government of the United States shall appoint in such manner as the Congress may direct: A number of electors of President and Vice President equal to the whole number of Senators and Representatives in Congress to which the District would be entitled if it were a state, but in no event more than the least populous state; they shall be in addition to those appointed by the states, but they shall be considered, for the purposes of the election of President and Vice President, to be electors appointed by a state; and they shall meet in the District and perform such duties as provided by the twelfth article of amendment.

Section 2. The Congress shall have power to enforce this article by appropriate legislation.

AMENDMENT XXIV

(1964) *Section 1.* The right of citizens of the United States to vote in any primary or other election for President or Vice President, for electors for President or Vice President, or for Senator or Representative in Congress, shall not be denied or abridged by the United States or any state by reason of failure to pay any poll tax or other tax.

Section 2. The Congress shall have power to enforce this article by appropriate legislation.

AMENDMENT XXV

(1967) *Section 1.* In case of the removal of the President from office or of his death or resignation, the Vice President shall become President.

Section 2. Whenever there is a vacancy in the office of the Vice President, the President shall nominate a Vice President who shall take office upon confirmation by a majority vote of both Houses of Congress.

Section 3. Whenever the President transmits to the President pro tempore of the Senate and the Speaker of the House of Representatives his written declaration that he is unable to discharge the powers and duties of his office, and until he transmits to them a written declaration to the contrary, such powers and duties shall be discharged by the Vice President as Acting President.

Section 4. Whenever the Vice President and a majority of either the principal officers of the executive departments or of such other body as Congress may by law provide, transmit to the President pro tempore of the Senate and the Speaker of the House of Representatives their written declaration that the President is unable to discharge the powers and duties of his office, the Vice President shall immediately assume the powers and duties of the office as Acting President.

Thereafter, when the President transmits to the President pro tempore of the Senate and the Speaker of the House of Representatives his written declaration that no inability exists, he shall resume the powers and duties of his office unless the Vice President and a majority of either the principal officers of the executive department or of such other body as Congress may by law provide, transmit within four days to the President pro tempore of the Senate and the Speaker of the House of Representatives their written declaration that the President is unable to discharge the powers and duties of his office. Thereupon Congress shall decide the issue, assembling within forty-eight hours for that purpose if not in session. If the Congress, within twenty-one days after receipt of the latter written declaration, or, if Congress is not in session, within twenty-one days after Congress is required to assemble, determines by two-thirds vote of both Houses that the President is unable to discharge the powers and duties of his office, the Vice President shall continue to discharge the same as Acting President; otherwise, the President shall resume the powers and duties of his office.

AMENDMENT XXVI

(1971) *Section 1.* The right of citizens of the United States, who are eighteen years of age or older, to vote, shall not be denied or abridged by the United States or any state on account of age.

Section 2. The Congress shall have the power to enforce this article by appropriate legislation.

AMENDMENT XXVII

(1992) No law varying the compensation for the services of the Senators and Representatives shall take effect until an election of Representatives shall have intervened.

TRANSCULTURAL EXAMPLES OF THE COMMON MORAL LAW

ETHIC STATEMENTS EXPRESSING THE MORAL LAW[1]

The general crosscultural agreement of ethical positions (evidence of the Moral Law) is manifest in the following quotations:

(1) The Law of General Beneficence

"Utter not a word by which anyone could be wounded" (Hindu).

"Never do to others what you would not like them to do to you" (Ancient Chinese).

"Men were brought into existence for the sake of men that they might do one another good" (Roman, Cicero).

(2) The Law of Special Beneficence

"Surely proper behavior to parents and elder brothers is the trunk of goodness" (Ancient Chinese).

"Love thy wife studiously. Gladden her heart all thy life long" (Ancient Egyptian).

"Natural affection is a thing right and according to Nature" (Greek).

"The union and fellowship of men will be best preserved if each receives from us the more kindness in proportion as he is more closely connected with us" (Roman, Cicero).

(3) Duties to Parents, Elders, Ancestors

"Has he despised Father and Mother?" (Babylonian).

"[There is a duty] to care for parents" (Greek).

"I tended the old man, I gave him my staff" (Ancient Egyptian).

(4) Duties to Children and Posterity

"Nature produces a special love of offspring" and "To live according to Nature is the supreme good" (Roman, Cicero).

"The Master said, Respect the young" (Ancient Chinese).

(5) The Law of Justice

"Has he drawn false boundaries?" (Babylonian).

"I have not stolen" (Ancient Egyptian).

"Justice is the settled and permanent intention of rendering to each man his rights" (Roman, Justinian).

"If the native made a 'find' of any kind (e.g. a honey tree) and marked it, it was thereafter safe for him, as far as his own tribesmen were concerned, no matter how long he left it" (Australian Aborigines).

"Whoso takes no bribe . . . well pleasing is this to Samas" (Babylonian).

(6) The Law of Good Faith and Veracity

"A sacrifice is obliterated by a lie and the merit of alms by an act of fraud" (Hindu).

"Whose mouth, full of lying, avails not before thee: thou burnest their utterance" (Babylonian).

"The Master said, Be of unwavering good faith" (Ancient Chinese).

"The foundation of justice is good faith" (Roman, Cicero).

(7) The Law of Mercy

"I have given bread to the hungry, water to the thirsty, clothes to the naked, a ferry boat to the boatless" (Ancient Egyptian).

"One should never strike a woman; not even with a flower" (Hindu).

"There, Thor, you got disgrace, when you beat women" (Old Norse).

"You will see them take care of . . . widows, orphans, and old men, never reproaching them" (Redskin).

(8) The Law of Magnanimity

"There are two kinds of injustice: the first is found in those who do an injury, the second in those who fail to protect another from injury when they can" (Roman, Cicero).

"To take no notice of a violent attack is to strengthen the heart of the enemy. Vigour is valiant, but cowardice is vile" (Ancient Egyptian).

"Nature and Reason command that nothing uncomely, nothing effeminate, nothing lascivious be done or thought" (Roman, Cicero).

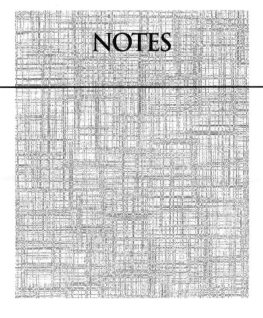

NOTES

PREFACE

1. Robert Bork, *Slouching Towards Gomorrah: Modern Liberalism and American Decline* (New York: Regan Books, HarperCollins, 1996, pbk. ed.), 5.

CHAPTER 1

1. William J. Bennett, *The Index of Leading Cultural Indicators* (New York: Simon & Schuster, 1994).
2. Richard Zoglin, "A Company Under Fire," *Time* (June 12, 1995).
3. Robert Pear, "House Panel Votes to Cut Food Stamps," *The New York Times* (March 8, 1995): 18.
4. A portion of the *Declaration of Independence*, emphasis added.
5. It is noteworthy that the *Declaration of Independence* was not based on a morality derived directly from the Bible, although moral law conclusions about Right and Wrong are in agreement with moral principles found in the Bible. In other words, even though many of the Founding Fathers were Christians who believed in the authority of the Bible (fifty-two of the fifty-five were professed members of orthodox churches), they appealed to the Moral Law to justify their independence, not the Bible.
6. Cited in Bennett, 36.

CHAPTER 2

1. See Mark Moore and Dean Gerstein, eds., *Alcohol and Public Policy: Beyond the Shadow of Prohibition* (n.p., 1981); and W. J. Rorabaugh, *The Alcoholic Republic* (n.p., 1979). Statistics cited by Norman H. Clark, "Prohibition and Temperance," *The Reader's Companion to American History* (n.p., 1991). Contained on Mindscape's Complete Reference Library CD (Novato, Calif.: Houghton Mifflin, 1994).
2. Ibid.
3. See "History of Alcohol Prohibition," National Commission on Marijuana and Drug Abuse at: http://www.druglibrary.org/schaffer/Library/studies/nc/nc2a.html.
4. Joseph Califano, "Fictions and Facts About Drug Legalization," *America* 171:0 (March 10, 1990). 7.
5. While pointing out many problems with enforcement of Prohibition, the commission was opposed to repealing the Eighteenth Amendment (Recommendation 1). Instead, the commission urged improved enforcement. Recommendation 9 reads as follows: "The Commission is of the opinion that the federal appropriations for enforcement of the Eighteenth Amendment should be substantially increased and that the vigorous and better organized efforts which have gone on since the Bureau of Prohibition Act, 1927, should be furthered by certain improvements in the statutes and in the organization, personnel, and equipment of enforcement, so as to give to enforcement the greatest practicable efficiency." (See Wickersham Commission Report: Conclusions and Recommendation at: http://www.druglibrary.org/schaffer/Library/studies/wick/index.html.)
6. For more on MADD's attempts to strengthen drunk driving laws see "Battles Brewing on Lowering Limit for Drunken Driving," *The Asbury Park Press*, January 2, 1998, A–17.
7. *The McLaughlin Group*, PBS, aired on August 5, 1995.
8. Cited in Bennett, *The Index of Leading Cultural Indicators*, 25.
9. As we shall see later in this chapter, laws can significantly influence attitudes toward a particular activity over the long term. Illegal activities that are suddenly declared legal often lose their immoral stigma over the long term. (For example, see later in this chapter our discussion on abortion and Prohibition.) And once something loses its immoral stigma, widespread acceptance and even greater widespread use are not far behind. Think about the debate over the legalization of other addictive drugs beyond alcohol and tobacco. If you think drug abuse is high now, wait for legalization. This would only encourage more drug abuse over the long term. Legalization would mean more sickness and deaths, more accidents, more lost productivity, more neglected children, and more broken families. In light of the problems we already have with excessive alcohol and tobacco use in this country, the acid test concerning the legalization of drugs lies with this question: "Do

we really believe it's morally right to pass down to future generations a culture that *openly* accepts scores of additional highly addictive substances; a culture that will only make it easier for our children to enslave themselves chemically; a culture that will dramatically increase the possibility that their lives and families will be destroyed?" We hope few would answer "yes."

CHAPTER 3

1. Joseph Fletcher, *Situation Ethics: The New Morality* (Philadelphia: The Westminster Press, 1966), 43–44.
2. Allan Bloom, *The Closing of the American Mind* (New York: Simon & Schuster, 1987), 26.
3. For a complete discussion on how to resolve conflicting moral absolutes, see Norman Geisler, *Christian Ethics: Options and Issues* (Grand Rapids, Mich.: Baker Book House, 1989), particularly chapter 7.

CHAPTER 4

1. Charley Reese, "Putting Profits Before Honor," *King Features Syndicate*, 1995.
2. "Prenatal Tests in China Threat to Girl Babies," *San Francisco Examiner*, April 24, 1994, A–7. Cited in Focus on the Family Newsletter, August 1995, by Dr. James Dobson.
3. "Fetuses: Health Food Fad in China," *Manila Bulletin*, April 13, 1995. See also "Human Fetuses Sold for Food, Says Report," *The Nikkei Weekly* [Japan's leading business newspaper], April 17, 1995, 24-A.
4. See *National Right to Life News*, April 24, 1995, p. 6.
5. *Manila Bulletin*, op. cit.
6. See Zheng Yi, I Cheng and T. P. Sym, [translator], *Scarlet Memorial: Tales of Cannibalism in Modern China*, Westview Press, 1996.
7. Sir Isaac Newton, *Mathematical Principles of Natural Philosophy*, book III, 1686, in Mortimer Adler, ed., *Great Books of the Western World*, vol. 34 (Chicago: Encyclopedia Britannica, Inc., 1952), 369.
8. Charles Darwin, *On the Origin of Species*, "Introduction," third edition.
9. Quoted in the *Encyclopedia of Philosophy*, vol. VIII, 276.
10. T. H. Huxley, *Evidence of Man's Place in Nature* (n.p., 1862), 107.
11. Assuming that something can come from nothing without intelligent intervention is only one of the many problems with total naturalistic evolutionary theory. A complete analysis of its problems are beyond the scope of this book but can be obtained elsewhere. See Michael J. Behe, *Darwin's Black Box: The Biochemical Challenge to Evolution* (New York: Free Press, 1996); Phillip Johnson, *Darwin on Trial*, rev. ed. (Downer's Grove, Ill.: InterVarsity Press, 1993); Phillip Johnson, *Defeating Darwinism by Opening Minds* (Downer's Grove, Ill: InterVarsity, 1997); Michael Denton, *Evolution: A Theory in Crisis* (Bethesda, Md.: Adler &

Adler, 1986); Norman Geisler and Ron Brooks, *When Skeptics Ask*, (Wheaton, Ill.: Victor Books, 1989) particularly chapter 10; and Norman Geisler and Kirby Anderson, *Origin of Science* (Grand Rapids, Mich.: Baker Book House), 1987.

12. Ernst Haeckel, *The Riddle of the Universe*, English trans., 1899 (New York: Harper and Brothers Pub., 1900), 337.

13. See *Marx and Engels on Religion*, Introduction by Reinhold Niebuhr (New York: Schoken Books, Inc., 1964), 295.

14. Charles Hodge, *What Is Darwinism?* (New York: Scribner, Armstrong, and Co., 1878), 177.

15. Friedrich Nietzsche, *Gay Science*, in Walter Kaufmann, *The Portable Nietzsche* (New York: The Viking Press, 1968), 95–96.

16. Adolf Hitler, *Mein Kampf* (London: Hurst and Blackett Ltd., Publishers, 4th printing, 1939), 239–240, 242.

17. Jerome Lawrence and Robert Lee, *Inherit the Wind* (New York: Random House, 1955). For a detailed analysis of the historical inaccuracies of *Inherit the Wind*, see Carol Iannone, "The Truth About Inherit the Wind," *Citizen* magazine (October 1997): 2–5. This is an article reprinted from *First Things* (Feb. 1997). It can be seen at http://www.firstthings.com. See also Phillip Johnson, *Defeating Darwinism by Opening Minds*, chapter 2, for an excellent discussion of the propagandist nature of *Inherit the Wind*.

18. Quoted by P. William Davis in *The World of Biology* (New York: McGraw-Hill Publishers, 1979), 610.

19. William Hillary and Oren Moetzger, *The World's Most Famous Court Trial* (Cincinnati, Oh.: National Book Co., 1925), 187.

20. See my eyewitness account in *The Creator in the Courtroom: "Scopes II"* (Mott Media, 1982). Although out-of-print, this book is now available from IMPACT at (704) 846–1226.

21. See Norman Geisler and Kirby Anderson, *Origin of Science* (Grand Rapids: Baker Book House, 1987), chapter 1.

22. Darwinists conveniently avoid the distinction between microevolution and macroevolution. By keeping their language imprecise, they can mislead many into thinking that any example of change within a species (e.g., beak variation in Darwin's finches) proves that one form of life can change itself into another and that bacteria can eventually change itself through successive species into a human being. In reality, examples of microevolution prove nothing about macroevolution. The former is observable; the latter has never been observed and goes against virtually everything we know from the fossil record, biology, and the origins of specified and complex systems. See the books listed in note 11 for more detail.

23. Quoted by John W. Whitehead and John Conlan, "The Establishment of the Religion of Secular Humanism and Its First Amendment Implications," *Texas Tech Law Review* (Winter 1978): 49.

24. Michael Behe, *Darwin's Black Box: The Biochemical Challenge to Evolution* (New York: Free Press, 1996), 193.

25. Phillip Johnson, "What Is Darwinism?" Bauman, ed., *Man and Creation: Perspectives on Science and Theology* (Hillsdale, Mich.: Hillsdale College Press, 1993). See also: http://www.mrccos.com/arn/johnson/wid.html.

26. *Texas Tech Law Review.*

27. Phillip Johnson, *Darwin on Trial* (rev. ed.) (Downer's Grove, Ill.: InterVarsity Press, 1993), 155.

28. Phillip Johnson, *The Religion of the Blind Watchmaker*. See: http://www.mrccos.com/arn/johnson/watchmkr.html.

29. See Norman Geisler and Ron Brooks, *When Skeptics Ask* (Grand Rapids, Mich.: Baker Book House, 1989), particularly chapter 10.

CHAPTER 5

1. Statistics adapted from *The Index of Leading Cultural Indicators*, by William Bennett (New York: Simon & Schuster, 1994).

2. See Paul Kurtz, ed., *Humanist Manifestoes I and II* (Buffalo, N.Y.: Prometheus Books, 1973), 8.

3. John Dewey, *A Common Faith* (New Haven, Conn.: Yale University Press, 1934), 87.

4. Julian Huxley, *Religion Without Revelation* (New York: Mentor, 1957).

5. Konstantin Kolenda, *Religion Without God* (Buffalo, NY: Prometheus Books), 1976.

6. J. Gales, ed., *1 Annals of Congress 434*, 1834. Cited by Robert L. Cord in H. Wayne House, ed., *Restoring the Constitution* (Dallas: Probe Books, 1987), 318.

7. William J. Federer, *America's God and Country Encyclopedia of Quotations* (Coppell, Tex.: 1994), 661 (see also note 77 on p. 827 for numerous additional references).

8. Ibid., 247.

9. Ibid., 10–11.

10. Actions of the Founding Fathers are documented in numerous places. See the chapter by Robert L. Cord in *Restoring the Constitution*. See also David Barton, *The Myth of Separation* (Aledo, Tex.: Wallbuilder Press, 1992) (Phone: 817–441–6044).

11. This illustrates how little today's Supreme Court justices care about the intentions of the Founding Fathers; the justices would rather rewrite the meaning of the Constitution to fit their own preferences. By doing this—legislating from the bench—the courts have taken control away from the people and have eroded the moral condition of this country. (Incidentally, while Congress voted to cease financial support for religious groups in 1896, today every session of Congress and the Supreme Court still begins with prayer.)

12. Federer, 654.

13. See Thomas Jefferson, Merrill D. Peterson, ed., *Jefferson Writings* (New York: Literary Classics of the United States, Inc., 1984), 510. See also *Reynolds v. U.S.*, 98 U.S. 164 (1878). See also David Barton, *The Myth of Separation* (Aledo, Tex.: Wallbuilders, 1992), particularly chapter 3 (Phone: 817–441–6044).
14. Cited in *Time* magazine (December 9, 1991): 63.
15. For example, Article 22 of Delaware's constitution reads: "Every person, who shall be chosen a member of either house, or appointed to any office or place of trust ... shall ... make and subscribe the following declaration, to wit: " 'I, _____ , do profess faith in God the Father, and in Jesus Christ, His only Son, and in the Holy Ghost, one God, blessed for evermore; and I do acknowledge the holy scriptures of the Old and New Testaments to be given by divine inspiration.' " Pennsylvania, Vermont, Massachusetts, and other states had similar requirements.

CHAPTER 6

1. Paul Blanshard, "Three Cheers for Our Secular State," *The Humanist* (Mar./Apr. 1976): 17. Quoted in H. Wayne House, ed., *Restoring the Constitution* (Dallas: Probe Books, 1987), 106.
2. *Engel v. Vitale* 370 U.S. 421, 422 (1962).
3. In 1647 what is now the state of Massachusetts required every town of more than fifty families to establish a school to teach the children how to read the Bible and to write. This became known as the "Old Deluder, Satan" law because these early American settlers believed that their children could better cope with that "Old Deluder, Satan" if they could read the Bible. This was essentially the beginning of public education in America.
4. *Roe v. Wade* 410 U.S. 159, 730 (1973).
5. See Norman Geisler and Frank Beckwith, *Matters of Life and Death: Calm Answers to Tough Questions About Abortion and Euthanasia* (Grand Rapids, Mich.: Baker Book House, 1991), particularly chapter 1. See also chapter 10 of this book.
6. William J. Federer, *America's God and Country Encyclopedia of Quotations* (Coppell, Tex.: 1994), 411.
7. G. Richard Bozarth, "On Keeping God Alive," *American Atheist* (Nov. 1977): 8. Cited in John Whitehead, *Texas Law Review* (Winter 1978): 40.
8. Source: *Congressional Quarterly*. Cited in William Bennett, *The Index of Leading Cultural Indicators* (New York: Simon & Schuster, 1994), 83.
9. For much more on the Court's legal schizophrenia, see David Barton, *The Myth of Separation* (Aledo, Tex.: Wallbuilder Press, 1992). Phone: 817-441-6044.
10. In a letter from Thomas Jefferson to Justice William Johnson on June 12, 1823. From Albert Bergh, ed., *Writings of Thomas Jefferson* (Washington, D.C.: Thomas Jefferson Memorial Association, 1904), XV: 449.

Quoted in Barton, 263. See also H. Wayne House, ed., *Restoring the Constitution* (Dallas: Probe Books, 1987), 237.

CHAPTER 7

1. Thomas Jefferson, *The Jefferson Bible: The Life and Morals of Jesus of Nazareth* (New York: Wilfred Funk, Inc., 1943), 132.
2. See Hebrews 8.
3. See Greg Bahnsen, *Theonomy in Christian Ethics* (Phillipsburg, N.J.: Presbyterian and Reformed Publishing Company, 1977), 444–445.
4. See also Norman Geisler, *Christian Ethics: Options and Issues* (Grand Rapids, Mich.: Baker Book House, 1989), particularly pp. 202–207.
5. Romans 2:14.
6. Romans 3:2.
7. Romans 9:4.
8. Deuteronomy 4:88.
9. Exodus 12:49.
10. Romans 2:12–15.
11. Ibid.
12. Romans 1:20.
13. Romans 2:12 and 3:19.
14. Rousas J. Rushdoony, "Government and the Christian," The Rutherford Institute, July-August, 1984, 7.
15. See John 18:36. Jesus is not simply referring to the source of His kingdom, but also to its nature. First, this is indicated by the use of the Greek word *ek* (from), which denotes the nature of His kingdom as well as its source. Second, the reference to His servants not "fight[ing]" to resist arrest reveals that He is contrasting His present kingdom with a political one. Third, the statement "But now my kingdom is from another place" indicates that at present His kingdom is spiritual, but later it will be political. Finally, Jesus refused being made an earthly king when the crowd tried to do so (John 6:15).
16. Matthew 28:19–20.
17. Matthew 13:24–30.
18. Charles Colson, *Kingdoms in Conflict* (Grand Rapids, Mich.: Zondervan Publishing Company, 1987), 305.
19. See theonomist Gary DeMar's *What's Wrong With the Christian Coalition?* at http://www.erols.com/mkturner/inet/ustp-va/notcc.html.
20. Robert Bork, *Slouching Towards Gomorrah: Modern Liberalism and American Decline* (New York: Regan Books, HarperCollins, 1996, pbk. ed.), 5.
21. John Dunphy, *The Humanist* (Jan./Feb. 1983), 26.
22. Joseph Fletcher, *Situation Ethics: The New Morality* (Philadelphia: The Westminster Press, 1966), 120.
23. Ibid., 134.
24. Ibid., 43–44.
25. See Paul Kurtz, *Humanist Manifestoes I and II*, 2:7, 18–19.

26. See William Watkins, *The New Absolutes* (Minneapolis, Minn.: Bethany House Publishers, 1996). We discuss the Left's "new absolutes" a bit more in chapter 8.

27. Bork, 155–157.

CHAPTER 8

1. *Planned Parenthood v. Casey*, 505 U.S. 851 (1992).

2. Bork, *Slouching Towards Gomorrah*, 111.

3. John Locke, "An Essay," 2.6, in *The Great Books*, vol. 35 (Chicago: Encyclopedia Britannia, Inc., 1952), 26.

4. Bork, 57.

5. C. S. Lewis, *Mere Christianity* (New York: Macmillan, 1952), 19.

6. Ibid.

7. For an excellent summary of Moral Law thought, see J. Budziszewski, *Written on the Heart: The Case for Natural Law* (Downer's Grove, Ill.: InterVarsity Press, 1997).

8. C. S. Lewis, *The Abolition of Man* (New York: Macmillan, 1947.)

9. Heraclitus, trans. by G. S. Kirk & J. E. Raven, cited in *The Presocratic Philosophers: A Critical History With a Selection of Texts* (Cambridge: Cambridge University Press, 1964), 188–189; 197–220.

10. See Plato, *Republic*, Books IV-VI (New York: Pantheon Books, 1964).

11. Cicero stated that "there is a true law, right reason in accord with nature; it is of universal application, unchanging and everlasting.... There is one law ... binding at all times upon all peoples." Cicero, *The Republic* 3.22, cited in Paul E. Sigmund, *Natural Law in Political Thought* (Cambridge, Mass.: Winthrop, 1971), 22.

12. Matthew 7:12.

13. Lewis, *The Abolition of Man*, 56 (in the 1947 edition).

14. Watkins, *The New Absolutes*, 45.

15. C. S. Lewis, *Mere Christianity* (New York: Macmillan, 1960, pbk. ed.), 25.

16. Ibid., 35.

17. *Jacobellis v. Ohio* 378 U.S. 194 (1964).

18. Budziszewski, *Written on the Heart*. See the chapter entitled "The Art of Teaching."

19. For a detailed analysis of all the major ethical systems, see Norman L. Geisler, *Christian Ethics: Options and Issues* (Grand Rapids, Mich.: Baker Book House, 1989). Chapter 7 describes "graded absolutism," or hierarchicalism.

20. Bork, *Slouching Towards Gomorrah*, 98.

21. Matthew 7:12.

22. Confucius, *Analects of Confucius* 25.23 cf. 12:2.

23. Ravi Zacharias, *Deliver Us From Evil* (Dallas: Word Publishing, 1996), 112.

24. Bork, 98.

25. Zacharias, *op. cit.*, 131.

26. Dennis Prager, "Blacks, Liberals, and The Los Angeles Riots," *Ultimate Issues*, 2 (1992): 15.

27. See Allan Bloom, *The Closing of the American Mind.*

CHAPTER 9

1. William J. Bennett, *The Index of Leading Cultural Indicators* (New York: Simon & Schuster, 1994).

2. Richard Tafel, Log Cabin Republicans: "Equal Rights in Marriage" web page.

3. Paul Cameron, Ph.D., William Playfair, M.D., and Stephen Wellum, "The Longevity of Homosexuals: Before and After the AIDS Epidemic," *Omega Journal of Death and Dying*, 29:3 (1994): 249–272.

4. Homosexual activists have criticized this study, claiming the findings are skewed toward a shorter life-span because not all homosexual deaths (particularly those who were "in the closet") are submitted to or reported by the newspapers from which the obituaries were drawn. On the other hand, the researchers note that the activists who run those newspapers are particularly eager to highlight the accomplishments of older homosexuals, thus potentially skewing the results the other way.

   Whatever the case may be, the relatively short life-spans discovered in the *Omega* study seem validated by other research, the most recent of which is a very large survey published by the University of Chicago Press. The survey was conducted in 1994 (after the *Omega* study) as part of a massive study detailed in *The Social Origins of Sexuality*, which was authored by Edward O. Laumann and others (a summary of the entire study also was published in the popular book *Sex in America*). In the survey, over 3,400 people of all adult age groups to age 59 were asked whether they considered themselves heterosexual, homosexual, or bisexual. *Respondents remained anonymous.* The findings for self-acknowledged homosexuals are found on p. 302 of *The Social Origins of Sexuality* as follows:

Age	Men	Women
18–29:	2.9%	1.6%
30–39	4.2%	1.8%
40–49	2.2%	1.3%
50–59	0.5%	0.4%

Where did all the homosexuals go between the ages of 40 and 59? Critics say that the older homosexuals were too embarrassed to answer truthfully. But this makes no sense because respondents remained anonymous. If homosexuals were living normal life-spans, we would expect to see a roughly uniform percentage throughout the age groups (especially if they were all "born that way"). However, the data show that the homosexual presence in the 50–59 age group *declined 840 per-*

cent relative to the 30–39 age group. Similar results were found by a National Opinion Research Center survey conducted in 1970. (See *Omega*, pp. 258–268 for additional corroborating data.) Either homosexuals are dying in dramatic numbers or nearly all of them are switching their "orientation" during that nineteen-year period.

While this survey data doesn't prove that the *Omega* life-span findings may not be skewed slightly one way or the other, we would expect to find very clear data to the contrary if the *Omega* findings were significantly in error. In other words, if the homosexual life-span really was closer to a normal life-span (75–79), it's reasonable to assume that the survey data would not reflect a *huge* 840 percent reduction in homosexuals from age 40 to 59. Common sense says the *Omega* findings can't be far from the truth.

One final note: While homosexual activists criticize the *Omega* study by personally attacking its coauthor, Dr. Paul Cameron (which is probably because they can't refute his findings with facts), to our knowledge no one has presented any scientific data that contradicts *Omega's* findings. Moreover, no one questions the *Social Origins of Sexuality* study, which, as we have seen, appears to affirm the findings of the *Omega* study.

5. U. S. Department of Health & Human Services, Office on Smoking and Health, "Cigarette Smoking-Related Mortality," Document #461123, April 24, 1996, 1.
6. Cameron, 249.
7. George Gilder, *Men and Marriage* (Bethesda, Md.: Adler & Adler, 1986).
8. See note #9.
9. The largest survey of homosexuals in the U.S., 13,000 of them, concluded in 1994 that "coupled" or "married" homosexuals reported the highest proportion of high-risk sexual activity. The largest Canadian survey (4,800) found the same. A British study concluded that "gay men in a closed relationship ... exhibit ... the highest risk of HIV transmission." A 1989 Italian study reported, "To our surprise, male prostitutes did not seem to be at increased risk, whereas homosexuals who reported a steady partner (i.e., the same man for the previous six months) carried the highest relative risk. Such individuals were also those who tended to practice both receptive and insertive anal sex." Finally, another study of 580 homosexuals found that "most 'unsafe' sexual activity occurs in steady relationships." Studies cited in A Special Report from the Family Research Institute, "What's Wrong With Gay Marriage," Colorado Springs, Colo., 1996.
10. David Dunlap, "In Age of AIDS, Love and Hope Can Lead to Risk," *New York Times*, July 27, 1996.
11. Ibid.
12. Ibid.
13. Ibid.

14. These goals are taken from the sixty-two platform demands of the march. The platform can be found in its entirety in the Official 1993 March on Washington for Lesbian, Gay, and Bi-Equal Rights and Liberation Program Guide, published by The Committee for the March on Washington, Inc., P.O. Box 34607, Washington, DC 20005–3406. See also: Richard Howe, *Homosexuality in America: Exposing the Myths* (Tupelo, Miss.: The American Family Association, 1994).
15. Carol Innerst, "Some kindergartners are taught about homosexuality," *The Washington Times*, National Weekly Edition (Dec. 7, 1997): 1.
16. William Byne, "The Biological Evidence Challenged," *Scientific American*, (May 1994): 55.
17. For more on the genetic debate, see Jeffrey Satinover, M.D., *Homosexuality and the Politics of Truth* (Grand Rapids, Mich.: Baker Book House, 1996). See also *Scientific American* (May 1994): 43–55 for both sides of this debate.
18. Out-of-wedlock births rose from 2 percent in 1940 to 31 percent in 1994 (and that figure doesn't illustrate the full increase in promiscuity because about a third of all pregnancies in 1994 ended in abortion).
19. Gilder, 74.
20. G. F. Lemp, et al., "HIV Seroprevalence and Risk Behaviors Among Lesbians and Bisexual Women in San Francisco and Berkeley, California," *American Journal of Public Health* (1995): 85:1549–1552. Cited in the Family Research Report from the Family Research Institute, P.O. Box 62640, Colorado Springs, CO 80962, Mar/Apr 1996, 8.

CHAPTER 10

1. Ravi Zacharias, Ravi Zacharias International Ministries: See at http:/www.rzim.com/jt/rthtp.html.
2. *Roe v. Wade* 410 U.S. 159, 730 (1973).
3. See Bork, *Slouching Towards Gomorrah* (1996), 175. See also Francis J. Beckwith, *Politically Correct Death: Answering Arguments for Abortion Rights* (Grand Rapids, Mich.: Baker, 1993), 44. See also *The Wonder of Life: A Video Journal of Life in the Womb* for absolutely amazing video footage of a new baby in the womb (2 weeks to 12 weeks gestation). This is an unbiased video documentary; abortion is not discussed. This video is produced by and available from The Health Science Curriculum Foundation, P.O. Box 480485, Kansas City, MO 64148. (Phone: 913–469–5116).
4. Beckwith, 42. This book is perhaps the best and most complete refutation of the pro-abortion position in print.
5. For these quotes, see The Human Life Bill—Hearings on S. 158, before the Subcommittee on Separation of Powers of the Senate Judiciary Committee, 97th Congress, 1st Session (1981).
6. Ibid.

7. See *The Wonder of Life: A Video Journal of Life in the Womb* (see note 3 above).
8. Bennett, *The Index of Leading Cultural Indicators,* 69. See also Bork, 180–81.
9. Stephen Schwarz, *The Moral Question of Abortion* (Chicago: Loyola University Press, 1990), 20, as quoted in Beckwith.
10. See Stephen M. Krason, *Abortion: Politics, Morality, and the Constitution* (Lanham, Md.: University Press of America, 1984), 164–66.
11. Ibid., 170–171. For documentation of the facts about the Fourteenth Amendment cited in the text, see pp. 168–73.
12. For more on the poor reasoning of the *Roe v. Wade* decision, see the critique by Francis Beckwith and Norman Geisler in *Matters of Life and Death: Calm Answers to Tough Questions About Abortion and Euthanasia* (Grand Rapids, Mich.: Baker Book House, 1991), chapter 2.
13. *Roe v. Wade* 410 U.S. 159, 737, (1973).
14. See Dr. Jacqueline Kasun, "The Population Bomb: A Look at the Facts," in Hensley, ed., *The Zero People* (Ann Arbor, Mich.: Servant Books, 1983), 33–41.
15. Beckwith and Geisler, 114.
16. A. Jackson, National Center of Child Abuse and Neglect, U.S. Dept. of Health and Human Services (1973, 1982), as cited in Willke, *Abortion,* 139–140.
17. Associated Press, "Kids Hurt in Scissors Attack at S.C. Mall," *The Charlotte Observer,* April 3, 1995, 3-C.
18. See Colin Fracome, *Abortion Practice in Britain and the United States* (New York: Allen and Unwin, 1986), 104.
19. Bernard Nathanson, M.D., *Aborting America* (New York: Doubleday, 1979), 193.
20. See table 35 from CDC's MMWR, August 8, 1997. See also Dr. and Mrs. John Wilke, *Abortion: Questions and Answers* (Cincinnati, Oh.: Hayes Publishing, 1985), 101–102.
21. See table 35 from CDC's MMWR, August 8, 1997.
22. The Commission on Professional and Hospital Activities found that in 1969 about 9,000 women were admitted to hospitals across the United States for treatment of injuries directly caused by abortions. In 1977, that figure had nearly doubled, to 17,000. See Todd Ackerman, " 'Pro-Choicers' Pushing Home Abortion Kits," *National Catholic Register* (September 3, 1989): 1.
23. Steven Waldman and Ginny Carroll, "Roe v. Roe," *Newsweek* (August 21, 1995).
24. See Barbara Kantrowitz, "Battle Over Partial-Birth Abortions: Did Pro-Choice Advocates Distort Statistics?" *Newsweek* (March 17, 1997). See also "Lies Sully Political Discourse," *Phoenix* magazine (March 2, 1997).
25. Bork, *Slouching Towards Gomorrah,* 182.

26. George F. Will, "Fanatics for Choice," *Newsweek* (December 11, 1995).
27. Jonathan Alter, "When Facts Get Aborted," *Newsweek* (October 7, 1996).
28. Schwarz, 148, as quoted in Beckwith.
29. As quoted in Beckwith, 71.
30. Ibid.
31. Having an induced abortion increases a woman's risk of developing breast cancer later in life by nearly one-third, according to a metanalysis of twenty-three studies of women with breast cancer, which appears in the October 1996 *Journal of Epidemiology and Community Health*, published by the British Medical Association.
32. Thanks to our friend Frank Beckwith for this anecdote.
33. Thanks to Mary Ellen Bork for this insightful observation. See Robert Bork, *Slouching Towards Gomorrah*, 176.
34. Beckwith, 98.
35. George F. Will as quoted in John Whitehead, *The Stealing of America* (Wheaton, Ill.: Crossway Books, 1983), 58.
36. See the *Milwaukee Sentinel*, May 14, 1984.
37. Janet McConnaughey, "Twin Born 95 Days After Brother," *The Charlotte Observer*, January 19, 1995, 8-A.
38. Ibid.
39. We'll describe and reference these gruesome events in more detail in the next chapter.
40. David C. Reardon, *Aborted Women: Silent No More* (Westchester, Ill.: Crossway Books, 1987), 13, 15, as quoted in Beckwith, 84.
41. Beckwith, 84.
42. *Roe v. Wade*, 728.
43. Norma McCorvey with Gary Thomas, *Won by Love* (Nashville: Thomas Nelson Publishers, 1998).
44. An excerpt from Mother Teresa's address at the National Prayer Breakfast, February 3, 1994. (A very uncomfortable President Clinton and Vice-President Gore were in attendance.) See *The Christian American* (March 1994): 29.

CHAPTER 11

1. *Time* (April 9, 1984).
2. This account is adapted from that of Dr. C. Everett Koop. See C. Everett Koop, *Koop: The Memoirs of America's Family Doctor* (Grand Rapids, Mich.: Zondervan Publishing House, 1992), 304–331.
3. Cited in William Brennan, *The Abortion Holocaust: Today's Final Solution* (St. Louis, Mo.: Landmark Press, 1983), 82.
4. Koop, 336.
5. *Medical World News* (June 8, 1973): 21.
6. John Whitehead, *The Stealing of America* (Wheaton, Ill.: Crossway Books, 1983), 52–53.

7. Brennan, 58–59.
8. See: F. I. Reyes, J. S. D. Winter, C. Raiman, "Studies on Human Sexual Development, I. Fetal Gonadal and Adrenal Sex Steriods," *Journal of Clinical Endocrinology and Metabolism* (July 1973): 37:1, 74–78; F. I. Reyes, R. S. Boroditsky, J. S. D. Winter, C. Faiman, "Studies on Human Sexual Development, II. Fetal and Maternal Serum Gonadotropin and Sex Steriod Concentrations," *Journal of Clinical Endocrinology and Metabolism* (April 1974): 38:4, 612–617; J. A. Clements, F. I. Reyes, J. S. D. Winter, C. Faiman, "Studies on Human Sexual Development, III. Fetal Pituitary and Serum, Amniotic Fluid Concentrations of LH, CG, and FSH" *Journal of Clinical Endocrinology and Metabolism* (January 1976): 42:1, 9–19; J. A. Clements, F. I. Reyes, J. S. D. Winter, C. Faiman, "Studies on Human Sexual Development, IV. Fetal Pituitary and Serum, Amniotic Fluid Concentrations of Prolactin," *Journal of Clinical Endocrinology and Metabolism* (February 1977): 44:3, 408–413; Garry I. Warne, Charles Faiman, F. I. Reyes, J. S. D. Winter, "Studies on Human Sexual Development, V. Concentrations of Testosterone, 17-Hydroxyprogesterone and Progesterone in Human Amniotic Fluid throughout Gestation, *Journal of Clinical Endocrinology and Metabolism* (May 1977): 44:5, 934–938; Garry L. Warne, F. I. Reyes, Charles Faiman, J. S. D. Winter, "Studies on Human Sexual Development, VI. Concentrations of Unconjugated Dehydroepiandrosterone, Estradiol, and Estriol in Amniotic Fluid throughout Gestation," *Journal of Clinical Endocrinology and Metabolism* (December 1978): 47:6, 1363–1367.
9. *Reuters News Agency*, June 12, 1972.
10. Bela A. Resch, et al., "Comparison of Spontaneous Contraction Rates of In Situ and Isolated Fetal Hearts in Early Pregnancy," *American Journal of Obstetrics and Gynecology*, 118:1 (January 1, 1974): 73–74.
11. *National Examiner* (August 19, 1980).
12. Ibid., 20.
13. *American College of Surgeons Bulletin* (August 1988): 4.
14. Associated Press, March 11, 1998.
15. Pat Buchanan, "Dr. Death and the 'Suicide Machine,'" *National Right to Life News* (June 25, 1990): 14.
16. Johanna H. Groenewoud, M.D., et al., "Physician-Assisted Death in Psychiatric Practice in The Netherlands," *New England Journal of Medicine*, 336:25 (June 19, 1997): 1795.
17. See John Horgan, "Seeking a Better Way to Die," *Scientific American*, 276:5 (May 1997): 105.
18. David C. Thomasma, "The Range of Euthanasia," *American College of Surgeons Bulletin*, 73:8, 4.
19. For a further discussion of "passive" euthanasia see J. P. Moreland and Norman L. Geisler, *The Life and Death Debate* (New York: Greenwood Press, 1990), chapters 3, 4, and 5; see also Francis J. Beckwith and Norman L. Geisler, *Matters of Life and Death* (Grand Rapids, Mich.: Baker

Book House, 1991, chapters 5, 6, and 7.

20. "Before the Court: The Sanctity of Life and Death," *The New York Times*, January 5, 1997.
21. Fletcher, *Situation Ethics*.
22. David C. Thomasma, "The Range of Euthanasia," *American College of Surgeons Bulletin*, 73:8, 4.
23. Koop, 369.
24. See *Washington v. Glucksberg*, nos. 96–110; and Johanna H. Groene-woud, M.D., et al., "Physician-Assisted Death in Psychiatric Practice in The Netherlands," *New England Journal of Medicine*, 336:25 (June 19, 1997): 1795.
25. See *American Medical News*, January 7, 1991, 12.
26. Ibid., 15.
27. While Oregon voters in November 1997 reaffirmed a law permitting doctor-assisted suicide, continued legal challenges and federal law may permanently sink its implementation. For example, doctors prescribing lethal drug dosages may run into trouble with the federal Drug Enforcement Agency, who have indicated that such practices are against federal law. It would seem that few doctors will risk losing their medical licenses to help someone commit suicide (other than Dr. Kevorkian, who has already been stripped of his). However, it was reported that at least one woman in Oregon was put to death under this law in late March 1998.
28. See *Washington v. Glucksberg*, nos. 96–110.
29. Ibid.
30. Bork, 189.
31. *American Medical News* (January 7, 1991): 15.
32. Ibid., 13.
33. Ibid., 15.
34. *National Right to Life News* (April 12, 1990): 5.
35. *The Chicago Tribune*, Sunday, November 30, 1975.
36. *National Right to Life News* (April 9, 1991): 8.
37. Ibid.
38. Letter to the editor, *Time* (January 25, 1993).
39. As quoted in Stephen Krason, *Abortion: Politics, Morality, and the Constitution* (Lanham, Md.: University Press of America, 1984), 132.
40. *American Medical News*, ibid., 15.
41. See *Washington v. Glucksberg*, nos. 96–110.
42. Ibid.
43. Ibid.
44. Groenewoud, "Physician-Assisted Death," 1795.
45. *Washington v. Glucksberg*.
46. John Horgan, "Seeking a Better Way to Die," *Scientific American*, 276:5 (May 1997): 101.
47. Bork, *Slouching Towards Gomorrah*, 187.

48. Horgan, 105.
49. Ibid.
50. See "Statement of the National Hospice Organization Opposing the Legalization of Euthanasia and Assisted Suicide," following a resolution approved by the delegates of the National Hospice Organization Annual Meeting, November 8, 1990, Detroit, Michigan.
51. *American Medical News,* 14.
52. Ibid., 15.
53. Ibid.
54. *American Medical News,* 14.
55. "Mercy Killing: A Position Statement Regarding David Rodriguez," The Hemlock Society, December 3, 1997.
56. "Hemlock Society Statement Proposes Euthanasia Decisions to Be Made by Guardians," National Right to Life Committee, Inc., December 9, 1997.
57. Bork, 189.
58. Groenewoud, 1795.
59. *National Right to Life News* (January 23, 1993): 5.
60. Bork, 185–186.
61. *American Medical News,* 14.
62. Ibid.
63. See Norman Geisler, *Is Man the Measure? An Evaluation of Contemporary Humanism* (Grand Rapids, Mich.: Baker Book House, 1983). (Currently out of print but available from IMPACT at (704) 846–1226.)
64. For an evaluation of atheism and the other six possible worldviews, see Norman L. Geisler, *Christian Apologetics* (Grand Rapids, Mich.: Baker, 1977). See also *When Skeptics Ask* (Grand Rapids, Mich.: Baker, 1990).
65. *National Right to Life News* (July 12, 1990): 8.
66. See *Cruzan v. Harmon,* nos. 88–1503 (1990).
67. *New England Journal of Medicine* (September 6, 1990): 670.
68. Bork, 192.

APPENDIX I

1. Taken from the Library of Congress website at: http://lcweb2.loc.gov.

APPENDIX II

1. Taken from the Library of Congress website at: http://lcweb2.loc.gov.

APPENDIX III

1. Excerpted from C. S. Lewis, *The Abolition of Man* (New York: Macmillan Publishing Co., Inc., 1947), 95–121.

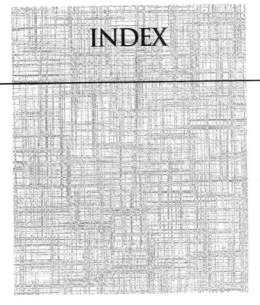

INDEX